Contents

		Page
Chapter 1	What is assurance?	1
Chapter 2	The rules and who sets them	27
Chapter 3	Corporate governance and internal audit	43
Chapter 4	Responsibilities	97
Chapter 5	Ethics and acceptance of appointment	113
Chapter 6	Planning	147
Chapter 7	Risk	195
Chapter 8	Systems and controls	213
Chapter 9	Audit evidence	267
Chapter 10	Audit procedures	313
Chapter 11	Completion and review	371
Chapter 12	Reporting	401

Contents

KAPLAN PUBLISHING

Paper Introduction

How to Use the Materials

These Kaplan Publishing learning materials have been carefully designed to make your learning experience as easy as possible and to give you the best chances of success in your examinations.

The product range contains a number of features to help you in the study process. They include:

(1) Detailed study guide and syllabus objectives

(2) Description of the examination

(3) Study skills and revision guidance

(4) Complete text or essential text

(5) Question practice

The sections on the study guide, the syllabus objectives, the examination and study skills should all be read before you commence your studies. They are designed to familiarise you with the nature and content of the examination and give you tips on how to best to approach your learning.

The **complete text or essential text** comprises the main learning materials and gives guidance as to the importance of topics and where other related resources can be found. Each chapter includes:

- The **learning objectives** contained in each chapter, which have been carefully mapped to the examining body's own syllabus learning objectives or outcomes. You should use these to check you have a clear understanding of all the topics on which you might be assessed in the examination.

- The **chapter diagram** provides a visual reference for the content in the chapter, giving an overview of the topics and how they link together.

- The **content** for each topic area commences with a brief explanation or definition to put the topic into context before covering the topic in detail. You should follow your studying of the content with a review of the illustration/s. These are worked examples which will help you to understand better how to apply the content for the topic.

- **Test your understanding** sections provide an opportunity to assess your understanding of the key topics by applying what you have learned to short questions. Answers can be found at the back of each chapter.

- **Summary diagrams** complete each chapter to show the important links between topics and the overall content of the paper. These diagrams should be used to check that you have covered and understood the core topics before moving on.

- **Question practice** is provided at the back of each text.

On-line subscribers

Our on-line resources are designed to increase the flexibility of your learning materials and provide you with immediate feedback on how your studies are progressing.

If you are subscribed to our on-line resources you will find:

(1) On-line referenceware: reproduces your Complete or Essential Text on-line, giving you anytime, anywhere access.

(2) On-line testing: provides you with additional on-line objective testing so you can practice what you have learned further.

(3) On-line performance management: immediate access to your on-line testing results. Review your performance by key topics and chart your achievement through the course relative to your peer group.

Ask your local customer services staff if you are not already a subscriber and wish to join.

Syllabus

Paper background

The aim of ACCA Paper F8 (INT), Audit and Assurance, is to develop knowledge and understanding of the process of carrying out the assurance engagement and its application in the context of the professional regulatory framework.

Objectives of the syllabus

- Explain the nature, purpose and scope of assurance engagements including the role of the external audit and its regulatory and ethical framework.

- Explain the nature of internal audit and describe its role as part of overall performance management and its relationship with the external audit.

- Demonstrate how the auditor obtains an understanding of the entity and its environment, assesses the risk of material misstatement, whether arising from fraud or other irregularities, and plans an audit of financial statements.

- Describe and evaluate information systems and internal controls to identify and communicate control risks and their potential consequences, making appropriate recommendations.

- Identify and describe the work and evidence required to meet the objectives of audit engagements and the application of the International Standards on Auditing.

- Evaluate findings and modify the audit plan as necessary.

- Explain how the conclusions from audit work are reflected in different types of audit report, explain the elements of each type of report.

Core areas of the syllabus

- Audit framework and regulation.

- Internal audit.

- Planning and risk assessment.

- Internal control.

- Audit evidence.

- Review.

- Reporting.

Syllabus objectives and chapter references

We have reproduced the ACCA's syllabus below, showing where the objectives are explored within this book. Within the chapters, we have broken down the extensive information found in the syllabus into easily digestible and relevant sections, called Content Objectives. These correspond to the objectives at the beginning of each chapter.

Syllabus learning objective

A AUDIT FRAMEWORK AND REGULATION

1 The concept of audit and other assurance engagements

(a) Identify and describe the objective and general principles of external audit engagements.[2] **Ch. 1**

(b) Explain the nature and development of audit and other assurance engagements.[1] **Ch. 1**

(c) Discuss the concepts of accountability, stewardship and agency.[2] **Ch. 1**

(d) Discuss the concepts of materiality, true and fair presentation and reasonable assurance.[2] **Ch. 1**

(e) Explain reporting as a means of communication to different stakeholders.[1] **Ch. 1**

(f) Explain the level of assurance provided by audit and other review assignments.[1] **Ch. 1**

2 Statutory audits

(a) Describe the regulatory environment within which statutory audits take place.[1] **Ch. 2**

(b) Discuss the reasons and mechanisms for the regulation of auditors. [2] **Ch. 2**

(c) Explain the statutory regulations governing the appointment, removal and resignation of auditors.[1] **Ch. 2**

(d) Discuss the types of opinion provided in statutory audits.[2] **Ch. 12**

(e) State the objectives and principal activities of statutory audit and assess its value (e.g. in assisting management to reduce risk and improve performance).[1] **Ch. 1**

(f) Describe the limitations of statutory audits.[1] **Ch. 1**

3 The regulatory environment and corporate governance

(a) Explain the development and status of International Standards on Auditing.[1] **Ch. 2**

(b) Explain the relationship between International Standards on Auditing and national standards.[1] **Ch. 2**

(c) Discuss the objective, relevance and importance of corporate governance.[2] **Ch. 3**

(d) Discuss the need for auditors to communicate with those charged with governance.[2] **Ch. 4**

(e) Discuss the provisions of international codes of corporate governance (such as OECD) that are most relevant to auditors.[2] **Ch. 3**

(f) Describe good corporate governance requirements relating to directors' responsibilities (e.g. for risk management and internal control) and the reporting responsibilities of auditors.[1] **Ch. 3**

(g) Analyse the structure and roles of audit committees and discuss their drawbacks and limitations.[2] **Ch. 3**

(h) Explain the importance of internal control and risk management.[1] **Ch. 4**

(i) Compare the responsibilities of management and auditors for the design and operation of systems and controls.[2] **Ch. 3**

4 Professional ethics and ACCA's Code of Ethics and Conduct

(a) Define and apply the fundamental principles of professional ethics of integrity, objectivity, professional competence and due care, confidentiality and professional behaviour.[2] **Ch. 5**

(b) Define and apply the conceptual framework.[2] **Ch. 5**

(c) Discuss the sources of, and enforcement mechanisms associated with, ACCA's Code of Ethics and Conduct.[2] **Ch. 5**

(d) Discuss the requirements of professional ethics and other requirements in relation to the acceptance of new audit engagements.[2] **Ch. 5**

(e) Discuss the process by which an auditor obtains an audit engagement. [2] **Ch. 5**

(f) Explain the importance of engagement letters and state their contents. [1] **Ch. 5**

B INTERNAL AUDIT

1 Internal audit and corporate governance

(a) Discuss the factors to be taken into account when assessing the need for internal audit.[2] **Ch. 3**

(b) Discuss the elements of best practice in the structure and operations of internal audit with reference to appropriate international codes of corporate governance.[2] **Ch. 3**

2 Differences between external and internal audit

(a) Compare and contrast the role of external and internal audit regarding audit planning and the collection of audit evidence.[2] **Ch. 4**

(b) Compare and contrast the types of report provided by internal and external audit.[2] **Ch. 4**

3 The scope of the internal audit function

(a) Discuss the scope of internal audit and the limitations of the internal audit function.[2] **Ch. 3**

(b) Explain the types of audit report provided in internal audit assignments. [1] **Ch. 3**

(c) Discuss the responsibilities of internal and external auditors for the prevention and detection of fraud and error.[2] **Ch. 4**

4 Outsourcing the internal audit department

(a) Explain the advantages and disadvantages of outsourcing internal audit.[1] **Ch. 3**

5 Internal audit assignments

(a) Discuss the nature and purpose of internal audit assignments including value for money, IT, best value and financial.[2] **Ch. 3**

(b) Discuss the nature and purpose of operational internal audit assignments including procurement, marketing, treasury and human resources management.[2] **Ch. 3**

C PLANNING AND RISK ASSESSMENT

1 Objective and general principles

(a) Identify and describe the need to plan and perform audits with an attitude of professional scepticism.[2] **Ch. 7**

(b) Identify and describe engagement risks affecting the audit of an entity. [1] **Ch. 7**

(c) Explain the components of audit risk.[1] **Ch. 7**

(d) Compare and contrast risk based, procedural and other approaches to audit work.[2] **Ch. 7**

(e) Discuss the importance of risk analysis.[2] **Ch. 7**

(f) Describe the use of information technology in risk analysis.[1] **Ch. 7**

2 Understanding the entity and knowledge of the business

(a) Explain how auditors obtain an initial understanding of the entity and knowledge of its business environment.[2] **Ch. 6**

3 Assessing the risks of material misstatement and fraud

(a) Define and explain the concepts of materiality and tolerable error. [2] **Ch. 6**

(b) Compute indicative materiality levels from financial information.[2] **Ch. 6**

(c) Discuss the effect of fraud and misstatements on the audit strategy and extent of audit work.[2] **Ch. 6**

4 Analytical procedures

(a) Describe and explain the nature and purpose of analytical procedures in planning.[2] **Ch. 6**

(b) Compute and interpret key ratios used in analytical procedures.[2] **Ch. 10**

5 Planning an audit

(a) Identify and explain the need for planning an audit.[2] **Ch. 6**

(b) Identify and describe the contents of the overall audit strategy and audit plan.[2] **Ch. 6**

(c) Explain and describe the relationship between the overall audit strategy and the audit plan.[2] **Ch. 6**

(d) Develop and document an audit plan.[2] **Ch. 6**

(e) Explain the difference between interim and final audit.[1] **Ch. 6**

6 Audit documentation

(a) Explain the need for and the importance of audit documentation.[1] **Ch. 9**

(b) Describe and prepare working papers and supporting documentation. [2] **Ch. 9**

(c) Explain the procedures to ensure safe custody and retention of working papers.[1] **Ch. 9**

7 The work of others

(a) Discuss the extent to which auditors are able to rely on the work of experts.[2] **Ch. 10**

(b) Discuss the extent to which external auditors are able to rely on the work of internal audit.[2] **Ch. 10**

(c) Discuss the audit considerations relating to entities using service organisations.[2] **Ch. 10**

(d) Discuss why auditors rely on the work of others.[2] **Ch. 10**

(e) Explain the extent to which reference to the work of others can be made in audit reports.[1] **Ch. 10**

D INTERNAL CONTROL

The following transaction cycles and account balances are relevant to this capability:

- revenue
- purchases
- inventory
- revenue and capital expenditure
- payroll
- bank and cash.

1 Internal control systems

(a) Explain why an auditor needs to obtain an understanding of internal control activities relevant to the audit.[1] **Ch. 8**

(b) Describe and explain the key components of an internal control system. [1] **Ch. 8**

(c) Identify and describe the important elements of internal control, including the control environment and management control activities. [1] **Ch. 8**

(d) Discuss the difference between tests of control and substantive procedures.[2] **Ch. 8**

2 The use of internal control systems by auditors

(a) Explain the importance of internal control to auditors.[1] **Ch. 8**

(b) Explain how auditors identify weaknesses in internal control systems and how those weaknesses limit the extent of auditors' reliance on those systems.[2] **Ch. 8**

3 Transaction cycles

(a) Explain, analyse and provide examples of internal control procedures and control activities.[2] **Ch. 8**

(b) Provide examples of computer system controls.[2] **Ch. 8**

4 Tests of control

(i) Explain and tabulate tests of control in the transaction cycles and account balances relevant to this sub-capability, suitable for inclusion in audit working papers.[2] **Ch. 8**

(ii) List examples of application controls and general IT controls.[2] **Ch. 8**

5 The evaluation of internal control components

(a) Analyse the limitations of internal control components in the context of fraud and error.[2] **Ch. 8**

(b) Explain the need to modify the audit strategy and audit plan following the results of tests of control.[1] **Ch. 8**

(c) Identify and explain management's risk assessment process with reference to internal control components.[1] **Ch. 8**

6 Communication on internal control

(a) Discuss and provide examples of how the reporting of internal control weaknesses and recommendations to overcome those weaknesses are provided to management.[2] **Ch. 8**

E AUDIT EVIDENCE

1 The use of assertions by auditors

(a) Explain the assertions contained in the financial statements.[2] **Ch. 9**

(b) Explain the principles and objectives of transaction testing, account balance testing and disclosure testing.[1] **Ch. 9**

(c) Explain the use of assertions in obtaining audit evidence.[2] **Ch. 9**

2 Audit procedures

(a) Discuss the sources and relative merits of the different types of evidence available.[2] **Ch. 9**

(b) Discuss and provide examples of how analytical procedures are used as substantive procedures.[2] **Ch. 10**

(c) Discuss the problems associated with the audit and review of accounting estimates.[2] **Ch. 10**

(d) Describe why smaller entities may have different control environments and describe the types of evidence likely to be available in smaller entities.[1] **Ch. 9**

(e) Discuss the quality of evidence obtained.[2] **Ch. 9**

3 The audit of specific items

For each of the account balances stated in this sub-capability:

- explain the purpose of substantive procedures in relation to financial statement assertions

- explain the substantive procedures used in auditing each balance, and

- tabulate those substantive procedures in a work program.

(a) Receivables:[2] **Ch. 10**

    (i) direct confirmation of accounts receivable

    (ii) other evidence in relation to receivables and prepayments, and

    (iii) the related income statement entries.

(b) Inventory:[2] **Ch. 10**

    (i) inventory counting procedures in relation to year-end and continuous inventory systems

    (ii) cut-off

    (iii) auditor's attendance at inventory counting

    (iv) direct confirmation of inventory held by third parties,

    (v) other evidence in relation to inventory.

(c) Payables and accruals:[2] **Ch. 10**

    (i) supplier statement reconciliations and direct confirmation of accounts payable

    (ii) obtain evidence in relation to payables and accruals, and

    (iii) the related income statement entries.

(d) Bank and cash:[2] **Ch. 10**

    (i) bank confirmation reports used in obtaining evidence in relation to bank and cash

    (ii) other evidence in relation to bank and cash, and

    (iii) the related income statement entries.

(e) Tangible non-current assets and long-term liabilities:[2] **Ch. 10**

    (i)   evidence in relation to non-current assets and

    (ii) non-current liabilities and

    (iii) the related income statement entries.

4 Audit sampling and other means of testing

(a) Define audit sampling and explain the need for sampling.[1] **Ch. 9**

(b) Identify and discuss the differences between statistical and non-statistical sampling.[2] **Ch. 9**

(c) Discuss and provide relevant examples of, the application of the basic principles of statistical sampling and other selective testing procedures. [2] **Ch. 9**

(d) Discuss the results of statistical sampling, including consideration of whether additional testing is required.[2] **Ch. 9**

5 Computer-assisted audit techniques

(a) Explain the use of computer-assisted audit techniques in the context of an audit.[1] **Ch. 10**

(b) Discuss and provide relevant examples of the use of test data and audit software for the transaction cycles and balances mentioned in sub-capability 3.[2] **Ch. 10**

(c) Discuss the use of computers in relation to the administration of the audit.[2] **Ch. 10**

6 Not-for-profit organisations

(a) Apply audit techniques to small not-for-profit organisations.[2] **Ch. 10**

(b) Explain how the audit of small not-for-profit organisations differs from the audit of for-profit organisations.[1] **Ch. 10**

F REVIEW

1 Subsequent events

(a) Explain the purpose of a subsequent events review.[1] **Ch. 11**

(b) Discuss the procedures to be undertaken in performing a subsequent events review.[2] **Ch. 11**

2 Going concern

(a) Define and discuss the significance of the concept of going concern. [2] **Ch. 11**

(b) Explain the importance of and the need for going concern reviews. [2] **Ch. 11**

(c) Explain the respective responsibilities of auditors and management regarding going concern.[1] **Ch. 11**

(d) Discuss the procedures to be applied in performing going concern reviews.[2] **Ch. 11**

(e) Discuss the disclosure requirements in relation to going concern issues.[2] **Ch. 11**

(f) Discuss the reporting implications of the findings of going concern reviews.[2] **Ch. 11**

3 Management representations

(a) Explain the purpose of and procedure for obtaining management representations.[2] **Ch. 11**

(b) Discuss the quality and reliability of management representations as audit evidence.[2] **Ch. 11**

(c) Discuss the circumstances where management representations are necessary and the matters on which representations are commonly obtained.[2] **Ch. 11**

4 Audit finalisation and the final review

(a) Discuss the importance of the overall review of evidence obtained. [2] **Ch. 11**

(b) Explain the significance of unadjusted differences.[1] **Ch. 11**

G REPORTING

1 Audit reports

(a) Describe and analyse the format and content of unmodified audit reports.[2] **Ch. 12**

(b) Describe and analyse the format and content of modified audit reports. [2] **Ch. 12**

2 Reports to management

(a) Identify and analyse internal control and system weaknesses and their potential effects and make appropriate recommendations to management.[2] **Ch. 8**

3 Internal audit reports

(a) Describe and explain the format and content of internal audit review reports and other reports dealing with the enhancement of performance. [1] **Ch. 3**

(b) Explain the process for producing an internal audit report.[1] **Ch. 3**

The superscript numbers in square brackets indicate the intellectual depth at which the subject area could be assessed within the examination. Level 1 (knowledge and comprehension) broadly equates with the Knowledge module, Level 2 (application and analysis) with the Skills module and Level 3 (synthesis and evaluation) to the Professional level. However, lower level skills can continue to be assessed as you progress through each module and level.

For a list of examinable documents, see the ACCA web site (www. accaglobal/pubs/students).

The Examination

Examination format

The examination is a three-hour paper covering five compulsory questions. The bulk of the questions will be discursive but some questions involving computational elements will be set from time to time.

The questions will cover all areas of the syllabus:

	Number of marks
Question 1 (scenario based)	30
Question 2 (knowledge based)	10
Questions 3-5 (each question will be worth 20 marks each)	60
	100

Total time allowed: reading and planning 15 minutes; writing 3 hours.

Paper-based examination tips

Spend the first few minutes of the examination reading the paper.

Divide the time you spend on questions in proportion to the marks on offer. One suggestion **for this examination** is to allocate 1.8 minutes to each mark available, so a 10-mark question should be completed in approximately 18 minutes.

Unless you know exactly how to answer the question, spend some time planning your answer. Stick to the question and tailor your answer to what you are asked. Pay particular attention to the verbs in the question.

Spend the last five minutes reading through your answers and making any additions or corrections.

If you **get completely stuck** with a question, leave space in your answer book and return to it later.

If you do not understand what a question is asking, state your assumptions. Even if you do not answer in precisely the way the examiner hoped, you should be given some credit, if your assumptions are reasonable.

You should do everything you can to make things easy for the marker. The marker will find it easier to identify the points you have made if your answers are legible.

Written questions: Your essay should have a clear structure. It should contain a brief introduction, a main section and a conclusion. Be concise. It is better to write a little about a lot of different points than a great deal about one or two points.

Reports, memos and other documents: some questions ask you to present your answer in the form of a report or a memo or other document. So use the correct format - there are easy marks to gain here.

Study skills and revision guidance

This section aims to give guidance on how to study for your ACCA exams and to give ideas on how to improve your existing study techniques.

Preparing to study

Set your objectives

Before starting to study decide what you want to achieve - the type of pass you wish to obtain. This will decide the level of commitment and time you need to dedicate to your studies.

Devise a study plan

Determine which times of the week you will study.

Split these times into sessions of at least one hour for study of new material. Any shorter periods could be used for revision or practice.

Put the times you plan to study onto a study plan for the weeks from now until the exam and set yourself targets for each period of study – in your sessions make sure you cover the course, course assignments and revision.

If you are studying for more than one paper at a time, try to vary your subjects as this can help you to keep interested and see subjects as part of wider knowledge.

When working through your course, compare your progress with your plan and, if necessary, re-plan your work (perhaps including extra sessions) or, if you are ahead, do some extra revision/practice questions.

Effective studying

Active reading

You are not expected to learn the text by rote, rather, you must understand what you are reading and be able to use it to pass the exam and develop good practice. A good technique to use is SQ3Rs – Survey, Question, Read, Recall, Review:

(1) **Survey the chapter** – look at the headings and read the introduction, summary and objectives, so as to get an overview of what the chapter deals with.

(2) **Question** – whilst undertaking the survey, ask yourself the questions that you hope the chapter will answer for you.

(3) **Read** through the chapter thoroughly, answering the questions and making sure you can meet the objectives. Attempt the exercises and activities in the text, and work through all the examples.

(4) **Recall** – at the end of each section and at the end of the chapter, try to recall the main ideas of the section/chapter without referring to the text. This is best done after a short break of a couple of minutes after the reading stage.

(5) **Review** – check that your recall notes are correct.

You may also find it helpful to re-read the chapter to try to see the topic(s) it deals with as a whole.

Note-taking

Taking notes is a useful way of learning, but do not simply copy out the text. The notes must:

- be in your own words

- be concise

- cover the key points

- be well-organised

- be modified as you study further chapters in this text or in related ones.

Trying to summarise a chapter without referring to the text can be a useful way of determining which areas you know and which you don't.

Three ways of taking notes:

Summarise the key points of a chapter.

Make linear notes – a list of headings, divided up with subheadings listing the key points. If you use linear notes, you can use different colours to highlight key points and keep topic areas together. Use plenty of space to make your notes easy to use.

Try a diagrammatic form – the most common of which is a mind-map. To make a mind-map, put the main heading in the centre of the paper and put a circle around it. Then draw short lines radiating from this to the main sub-headings, which again have circles around them. Then continue the process from the sub-headings to sub-sub-headings, advantages, disadvantages, etc.

Highlighting and underlining

You may find it useful to underline or highlight key points in your study text – but do be selective. You may also wish to make notes in the margins.

Revision

The best approach to revision is to revise the course as you work through it. Also try to leave four to six weeks before the exam for final revision. Make sure you cover the whole syllabus and pay special attention to those areas where your knowledge is weak. Here are some recommendations:

Read through the text and your notes again and condense your notes into key phrases. It may help to put key revision points onto index cards to look at when you have a few minutes to spare.

Review any assignments you have completed and look at where you lost marks – put more work into those areas where you were weak.

Practise exam standard questions under timed conditions. If you are short of time, list the points that you would cover in your answer and then read the model answer, but do try to complete at least a few questions under exam conditions.

Also practise producing answer plans and comparing them to the model answer.

If you are stuck on a topic find somebody (a tutor) to explain it to you.

Read good newspapers and professional journals, especially ACCA's Student Accountant – this can give you an advantage in the exam.

Ensure you know the structure of the exam – how many questions and of what type you will be expected to answer. During your revision attempt all the different styles of questions you may be asked.

Further reading

You can find further reading and technical articles under the student section of ACCA's website.

Icon Explanations

Definition – these sections explain important areas of Knowledge which must be understood and reproduced in an exam environment.

Key Point – identifies topics which are key to success and are often examined.

New – identifies topics that are brand new in papers that build on, and therefore also contain, learning covered in earlier papers.

Expandable Text – within the online version of the work book is a more detailed explanation of key terms, these sections will help to provide a deeper understanding of core areas. Reference to this text is vital when self studying.

Test Your Understanding – following key points and definitions are exercises which give the opportunity to assess the understanding of these core areas. Within the work book the answers to these sections are left blank, explanations to the questions can be found within the online version which can be hidden or shown on screen to enable repetition of activities.

Illustration – to help develop an understanding of topics and the test your understanding exercises the illustrative examples can be used.

Exclamation Mark – this symbol signifies a topic which can be more difficult to understand, when reviewing these areas care should be taken.

1

What is assurance?

Chapter learning objectives

Upon completion of this chapter you will be able to:

- state the objectives and principal activities of statutory audit and assess its value (e.g. in assisting management to reduce risk and improve performance)
- describe the limitations of statutory audits
- explain the level of assurance provided by audit assignments
- explain the level of assurance provided by other review assignments
- explain reporting as a means of communication to different stakeholders
- explain the nature and development of audit and other assurance engagements
- discuss the concept of stewardship
- discuss the concept of accountability
- discuss the concept of agency
- identify and describe the objective and general principles of external audit engagements
- explain the concept of materiality
- explain the concept of true and fair
- explain the concept of presentation and reasonable assurance.

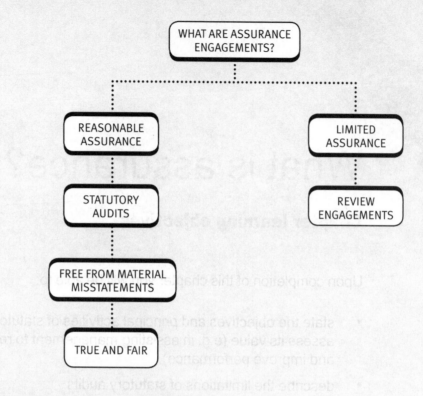

1 Why we need assurance

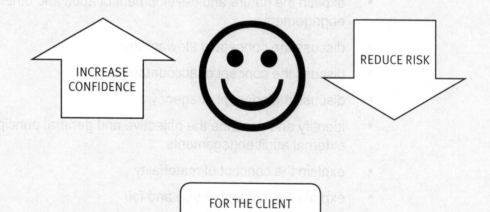

The purpose of assurance services is to:

- increase the confidence
- reduce the risk

of the user of those services.

2 How does assurance work?

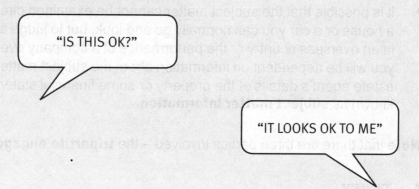

"IS THIS OK?"

"IT LOOKS OK TO ME"

Consider almost any purchase you have made, of almost anything – certainly anything which is important to you.

You will probably ask someone else's **opinion** before you buy.

- Do I look OK in these clothes?
- What does it taste like?

If the purchase is for something more expensive:

- a new computer
- a new car

you may well do some research in computer or motoring magazines first.

If the purchase was a new house, you would almost certainly get a surveyor to look at it to give you some confidence that it was structurally sound before you committed yourself to buy it.

All of these transactions have similar elements. The most obvious ones are:

- you – the potential **user** of the thing you want to buy
- the thing you want to buy – the **subject matter** of the transaction
- your friend, the magazine or the surveyor who tells you what they think – in a formal assurance context known as the **practitioner.**

However, there are at least two other elements to the transaction:

- the person supplying the goods or services – the **responsible party**
- your expectations – the **criteria** against which you will decide whether your purchase is worthwhile.

There **may** be one more thing:

- it is possible that the subject matter cannot be examined directly – with a house or a car you can normally go and look, but to judge a property in an overseas country or the performance of a company over a year, you will be dependent on information about the subject matter – the real estate agent's details of the property or some financial statements – known as **subject matter information.**

Note that there are three parties involved – the **tripartite engagement:**

- the user
- the responsible party
- the practitioner.

Note also that because the practitioner is offering a professional service (there is rather more to it than the "is this OK?" question above for which he or she expects to be paid a number of other issues arise:

- the need for competence
- the need for objectivity and independence
- the need for work to be carried out to expected standards.

All of these issues will be considered in the chapters which follow.

KAPLAN PUBLISHING

3 Assurance engagements

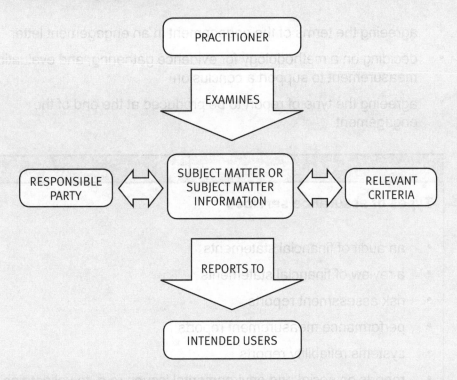

Expandable text - Assurance engagements

The International Framework for Assurance Engagements (the Framework) provides the overall guidance for carrying out assurance engagements. It states that the objective of an assurance engagement is:

- for a **practitioner** (usually a professional accountant) to evaluate or measure **subject matter** (e.g. the financial statements or an environmental report), that is the responsibility of another party (the **responsible party**, e.g. the board of directors of a company) against identified suitable **criteria**, (e.g. compliance with standards) so they can express a conclusion that provides the intended user with a level of assurance about that subject matter.

The engagement process usually involves:

- agreeing the terms of the engagement in an engagement letter

- deciding on a methodology for evidence gathering, and evaluation and measurement to support a conclusion

- agreeing the type of report to be produced at the end of the engagement.

Illustration 1 – Assurance engagements

Types of assurance services

- an audit of financial statements

- a review of financial statements

- risk assessment reports

- performance measurement reports

- systems reliability reports

- reports on social and environmental issues (e.g. to validate an employer's claims about being an equal opportunities employer or a company's claims about how 'green' it is)

- reviews of internal control

- best value/value for money work in private/public sector organisations.

4 Types of assurance engagement

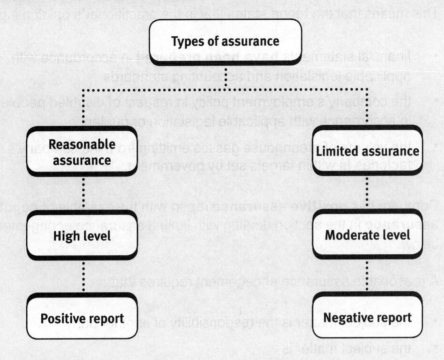

The Framework permits only two types of assurance engagement to be performed:

- a reasonable assurance engagement
- a limited assurance engagement.

Reasonable assurance engagements

In a reasonable assurance engagement, the practitioner

- gathers **sufficient appropriate evidence**

  We will look at this in detail in the chapters on audit evidence and audit procedures, but for now let us accept that it means that the practitioner has to do enough work to be able to draw rational conclusions

- concludes that the subject matter conforms in **all material respects** with identified suitable criteria

  Materiality is another concept which we will consider in detail later. The important point for you to understand is that the practitioner is not saying that everything is absolutely correct, but that, broadly speaking, the information given is reliable

- gives his report in the form of **positive assurance.**

Illustration 2 – Types of assurance engagement

This means that the report states that in the practitioner's opinion e.g.:

- financial statements **have been prepared** in accordance with applicable legislation and accounting standards
- the company's employment policy in respect of disabled people **is** in accordance with applicable legislation or guidance
- the volume of greenhouse gasses emitting from the company's factories **is** within targets set by government.

Compare this **positive assurance** report with the example of **negative assurance** in the section dealing with limited assurance engagements below.

A reasonable assurance engagement requires that:

- the subject matter is the responsibility of another party
- the subject matter is
    - identifiable
    - in a form that can be subjected to evidence gathering procedures
    - the practitioner is not aware of any reason for believing that a conclusion expressing a reasonable level of assurance about the subject matter based on suitable criteria cannot be expressed.

Limited assurance engagement

The practitioner:

- gathers sufficient appropriate evidence to be satisfied that the subject matter is plausible in the circumstances
- gives his report in the form of **negative assurance.**

A negative assurance report takes the form:

'nothing has come to our attention that causes us to believe that the financial statements are not prepared, in all material respects, in accordance with an applicable financial reporting framework'.

Not absolute assurance

It is not possible to give an absolute level of assurance due to:

* the lack of precision often associated with the subject matter – e.g. financial statements are often subject to estimation and judgement

* the nature, timing and extent of procedures

* the fact that evidence is usually persuasive rather than conclusive

* the fact that evidence is gathered on a test basis.

Even if everything reported on was examined and found to be satisfactory, there may be other items which should have been included – the **completeness** problem.

Illustration – reasonable assurance engagement

The most common example of a reasonable assurance engagement is an external audit. Using the terminology of the earlier paragraphs in this section, we can identify the elements of an audit engagement and the elements of an audit report.

The elements of an audit engagement are:

* a three party relationship between
    - a professional accountant (the auditor)
    - a responsible party (the board of directors of the company being audited)
    - intended users (the readers of the financial statements)

* a subject matter (the performance of the company)

* subject matter information (the annual financial statements)

* suitable criteria (the applicable financial reporting framework, e.g. national or international accounting standards and relevant law)

* sufficient appropriate evidence (the results of the tests that the auditor carries out to reach his conclusion)

* a written report (the audit report that is contained within the published financial statements).

External, statutory audit is the subject of the majority of the rest of this chapter, and, indeed, the majority of the syllabus and will therefore be dealt with in depth in the chapters that follow.

Illustration – limited assurance engagement

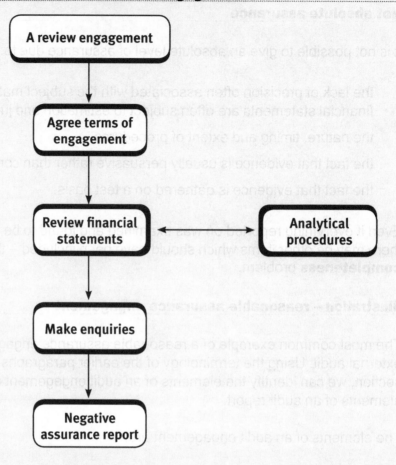

An example of a limited assurance engagement is an engagement to review financial statements.

Expandable Text - The objective of a review engagement

The IAASB has published an International Standard on Review Engagements 2400 (ISRE 2400) which sets out the terms of engagement and the type of procedures required for such an engagement.

The objective of a review engagement

The objective of a **review engagement** is to enable a practitioner to state whether, on the basis of procedures which do not provide all the evidence that would be required in an audit, anything that has come to the practitioner's attention that causes the practitioner to believe that the financial statements are not prepared, in all material respects, in accordance with an applicable financial reporting framework.

ISRE 2400

In a review engagement, therefore, the auditor gives **negative assurance**, reporting that he is not aware that anything is materially wrong.

Characteristics of a review engagement

A review engagement has all the attributes of any assurance engagement:

- the **practitioner** who conducts the work
- the **user** who commissioned the work
- a **responsible party**
- the **subject matter**
- the **subject matter information**
- **criteria**
- **sufficient appropriate evidence** which needs to be **documented**
- a **report.**

However, there are important differences between a review engagement and an audit.

- The practitioner is **not** carrying out an audit

- For an audit the user will always be the company's shareholders. Whereas for review engagement, the user could be whoever commissions the work e.g.:
  - a bank wanting to know whether to maintain existing or extend further credit facilities
  - the directors of the predator company in a takeover situation.

Expandable Text - Subject matter

- The subject matter will be the performance of the business and the subject matter information will be financial statements, but:
  - the period reviewed could be any period determined in the terms of engagement rather than the statutory reporting period subject to audit

  - the financial statements could be management accounts, profit forecasts or similar reports, rather than the statutory financial statements prepared under applicable law and accounting standards which are the subject of an audit.

- The criteria for audited financial statements are applicable law and accounting standards, but for a review engagement, the criteria will be whatever is agreed in the terms of engagement.

- What exactly constitutes sufficient appropriate evidence for an audit will take up the whole of chapters 9 and 10 and needs to be of the necessary quantity and quality to enable the auditor to form a positive opinion. For a review engagement the procedures undertaken will normally be:

    – analytical procedures on the financial statements – i.e. ensuring the figures and the relationships between them are in accordance with the reviewer's informed expectations

    – enquiries of management and other relevant parties

    – follow up procedures where analytical procedures and enquiries, indicate that material misstatements might be included in the financial statements

- An audit report gives positive assurance whereas the report after a review engagement gives negative assurance.

The level of assurance

The framework states that the level of assurance given by a reasonable assurance engagement is **high**, whereas a limited assurance engagement gives a **moderate** level of assurance.

There is no precise definition of what is meant by high or moderate in this context.

What is clear is that the confidence inspired in the user by the report produced after a reasonable assurance engagement is designed to be greater than the outcome of a limited assurance engagement.

It follows therefore that

- the procedures carried out will be more intensive
- the evidence gathered needs to be of higher quality

for a reasonable assurance engagement and this is reflected in the nature of the opinion given.

Test your understanding 1

What is the difference between a review and an audit?

(10 marks)

5 Reporting the outcome of assurance engagements

Expandable Text - Reporting to stakeholders

Reporting to stakeholders

We have seen that the outcome from any assurance engagement will be a report by the practitioner to the user.

We know that this report may give either:

*   positive or
*   negative

assurance.

We have also seen that the most common assurance engagement is the audit of a company's annual, statutory, financial statements.

The International Accounting Standards Board describes these financial statements as **'General Purpose'** financial statements, which recognises that, although, strictly speaking the auditor is reporting to the shareholders, many other **stakeholder** groups are interested in the outcome of the audit.

We will briefly consider who these stakeholders are and what other forms of report may be appropriate for their needs.

Who are the stakeholders of a company?

The **stakeholders** of a company are all those who are influenced by, or can influence, the company's decisions and actions. Examples of stakeholder groups are:

*   shareholders
*   management, i.e. the directors or other senior officials with an executive role
*   other employees
*   those charged with governance, i.e. those whose role is to supervise management to ensure that they operate the business in the interests of the shareholders and other stakeholders and not, purely in their own, personal interests. This will be dealt with in more depth in chapter 3.
*   customers

- suppliers
- the government
- lenders of funds
- community organisations, especially in the local neighbourhood.

Expandable Text - Other types of report

Other types of report

The financial statements give an account of the performance of the company over the relevant period and of management's stewardship of the company. As such they contain a great deal of information which is useful to many stakeholder groups other than the shareholders for whom they are intended.

Expandable Text - Reporting the outcome of assurance

Illustration – Reporting the outcome of assurance engagements

- Employees may be able to judge whether they think their levels of pay are adequate compared to the directors and results of the company.

- Those charged with governance can see whether they think management have struck the right balance between their own need for reward (remuneration, share options etc) and the needs of other stakeholders.

- Customers' suppliers and lenders can make judgements about whether the company has sufficient financial strengths for business relationships with it to be worthwhile.

- The government can decide whether the right amounts of tax have been paid etc.

Expandable Text - Reporting the outcome of assurance

Illustration – Reporting the outcome of assurance engagements

However, other forms of report may be more appropriate to some stakeholders in particular circumstances:

KAPLAN PUBLISHING

- Management and those charged with governance may need reports about how effective the company's systems are as a mechanism for producing financial statements, showing a true and fair view and safeguarding the company's assets – a systems or internal control review. The auditors usually produce a report like this, often called a management letter, as a by-product of the audit. (See chapter 8 on systems and controls.)

- Lenders may commission a report (often on a limited assurance basis) on the financial viability of a company seeking loan finance.

- The company's management may commission reports on the company's employment or environmental practices to satisfy the demands of employees and local community groups. (You may like to give some brief thought to the degree of objectivity of such reports and the real benefits of having an independent practitioner involved.)

6 The development of audit and other assurance engagements

Expandable Text - Historical background

Historical background

Although the role of the auditor has become much more sophisticated in recent times, the concept of auditing goes back many hundreds of years. There are records from ancient Egypt and Rome, showing that people were employed to review work done by tax collectors and estate managers. In medieval Britain, an independent auditor was employed by the feudal Barons to ensure that returns from tenant farmers accurately reflected revenues received from the estates. The emphasis was very much on the detection of fraud and other irregularities.

Incorporation and the relationship between the owners and managers of a business

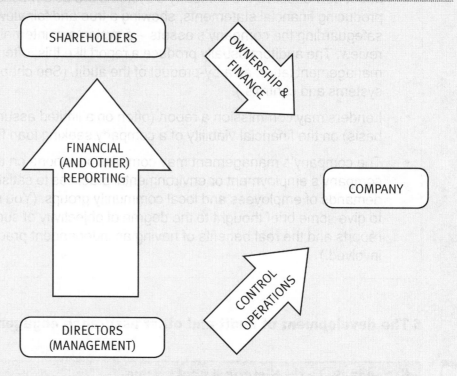

In most countries it is possible for businesses to be operated through companies – a process known as **incorporation.**

Incorporation may have two implications:

- the creation of a distinction between the owners of the business and the business itself, which may in turn lead to the business being run by managers who are distinct from its owners

- the granting of limited liability status so that, if the business fails, the owners only stand to lose a specific amount of money – hence the term **'limited'.** It is possible to have companies without limited liability status, but they are uncommon.

A legal framework was therefore needed for how companies should be operated

- to protect business owners from unscrupulous managers

- to protect the business world and the public at large from owners taking unfair advantage of limited liability status.

This in turn had two results:

- the legal requirement for accounts to be produced by management on a regular basis to account to the shareholders for their **stewardship** of the business

- the recognition of the need for these accounts to be checked in some way by someone independent of the managers – the auditor.

In most countries, therefore, companies generally require an audit. However, small or owner-managed companies are often exempt.

Stewardship is the responsibility to take good care of resources. A steward is a person entrusted with management of another person's property, for example, when one person is paid to look after another person's house while the owner goes abroad on holiday.

This relationship, where one person has a duty of care towards someone else is known as a **'Fiduciary relationship'.**

The steward is **accountable** for the way he carries out his role.

A fiduciary relationship is a relationship of 'good faith' such as that between the directors of a company and the shareholders of the company. There is a 'separation of ownership and control' in the sense that the shareholders own the company, while the directors take the decisions. The directors must take their decisions in the interests of the shareholders rather than in their own selfish personal interests.

Accountability means that people in positions of power can be held to account for their actions, i.e. they can be compelled to explain their decisions and can be criticised or punished if they have abused their position.

In a company this works as follows:

- It is the **shareholders** of the company who own the shares in the company and thus indirectly own the assets of the company.

- The **directors** are accountable to the shareholders and to society at large for:
  - making decisions on behalf of the company's owners (the shareholders)
  - using the assets of the company efficiently and effectively.

- The shareholders in turn have the right to remove the directors by voting in a general meeting and are likely to do this if they are dissatisfied with the decisions taken.

- Additionally, if the directors have acted illegally while running the company, they can be fined or even sent to jail.

Accountability is thus central to the concept of good **corporate governance** – the process of ensuring that companies are well run – which we will look at in more detail in chapter 3.

The concept of agency

Agency relationships occur when one party, the **principal**, employs another party, the **agent**, to perform a task on their behalf.

Modern organisational theory views an organisation as comprising various interest groups often called **stakeholders** (see above). The relationships between the various stakeholders in a company are often described in terms of **agency theory**. For example, directors can be seen as the agents of shareholders, employees as the agents of directors and external auditors as agents of shareholders.

Each principal needs to recognise that, although he is employing the agent, the agent will have interests of his own to protect and thus may not fully carry out the requirements of the principal – a conflict of interests may arise.

> ### Illustration 3 – Agency theory considerations
>
> For example, the directors have a duty of stewardship of the company's assets. However, they are also interested in their level of remuneration and, if this increases, the assets of the company go down. The decision to award directors pay increases may be in the hands of the directors themselves.

The role of the auditor

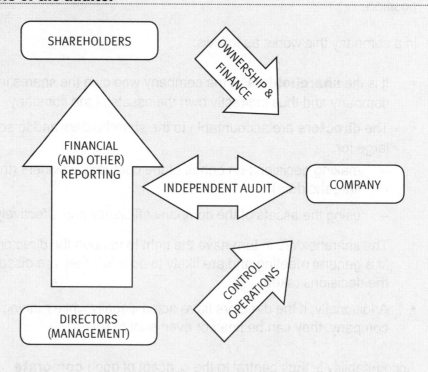

The concepts of:

- stewardship
- fiduciary duty
- accountability

are all very well.

The requirement for a company's management to produce financial statements giving an account of their stewardship of the company at regular intervals, certainly helps with the accountability concept.

But what if the financial statements contain errors, or worse, are fraudulent?

Clearly there was a need for some kind of independent validation of the financial statements – there was a need for **independent audit.**

There is a problem, however, in getting the balance right. If the auditors are expected to verify that the financial statements are correct this:

- may prove to be very expensive because of the amount of work required
- may prove to be unduly disruptive to the operation of the business.

Over time, therefore, the role of the auditor has been established as forming an independent opinion about:

- the truth and fairness of the financial statements (see below about true and fair)
- their compliance with legal and regulatory requirements.

In other words the audit

- has all the characteristics of an assurance engagement
- cannot provide absolute assurance.

The statutory audit is going through a period of criticism and change. Part of this is due to the perceived failure of auditors to notice companies about to collapse, often due to massive frauds and accounting irregularities – the obvious examples in the past decade are Barings Bank, Enron, WorldCom and Parmalat. Linked in to this, is the growing belief that many firms of auditors are unable to make objective judgements, because they are too close to the companies they audit. As objectivity is vitally important to any opinion which the auditor gives on the 'truth and fairness' of the financial statements, this is extremely important and will be looked at in depth in chapter 5 Ethics.

The contrast between the objective of the audit as a reasonable assurance engagement and the expectation that it should lead to the discovery of all errors and fraud is a phenomenon known as the **'expectation gap'**.

Test your understanding 2

What is the purpose of an audit?

(2 marks)

---

7 Audit engagements

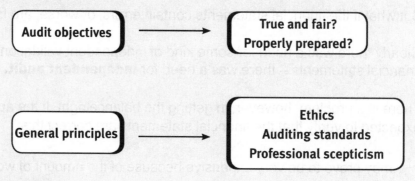

External audit

In most developed countries, all publicly quoted companies and all large companies are required by law to produce annual financial statements and have them audited by an external auditor. The majority of the syllabus is designed around this process.

Other organisations (e.g. small private companies, partnerships, etc.) may choose to be audited even if there is no legal requirement.

Objective of an external audit

The objective of an external audit engagement is to enable the auditor to express an opinion on whether the financial statements

- give a true and fair view (or present fairly in all material respects)

- are prepared, in all material respects, in accordance with an applicable financial reporting framework.

The financial reporting framework to be applied will vary from country to country.

General principles to be followed

The auditor should follow certain general principles in the conduct of an external audit.

- Compliance with applicable ethical principles, i.e. the IFAC Code of Ethics for Professional Accountants and the ethical pronouncements of the auditor's professional body (e.g. the ACCA's Rules of Professional Conduct) (See chapter 5).

- Compliance with applicable auditing standards, i.e. the International Auditing and Assurance Standards Board's (IAASB's) International Standards on Auditing (ISAs).

- Planning and performing the audit with an attitude of **professional scepticism** that recognises that the financial statements being audited may be materially misstated. For example, the auditor should not simply accept an explanation about a matter given by management. The auditor should seek further evidence about the matter that confirms or contradicts management's explanation.

8 Key concepts in the process of auditing

IT MAY BE TRUE

BUT IS IT FAIR?

AND WHAT IS THIS MATERIALITY STUFF ANYWAY?

As stated earlier in this chapter, an audit is designed to provide reasonable assurance that the financial statements taken as a whole are free from material misstatement and give a true and fair view.

The purpose of this section is to investigate the meaning of 'material misstatement' and 'true and fair view'. These are vitally important concepts, both in practice and for the purposes of the exam.

Materiality

Information is **material** if its omission or misstatement could influence the economic decisions of users taken on the basis of the financial statements.

IAASB Glossary of Terms

You have already seen that it is impossible for anyone to state that financial statements are precisely and absolutely correct. By stating that the accounts are free from material misstatement the auditor is saying that there are no alterations required that could alter the way in which someone might view/read the accounts (in other words, they are close enough to the truth!).

Expandable Text - Key concepts in the process of auditing

Illustration – Key concepts in the process of auditing

Material misstatement

Suppose that the correct income statement for Company X for the year just ended is as follows:

	$
Revenue	1,000,000
Cost of sales	(600,000)
Gross profit	400,000
Expenses	(300,000)
Net profit	100,000

If the accountant had added up the sales figure incorrectly for the year by $1,000, he would submit the following income statement to the auditors to be audited:

	$
Revenue	1,001,000
Cost of sales	(600,000)
Gross profit	401,000
Expenses	(300,000)
Net profit	101,000

When the auditors discover the error, they must decide whether this is a material misstatement.

- Will it influence the economic decisions of users?
- Will new investors be attracted to buy shares in the company because they are deceived by the over-statement of profits?

A judgement must be made in each particular circumstance, but a rule of thumb is that a misstatement of less than 10% of profit before tax is probably not material, while any amount greater than 10% of profit before tax is probably material. Here we have a misstatement of 1% of profit before tax, so it is very unlikely to be material in size.

We will look at audit materiality and how it might be calculated in more detail in chapter 6 Planning.

True and fair

In most countries the directors have a statutory duty to produce financial statements which give a true and fair view, and the auditors are required by law to report whether, in their opinion, the financial statements give a true and fair view. However, there is no official definition in the IAASB Glossary of Terms or in any individual ISA of the meaning of 'true and fair'.

'Truth' in accounting terms can be taken to mean not factually incorrect.

The word **fair** can have the following meanings:

- on the one hand clear, distinct and plain; and
- on the other impartial/unbiased, just and equitable.

Both can be considered relevant when fair is used in an accounting context.

Auditors should attempt to ensure that the financial statements which are the subject of the audit, present clearly and equitably the financial state of affairs of the enterprise. This suggests that in order to achieve the statutory true and fair view, it is necessary:

- to present certain information impartially
- that this data is shown in such a way that it is clearly understood by the user.

Limitations and benefits of statutory audits

Benefits

- High quality, reliable information circulates the market (gives investors faith and improves reputation of the market).

- Independent verification (management value having their business scrutinised).

- Reduces the risk of management bias, fraud and error (by acting as a deterrent).

- Enhances the creditability of the information (especially for raising finance and for the tax authorities).

- Deficiencies may be highlighted in the management letter.

Limitations

- Financial information includes subjective and judgemental matters.

- Inherent limitations of controls used as audit evidence.

- Representations from management may have to be relied upon as the only source of evidence in some areas.

- Evidence is persuasive not conclusive.

- Do not review 100% of the transactions.

9 Chapter summary

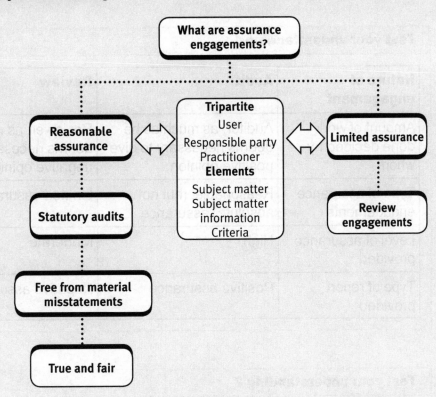

Test your understanding answers

Test your understanding 1

Nature of engagement	Audit	Review
Amount of work done decided by whom	Auditor, as much as he deems necessary to give positive opinion	Reviewer, as much as he deems necessary to give negative opinion
Type of assurance engagements	Reasonable, (but not absolute) assurance	Limited assurance
Level of assurance provided	High	Moderate
Type of report provided	Positive assurance	Negative assurance

Test your understanding 2

What is the purpose of an audit?	To provide confidence for the shareholders that the financial statements are true and fair. To reduce the risk of misstatement, as someone independent, qualified reviews and gives an opinion on the truth and fairness of the financial statements.

2

The rules and who sets them

Chapter learning objectives

Upon completion of this chapter you will be able to:

- describe the regulatory environment within which statutory audits take place

- explain the development and status of International Standards on Auditing

- explain the relationship between International Standards on Auditing and national auditing standards

- discuss the reasons and mechanisms for the regulation of auditors

- explain the statutory regulations governing the appointment, removal and resignation of auditors

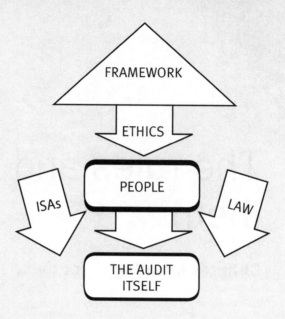

1 Conduct of audit

The conduct of audits is governed by three sets of rules:

- Codes of ethics
- Auditing Standards (ISAs)
- Company law.

In addition, Governments have increasingly tried to ensure that audits are conducted by people who are suitably qualified and whose work is of satisfactory quality – a process known as Audit Regulation.

2 Setting auditing standards

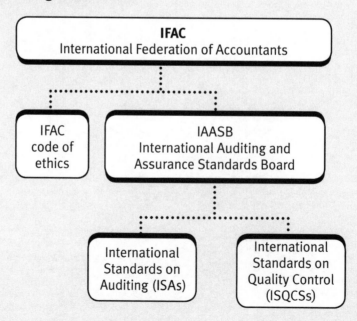

IFAC

The International Federation of Accountants (IFAC) is the global organisation for the accountancy profession. It was formed in 1977 and is based in New York. IFAC has more than 160 member bodies of accountants (including the ACCA), representing 2.5 million accountants from 120 separate countries.

IFAC's overall mission is to serve the public interest, strengthen the worldwide accountancy profession, and contribute to the development of strong international economies by establishing and promoting adherence to high-quality professional standards.

International standards on auditing (ISAs)

- Set by: **International Auditing and Assurance Standards Board (IAASB)**.

- IAASB is a subsidiary of the **International Federation of Accountants (IFAC)**.

- There are more than 30 ISAs.

All audits carried out under the laws of member states of the EU have had to be conducted under ISAs for all accounting periods beginning on or after 1 January 2005.

Expandable Text - The standard setting process

The standard setting process

- IAASB identifies new projects based on a review of auditing developments and suggestions from interested parties.

- IAASB then appoints a project task force to work up the detail of the standard.

- There may be consultation through a round table meeting or the issue of a consultation paper for comment.

- A draft standard is then produced for public exposure, usually for a period of 120 days, during which interested parties may submit their comments. Comments are a matter of public record and posted on the IAASB's website.

- The project task force considers the comments and amends the draft standard as appropriate.

> - If there are significant changes there may be another exposure period.
> - When the standard is finalised it is formally approved by a meeting of the IAASB at which there must be a quorum (minimum) of 12 members.

Other IFAC and IAASB activities

- IFAC publishes a code of ethics governing all assurance engagements carried out under IAASB standards.
- IAASB publishes International Standard on Quality Control 1 (ISQC1) setting out quality control principles for all assurance engagements (including audits) conducted under its standards.
- IAASB sets standards for other types of assurance engagements in addition to audits.

The relationship between international and national standards and regulation

Because IFAC is simply a grouping of accountancy bodies, it has no legal standing in individual countries. Countries therefore need to have arrangements in place for:

- regulating the audit profession
- implementing auditing standards.

National Regulatory bodies:

- enforce the implementation of auditing standards
- have disciplinary powers to enforce quality of audit work
- have rights to inspect audit files to monitor audit quality.

There are two possible schemes for regulation at the national level:

- self regulation by the audit/accountancy profession
- regulation by government or by some independent body set up by government for the purpose.

National standard setters

- may set their own auditing standards
- may adopt and implement ISAs, possibly after modifying them to suit national needs.

Following the decision by the EU to implement ISAs in all member states for all accounting periods beginning on or after 1 January 2005, countries with their own standard setting bodies such as the UK had to decide whether to:

- modify their own standards to bring them into line with ISAs

- adopt ISAs and modify them to suit national requirements.

In the UK the national standard setter – The Auditing Practices Board – decided to adopt and modify ISAs.

Test your understanding 1

(1) Describe the role of the IFAC?

(3 marks)

(2) Describe how ISAs and national auditing standards influence each other.

(2 marks)

3 The Law

Who needs an audit and why?

In most countries it is possible for businesses to be operated through companies – a process known as **incorporation**.

Expandable Text - Incorporation

Incorporation may have two implications.

- The creation of a distinction between the owners of the business and the business itself, which may in turn lead to the business being run by managers who are distinct from its owners.

- The granting of limited liability status so that, if the business fails, the owners only stand to lose a specific amount of money – hence the term '**limited**'. It is possible to have companies without limited liability status, but they are uncommon.

A legal framework was therefore needed for how companies should be operated.

- To protect business owners from unscrupulous managers.

- To protect the business world and the public at large from owners taking unfair advantage of limited liability status.

> This in turn had two results.
>
> - The legal requirement for accounts to be produced by management on a regular basis to account to the shareholders for their stewardship of the business.
>
> - The recognition of the need for these accounts to be checked in some way by someone independent of the managers – the auditor.

In most countries companies are generally required to carry out an audit, as it is a legal requirement. However, small or owner managed companies are often exempt (e.g. in UK, companies with annual turnover < £6.5 million).

Audit exemption

The main reasons for exempting small companies are:

- for owner-managed companies, those receiving the audit report are those running the company (and hence preparing the accounts!)

- the advice/value which accountants can add to a small company is more likely to concern other services, such as accounting and tax, rather than audit and which may also give rise to a conflict of interest under the ethics rules

- the impact of misstatements in the accounts of small companies is unlikely to be material to the wider economy

- given the above points, the audit fee and related disruption are seen as too great a cost for any benefits the audit might bring.

The auditor's duties

Fundamental duties are to:

- form an opinion on whether the financial statements give a true and fair view and are prepared in accordance with applicable reporting framework

- issue an audit report.

Matters implicit in the audit report and which the auditors therefore have a duty to check are as follows.

- Proper **R**eturns received from branches not visited by the auditor.

- The company's financial statements agree with the underlying **A**ccounting records.

- **P**roper accounting records have been kept.

- All necessary Information and explanations have been obtained.

- Information issued with the financial statements is consistent with the financial statements.

- Other information required by law, if not included in the financial statements, is included in the auditors' report.

   For example, in Britain this includes information about directors' pay and benefits and any amounts owed by the directors to the company.

The above are often called **exception reporting**.

The above 5 points will not be included in the audit report unless there is a problem.

Expandable Text - Other work required by Law

Other work required by law

Some countries require the auditors to carry out and report on other matters, e.g.:

- in Ireland – to check that the company's capital has not been eroded beyond certain limits

- in the UK, for listed companies, to report on compliance with the rules for the disclosure of Directors' Remuneration.

---

4 Who may act as auditor?

To be eligible to act as auditor, a person must be:

- a member of a Recognised Supervisory Body (RSB), e.g. ACCA

and

- allowed by the rules of that body to be an auditor

or

- someone directly authorised by the state.

Individuals who are authorised to conduct audit work may be:

- sole practitioners
- partners in a partnership
- members of an LLP
- directors of an audit company.

To be eligible to act as auditor, a firm must be:

- controlled by members of a suitably authorised supervisory body

or

- a firm directly authorised by the state.

NB. In some countries only individuals can be authorised to act as auditor and need to be directly authorised by the state.

5 Who may not act as auditor?

Excluded by law

The law in most countries excludes those involved with managing the company and those who have business or personal connections with them.

For example, in Britain the following are excluded by company law:

- an officer (Director or secretary) of the company
- an employee of the company
- a business partner or employee of the above.

Excluded by the ethics rules (See chapter 5 for more detail)

The IFAC and ACCA ethics rules and the APB Ethics Standards require Auditors to consider whether their objectivity and independence might be questioned by external parties because of:

- business relationships
- personal relationships
- long association with the client
- fee dependency
- non audit services provided.

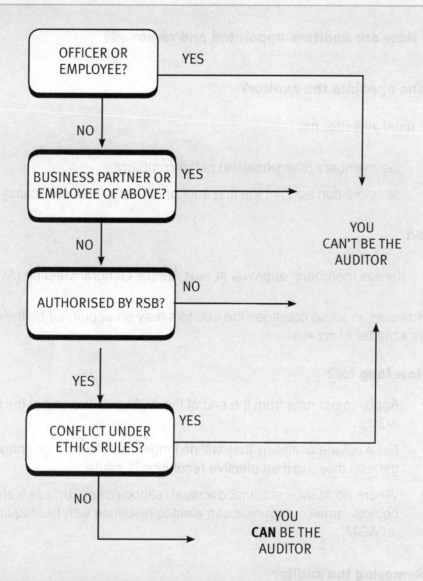

Who may and who may not be the auditor – some examples

- Mr Blue is a very experienced accountant and business consultant. He has a degree but no professional qualifications. He is **not** allowed to act as an auditor.

- Ms Green is a qualified ACCA but has always worked in the accounting and finance departments of large companies. She is **not** allowed to act as an auditor.

- Mr Red, FCCA is a partner in an accounting practice and is authorised by the ACCA to conduct audits. He **may be** allowed to act as an auditor.

- Mr Red's brother runs a successful company in the town and asks Mr Red to become his auditor. Mr Red must refuse because the relationship with his brother would bring his independence into question.

- Mr Red is also a non-executive director of a large local company Euphonium Ltd. Neither he, his firm, his partners, nor any members of his staff, may act as auditor for Euphonium Ltd.

6 How are auditors appointed and removed?

Who appoints the auditor?

In most jurisdictions:

- the members (shareholders) of the company
- directors can appoint the first auditor and fill a 'casual vacancy'

but

- needs members' approval at next Annual General Meeting (AGM).

However, in some countries the auditors may be appointed by the directors as a matter of course.

How long for?

- Appointment runs from the end of the AGM until the end of the next AGM.
- For a private company they will no longer have to hold an annual general meeting if an elective resolution is made.
- Where no AGM – automatic annual reappointment unless a shareholder objects (small companies can elect to dispense with the requirement for an AGM).

Removing the auditor

Arrangements for removing the auditor have to be structured in such a way that:

- the auditor has sufficiently secure tenure of office, to maintain independence of management
- incumbent auditors can be removed if there are doubts about their continuing abilities to carry out their duties effectively.

To enable this balance to be maintained, the removal of auditors can usually be achieved by a simple majority at a general meeting of the company, but with some safeguards such as a specified notice period, to prevent the resolution to remove the auditors being 'sprung' on the meeting.

In practice, if the auditors and management find it difficult to work together, the auditors will usually resign.

To prevent the circumstances of the resignation being hidden from the company's members, the auditors have to submit a statement of the circumstances surrounding their resignation.

The details which follow about the appointment and removal of the auditors are taken from UK law and practice, but give an example of the way these things are usually handled.

The auditor's responsibilities on appointment and removal

On appointment

- Obtain clearance from the client to write to the existing auditor (if denied, appointment should be declined).

- Write to the existing auditor asking if there are any reasons why the appointment should not be accepted

On removal/resignation

- Deposit at the company's registered office a statement of the circumstances connected with the removal/resignation or
- A statement that there are no such circumstances
- Deal promptly with requests for clearance from new auditors.

7 The auditor's rights

During the audit/continued appointment

- Access to the company's books and records.
- To receive information and explanations necessary for the audit.
- To receive notice of and attend any general meeting of members of the company.
- To be heard at such meetings on matters of concern to the auditor.

On resignation

- To request an Extraordinary General Meeting (EGM) of the company to explain the circumstances of the resignation.
- To require the company to circulate the notice of circumstances relating to the resignation.

Test your understanding 2

(1) List the statutory duties of the auditor?

(3 marks)

(2) Who may act as auditor of a company?

(2 marks)

(3) Who may not act as the auditor of a company?

(3 marks)

(4) Who may appoint the first auditors of a company?

(1 mark)

(5) What action should a company take if the auditor resigns prior to completion of his term of office?

(1 mark)
(10 marks)

---

8 Chapter summary

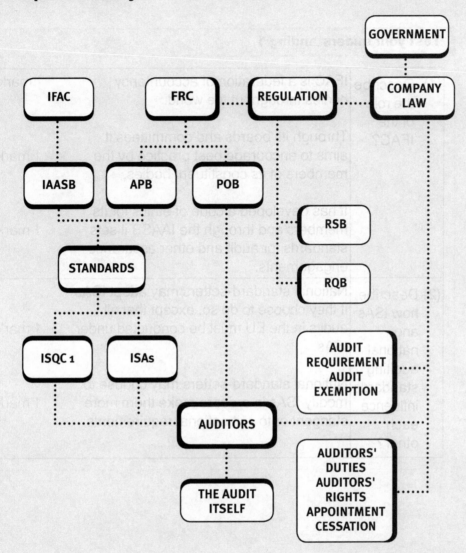

GOVERNMENT

IFAC — FRC — REGULATION — COMPANY LAW

IAASB — APB — POB

RSB

RQB

STANDARDS

ISQC 1 — ISAs

AUDIT REQUIREMENT / AUDIT EXEMPTION

AUDITORS

THE AUDIT ITSELF

AUDITORS' DUTIES / AUDITORS' RIGHTS / APPOINTMENT / CESSATION

Test your understanding answers

Test your understanding 1		
(1) Describe the role of the IFAC?	IFAC is a federation of accountancy bodies throughout the world.	1 mark
	Through its boards and committees it aims to encourage best practice by the members of its constituent bodies.	1 mark
	It has developed a code of ethics for its members and through the IAASB it sets standards for audit and other assurance engagements.	1 mark
(2) Describe how ISAs and national auditing standards influence each other?	National standard-setters may adopt ISAs if they choose to do so, except that all audits in the EU must be conducted under ISAs.	1 mark
	National standard-setters may choose to modify ISAs in order to make them more stringent or to suit national requirements.	1 mark

KAPLAN PUBLISHING

Test your understanding 2

(1)	List the statutory duties of the auditor?	To form an opinion on the financial statements of the company To issue an audit report Other duties imposed by law, e.g. to report if: • returns from branches have not been received • accounting records are inconsistent with the financial statements • information or explanations have not been received • proper accounting records have not been kept • disclosures regarding directors' pay and balances with the company have not been made • other information issued with the financial statements conflicts with those statements.	½ mark per point
(2)	Who may act as auditor of a company?	An individual authorised by the state to be an auditor or the members of a professional body authorised by the state.	1 mark 1 mark

(3)	Who may not act as the auditor of a company?	Those who are unable to comply with ethics rules with respect to independence, objectivity and competence to act as auditor for any particular client.	1 mark
		Those who are prohibited by law from acting as auditor for particular clients:	1 mark
		e.g. officers and employees of the company being audited and those closely associated with them – business partners, close relatives, etc.	1 mark
(4)	Who may appoint the first auditors of a company?	The directors or the members.	1 mark
(5)	What action should a company take if the auditor resigns prior to completion of his term of office?	Hold an EGM if so requested by the auditor	½ mark
		Circulate the auditors' notice of the circumstances surrounding the resignation.	½ mark

KAPLAN PUBLISHING

3

Corporate governance and internal audit

Chapter learning objectives

Upon completion of this chapter you will be able to:

- discuss the objective, relevance and importance of corporate governance

- discuss the provisions of international codes of corporate governance (the OECD Principles) that are most relevant to auditors

- describe good corporate governance requirements relating to directors' responsibilities and reporting responsibilities of auditors

- analyse the structure and roles of audit committees and discuss their drawbacks and limitations

- explain the importance of internal control and risk management

- discuss the factors to be taken into account when assessing the need for internal audit

- discuss the elements of best practice in the structure and operations of internal audit with reference to appropriate international Codes of Corporate Governance

- discuss the scope of internal audit and the limitations of the internal audit function

- explain the advantages and disadvantages of outsourcing internal audit

- describe and explain the format and content of internal audit review reports and other reports dealing with the enhancement of performance

- discuss the nature and purpose of internal audit assignments including:
  - value for money
  - IT
  - best value
  - financial
- discuss the nature and purpose of operational internal audit assignments including:
  - procurement
  - marketing
  - treasury
  - human resources management
- explain the types of audit report provided in internal audit assignments
- explain the process for producing an internal audit report.

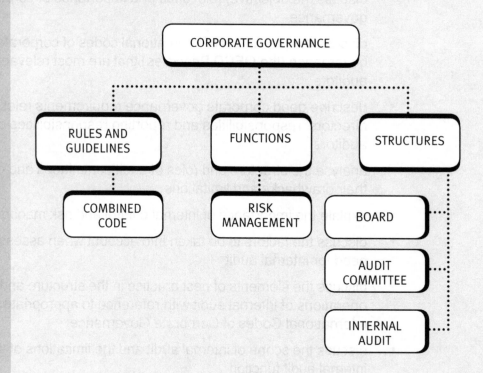

1 Introduction

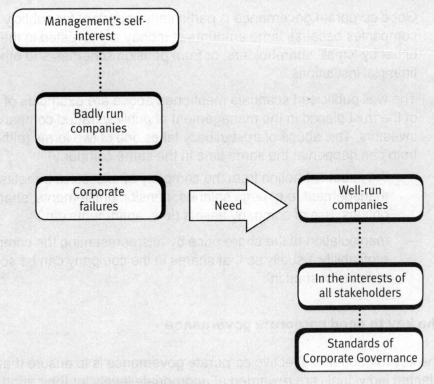

What is corporate governance?

Corporate governance is the means by which a company is operated and controlled.

It concerns such matters as:

- the responsibilities of directors
- the appropriate composition of the board of directors
- the necessity for good internal control – the necessity for an audit committee
- relationships with the external auditors.

Corporate governance is about ensuring that companies are run well in the interests of their shareholders and the wider community.

- The need to improve corporate governance came to prominence in the UK in the 1980s, following the high profile collapses of a number of large companies (Maxwell, Polly Peck, BCCI, etc).

- Poor standards of corporate governance had led to insufficient controls being in place to prevent wrongdoing in the US in the 1990s, as demonstrated by the collapses at Enron and WorldCom.

- The authorities internationally have now been working for a number of years to tighten up standards of corporate governance (see the section on OECD Principles below).

- Good corporate governance is particularly important for publicly traded companies because large amounts of money are invested in them, either by 'small' shareholders, or from pension schemes and other financial institutions.

- The well publicised scandals mentioned above are examples of abuse of the trust placed in the management of publicly traded companies by investors. This abuse of trust usually takes one of two forms (although both can happen at the same time in the same company):

  - the direct extraction from the company of excessive benefits by management, e.g. large salaries, pension entitlements, share options, use of company assets (jets, apartments etc.)

  - manipulation of the share price by misrepresenting the company's profitability, usually so that shares in the company can be sold or options 'cashed in'.

The key to good corporate governance

The key to good and effective corporate governance is to ensure that talented individuals are rewarded at appropriate levels for their effort and skill, whilst ensuring that they act in the best interests of the company and its stakeholders.

Responsibilities

- Maintaining satisfactory standards of corporate governance is the responsibility of those operating a company – its management and those appointed for the purpose of ensuring that it is well managed.

- Whilst the external auditors do **not** have responsibility for standards of corporate governance at audit clients, they **do** have an interest in a company's attitude and approach to the subject because:

  - they are concerned with the risk that a company's financial statements might be misstated – we will consider the technical meaning of assurance and audit risk later, but for now let us accept that it simply means the likelihood that a company's financial statements will contain errors.

  - if a company has good standards of corporate governance and is well managed, the risk of errors in the financial statements is reduced.

Auditors responsibility for reporting on corporate governance

- Listed companies following the Combined Code in the UK, or other applicable guidance in respect of corporate governance, must include a corporate governance statement in the annual report.

- The auditors are not required to 'audit' this statement but must review it for inconsistencies with other information contained within the annual report.

- If inconsistencies are found, there may be an impact on the audit report in two ways:
  - if the inconsistency highlights an error in the financial statements and the directors refuse to amend the error, the auditor will issue a qualified report

  - if the inconsistency highlights an error or misleading information in the corporate governance statement, the auditor will add an emphasis of matter paragraph to their report. This is not a qualification. It is included to bring the reader's attention to the matter.

- In the US, the requirements are more stringent. Sarbanes Oxley states that the auditors must attest as to whether the company has complied with corporate governance requirements. Therefore, they must give an opinion as to the effectiveness of the company's internal control system amongst other things. Therefore there is significantly more risk involved with auditing US listed companies who are covered by Sarbanes Oxley.

2 The OECD Principles of Corporate Governance

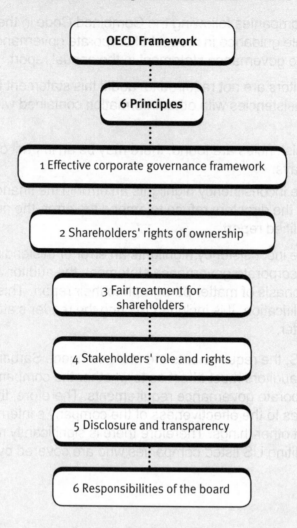

OECD Framework

6 Principles

1 Effective corporate governance framework

2 Shareholders' rights of ownership

3 Fair treatment for shareholders

4 Stakeholders' role and rights

5 Disclosure and transparency

6 Responsibilities of the board

Although there have always been well run companies as well as those where scandals have occurred, the fact that scandals **do** occur has led to the development of codes of practice for good corporate governance.

Often this is done by pressures exerted by stock exchanges on the companies whose shares are traded. In 1999 the Organisation for Economic Co-operation and Development, OECD, took a hand.

The OECD Principles of Corporate Governance are intended to:

- assist Member and non-Member governments in their efforts to evaluate and improve the legal, institutional and regulatory framework for corporate governance in their countries

- to provide guidance and suggestions for stock exchanges, investors, corporations, and other parties that have a role in the process of developing good corporate governance.

There are six Principles, each backed up by a number of sub principles. The Principles are reproduced below. Sub-principles relevant to the auditor are considered in section 'The OECD Principles and the audit' below`.

The OECD principles of corporate governance were first published in 1999 and were revised in 2004. Their focus is on publicly traded companies. However, to the extent they are deemed applicable, they are a useful tool to improve corporate governance in non-traded companies.

Expandable Text - Structure of the principles

Structure of the Principles

The six Principles:

(i) **Ensuring the basis for an effective corporate governance framework**

The corporate governance framework should promote transparent and efficient markets, be consistent with the rule of law and clearly articulate the division of responsibilities among different supervisory, regulatory and enforcement authorities. In other words, making sure everyone involved is aware of their individual responsibilities so no party is in doubt as to what they are accountable for.

(ii) **The rights of shareholders and key ownership functions**

The corporate governance framework should protect and facilitate the exercise of shareholders' rights. As we saw in chapter 1, the directors are the stewards of the company and should be acting in the best interests of the shareholders. However, the existence of the corporate collapses mentioned above proves that this isn't always the case and shareholders need protecting from such people.

(iii) **The equitable treatment of shareholders**

The corporate governance framework should ensure the equitable treatment of all shareholders, including minority and foreign shareholders. All shareholders should have the opportunity to obtain effective redress for violation of their rights.

(iv) **The role of stakeholders in corporate governance**

The corporate governance framework should recognise the rights of stakeholders established by law or through mutual agreements and encourage active co-operation between corporations and stakeholders in creating wealth, jobs, and the sustainability of financially sound enterprises.

(v) **Disclosure and transparency**

The corporate governance framework should ensure that timely and accurate disclosure is made on all material matters regarding the corporation, including the financial situation, performance, ownership and governance of the company. Therefore, the annual financial statements should be produced on a timely basis and include all matters of interest to the shareholders. For any matters of significance arising during the year, these should be communicated to the shareholders as appropriate.

(vi) **The responsibilities of the board**

The corporate governance framework should ensure the strategic guidance of the company, the effective monitoring of management by the board, and the board's accountability to the company and the shareholders. The introduction of audit committees and non executive directors on the board is the usual way for monitoring management. Non executive directors are not involved in the day to day running of the company and are therefore more independent. They can evaluate the effectiveness of the executive board on its merits and make sure they are carrying out their duties properly.

Expandable Text - The OECD principles and the audit

The OECD Principles and the audit

The principles suggest that external audit, conducted to professional standards, helps to maintain standards of corporate governance.

External audit is mentioned in sub-principles V.C. and V.D., within 'disclosure and transparency'.

Sub principle VC

'An annual audit should be conducted by an independent, competent and qualified auditor in order to provide an external and objective assurance to the board and shareholders that the financial statements fairly represent the financial position and performance of the company in all material respects.'

Sub principle VD

'External auditors should be accountable to the shareholders and owe a duty to the company to exercise due professional care in the conduct of the audit.'

Expandable Text - The OECD principles and the board

The OECD Principles and the board

The key responsibilities of the board are described in sub-principle VI.D (within 'the responsibilities of the board') as follows:

- **Reviewing and guiding corporate strategy**, major plans of action, risk policy, annual budgets and business plans; setting performance objectives; monitoring implementation and corporate performance, and overseeing major capital expenditures, acquisitions and divestitures.

- **Monitoring the effectiveness of the company's governance practices** and making changes as needed.

- **Selecting, compensating, monitoring and, when necessary, replacing key executives** and overseeing succession planning.

- **Aligning key executive and board remuneration** with the longer term interests of the company and its shareholders ensuring a formal and transparent board nomination and election process.

- Monitoring and managing **potential conflicts of interest of management, board members and shareholders**, including misuse of corporate assets and abuse in related party transactions.

- Ensuring the **integrity of the corporation's accounting and financial reporting systems**, including the independent audit, and that appropriate systems of control are in place, in particular, systems for risk management, financial and operational control, and compliance with the law and relevant standards.

- Overseeing the process of **disclosure and communications**.

The OECD principles use the term 'Board' primarily to mean the Supervisory board in a two tier board arrangement or the Non-executive directors and relevant sub committees in a unitary board structure (see below).

You can see from the bullet points above that the overall concern is with ensuring that the company is run for the benefit of its stakeholders and that management should be fairly rewarded for doing so.

Note also the reference to accounting and financial systems and external audit in the penultimate bullet point.

Expandable Text - The status of the OECD principles

The status of the OECD Principles

- The Principles represent a common basis that OECD Member countries consider essential for the development of good governance practice.

- They are intended to be concise, understandable and accessible to the international community.

- They are not intended to be a substitute for government or private sector initiatives to develop more detailed 'best practice' in governance.

For example, the International Corporate Governance Network (ICGN), founded in 1995 at the instigation of major institutional investors, represents investors, companies, financial intermediaries, academics and other parties interested in the development of global corporate governance practices. Its objective is to facilitate international dialogue on the issues concerned.

3 How companies are run

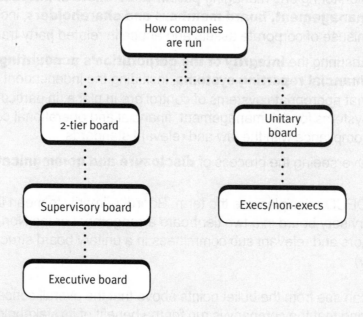

Boards of directors

Fundamentally corporate governance is about how a company is run by its management.

There are two basic models of board structure:

- The two tier board
- The unitary board.

Two tier board

In continental Europe, the 'two tier' board is common. This comprises:

- the executive board which takes day to day decisions in the running of the company.

- the supervisory board, which oversees the executive board and is made up of representatives of employees, investors and others. Major decisions are referred to the supervisory board for approval and which acts as a check on the actions of the executive board.

Disadvantage of this structure:

- The structure can be cumbersome and difficult to administer.

- The supervisory board may not have access to the information it needs on a sufficiently timely basis.

- It has been suggested that investors and some of the other stakeholders represented are reluctant to discuss many key issues in the presence of employees' representatives.

Unitary board

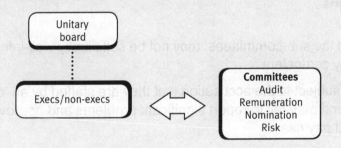

The structure of boards of directors is different in the UK and many other English-speaking countries.

The main points to note are:

- Single board of directors ('unitary' board).

- Distinction between executive and non-executive directors. (Executive directors are often referred to as 'management').

- Oversight of management's actions is by non-executive directors and by sub-committees, e.g. audit committee, remuneration committee.

Non-executive directors

Non-executive directors are usually employed on a part-time basis and do not take part in the routine executive management of the company.

Their role is as follows.

- Participation at board meetings.

- To provide experience and business contacts which strengthen the board.

- Membership of sub-committees, e.g. audit committee, which should be by independent and knowledgeable non-executive directors.

  Almost all listed companies in the UK and USA now have audit and remuneration committees as they are effectively a requirement of stock exchanges.

Advantages of participation by non-executive directors

- Oversight of the whole board.
- Often act as a 'corporate conscience'.
- They bring external expertise to the company.

Disadvantages

- They, and the sub-committees, may not be sufficiently well-informed or technically competent.

- They are subject to the accusation that they are staffed by an 'old boy' network and may fail to report significant problems and approve unjustified pay rises.

Enron provides a cautionary note as its audit committee proved incapable of preventing the wrongdoing of the executive directors.

4 Corporate governance in action

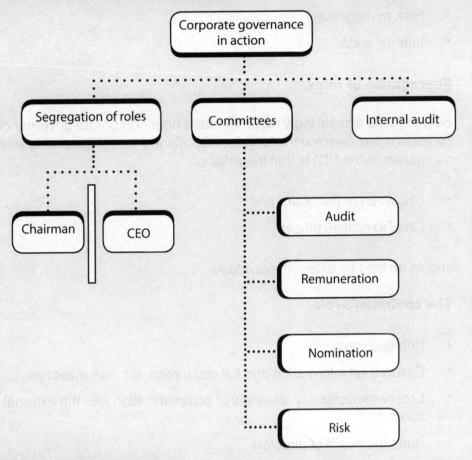

Challenges for companies

Some companies are struggling more than others to deal with an increasingly demanding corporate governance environment. For example:

- the need for an ongoing mechanism for managing risks presents challenges for the organisation
- no longer is it enough to send a checklist around once a year to meet corporate governance requirements, there must be evidence of an appropriate control culture and evidence of ongoing review
- this has resulted in increased importance of Audit Committees and the need for greater information to be made available to the Board and to the Audit Committee.

We will now look at four aspects of corporate governance in action which are regarded as crucial if public companies are to be well run.

- Segregation between the roles of chairman and chief executive officer (CEO).
- Audit Committees.

- Other Committees, e.g. nominations and remuneration.
- Risk management.
- Internal audit.

Segregation of roles

Best practice and strongly recommended under corporate governance codes in many jurisdictions (e.g. the 'Combined Code' governing listed companies in the UK) is that the roles of:

- Chairman of the board and
- Chief executive officer.

should be held by different individuals.

The chairman's role

- Non executive.
- Ensures full information and full discussion at board meetings.
- Ensures satisfactory channels of communication with the external auditors.
- Runs the board of directors.
- Ensures the effective operation of sub-committees of the board.

The Chief executive's role

- Ensures the effective operational functioning of the company.
- It is important that there is a distinction between the chief executive and chairman as effectively one person assuming both roles is a conflict of interests. The chief executive heads up the executive directors and the chairman heads up the non executives.
- Not only that, but having one person in both roles means there is a lot of power vested in that one person. They would be able to sway the decisions taken by the board. Those decisions may not be made in the best interests of the shareholders but in the best interests of the directors.

Audit committees

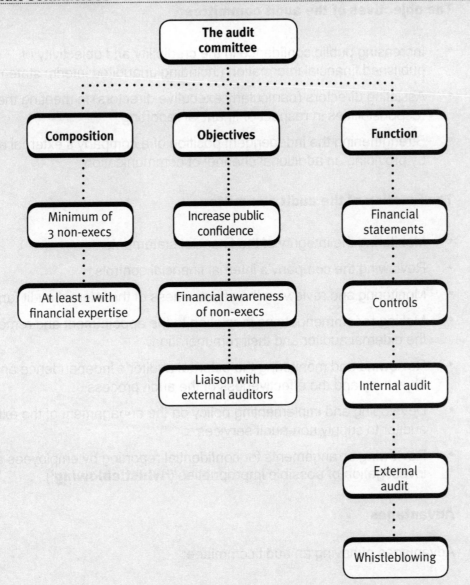

An audit committee is a committee consisting of non-executive directors which is able to view a company's affairs in a detached and independent way and liaise effectively between the main board of directors and the external auditors.

Best practice for listed companies:

- The company should have an audit committee of at least three non-executive directors (or, in the case of smaller companies, two).

- At least one member of the audit committee should have recent and relevant financial experience.

The objectives of the audit committee

- Increasing public confidence in the credibility and objectivity of published financial information (including unaudited interim statements).

- Assisting directors (particularly executive directors) in meeting their responsibilities in respect of financial reporting.

- Strengthening the independent position of a company's external auditor by providing an additional channel of communication.

The function of the audit committee

- Monitoring the integrity of the financial statements.

- Reviewing the company's internal financial controls.

- Monitoring and reviewing the effectiveness of the internal audit function.

- Making recommendations in relation to the appointment and removal of the external auditor and their remuneration.

- Reviewing and monitoring the external auditor's independence and objectivity and the effectiveness of the audit process.

- Developing and implementing policy on the engagement of the external auditor to supply non-audit services.

- Reviewing arrangements for confidential reporting by employees and investigation of possible improprieties (**'Whistleblowing'**).

Advantages

Advantages of having an audit committee:

- It provides the internal audit department with an independent reporting mechanism compared to reporting to the directors who may wish to hide or amend unfavourable internal audit reports.

- The audit committee will assist the internal auditor by ensuring that recommendations in internal audit reports are auctioned.

- Shareholder and public confidence in published financial information is enhanced because it has been reviewed by an independent committee.

- The committee helps the directors fulfil any obligations under corporate governance to implement and maintain an appropriate system of internal control within the company.

- The committee should assist in providing better communication between the directors, external auditors and management arranging meetings with the external auditor.

- Strengthens the independence of company's external auditor by providing a clear reporting structure and separate appointment mechanism from the board.

Disadvantages

Audit committees may lead to:

- fear that their purpose is to catch management out

- non-executive directors being over-burdened with detail

- a 'two-tier' board of directors

- additional cost in terms, at least, of time involved.

The audit committee and internal audit

Clearly, the functions of the audit committee are quite wide-reaching, therefore, it may be necessary to establish an internal audit function in order to help them fulfil their responsibilities.

Best practice is that the audit committee should:

- Ensure that the internal auditor has direct access to the board chairman and to the audit committee and is accountable to the audit committee.

- Review and assess the annual internal audit work plan.

- Receive periodic reports on the results of internal audit work.

- Review and monitor management's responsiveness to the internal auditor's findings and recommendations.

- Meet with the head of internal audit at least once a year without the presence of management.

- Monitor and assess the effectiveness of internal audit in the overall context of the company's risk management system.

Expandable Text - Other committees (outside the syllabus)

For completeness you should understand something about:

- The nomination committee.

- The remuneration committee.

Both of these committees have a crucial role in corporate governance because they determine who will run the company and how much they will be paid.

The intention is to introduce a measure of independence into the whole process.

There is an argument, however, that as the community of non-executive directors, even on a global basis, is a comparatively small one, it may happen that a non-executive director of company A may be the chief executive of company B, whose non-executive directors may include the CEO of company A. Hence the accusation that the community of non-executive directors is something of an 'old boys club'.

The nomination committee

The function of the nomination committee is to suggest suitable candidates for appointment to the board and other senior posts.

The nomination committee should ensure that the best person is chosen for the job. If there was not such a committee in place and the decision was down to one person, an inappropriate appointment could be made. It could be just that the person is not the most suitable. However, it could be that appointment is made of someone who will back up the person making the appointment in board decisions and it could be a way of fixing board votes.

The remuneration committee

The function of the remuneration committee is to determine fair rates of pay and other compensation – pension rights, share options etc – for management and other senior employees.

- The remuneration committee should ensure that directors are not paid excessive amounts.

- They should be paid enough to attract good people to the role but not too much.

- We have all seen stories in the newspaper where chief executives are paying themselves $10m salary per year and we might assume that to be excessive. However, if they could move to another company and be paid the same or more, the company is going to have to pay that amount of money to retain them.

- However, it is now deemed beneficial to pay people for good performance. Therefore many directors now receive a much lower salary, maybe $2m, which is topped up with a performance related bonus, which usually brings them back up to their $10m.

Again, it is beneficial to use a committee to set salaries so that the decision does not rest with one person. That person could take bribes from other directors for giving undeserved payrises.

5 Risk management

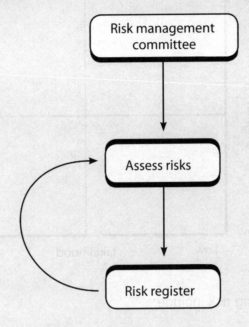

Business risk

All companies face risks of many kinds.

- The risk that products may become technologically obsolete.
- The risk of losing key staff.
- The risk of a catastrophic failure of IT systems.
- The risk of changes in government policy.
- The risk of fire or natural disaster.

Companies therefore need to:

- Identify potential risks and
- Decide on appropriate ways to minimise those risks.

Risk management in practice

The following are practical ways a company may address the issue:

- Identify the risks a company faces and maintain a risk register.
- Risks can be of many types – e.g. operational, financial, legal.
- The company should then assess the relative importance of each risk by scoring it on a combination of its likelihood and potential impact. This could take the form of a 'risk map'.

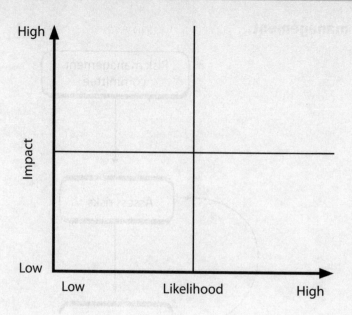

Ways of reducing risk include:

- insurance
- implementing better procedures, e.g. health and safety provisions outsourcing
- discontinuing especially risky activities
- improving staff training.

Sometimes the company may be forced to accept the risk as an inevitable part of its operations.

Internal controls and risk management

One way of minimising risk is to incorporate internal controls into a company's systems and procedures.

It is the director's responsibility to implement internal controls and the internal auditors role to monitor that these controls are being adhered to.

The external auditors test the systems to help confirm the financial statements.

We will look at internal controls in detail in chapter 8. Here it is sufficient for you to know that internal controls are any mechanisms built into a company's systems and procedures to reduce the risk of error or fraud.

Examples might be as follows.

- one person checking another person's work.
- locking important documents in a safe.
- restricting access to places with security systems.

- restricting access to information and systems held on computers through passwords etc.

- an internal audit department which checks that procedures and systems are operating as they should.

In other words, internal controls are a means of minimising risk. They may not be able to:

- prevent an earthquake destroying a factory

- prevent a competitor coming up with a product which makes your product obsolete.

But they may be able to:

- reduce the risk that financial statements contain material errors

- reduce the risk of theft of the company's assets

- reduce the risk that your business secrets might be handed over to a competitor.

Test your understanding 1

(1) **What is meant by corporate governance?**

(3 marks)

(2) **Why are external auditors interested in corporate governance?**

(3 marks)

(3) **What are the key things the OECD principles are intended to deliver?**

(5 marks)

(4) **Explain the difference between a unitary board of directors and a two-tier board.**

(2 marks)

(5) **Who should make up a typical audit committee?**

(1 mark)

(6) **What is the committee's role?**

(2 marks)

(7) **Why would a company need an audit committee if it has a good relationship with its external auditors?**

(4 marks)

(8) **A company has identified one of its major risks as loss of key staff. Explain:**

    (a) **what they should do as a result of this?**

    (b) **how they might reduce or even eliminate the risk?**

    (c) **why the auditor is interested in this, given that it is not a direct financial risk?**

(5 marks)

6 Internal audit and corporate governance

Expandable Text - Introduction - The need for internal audit

Introduction – the need for internal audit

We have seen that Corporate Governance is about ensuring that companies are run well in the interest of all stakeholders.

We have seen that two factors which contribute strongly to good corporate governance are:

- the way the board is structured
- mechanisms to ensure that management is subject to checks and balances which ensure that management's actions are reviewed either by:
  - a supervisory board or
  - non-executive directors acting through board sub-committees.

These mechanisms are referred to in the ISAs as 'Those charged with governance' and **ISA 260 Communication of audit matters with those charged with governance** is designed to ensure that the necessary channels of communication exist between the external auditors and those charged with governance.

All of this is all very well, however:

- the external auditors' role is to form an opinion on whether or not the statutory financial statements give a true or fair view and they cannot, indeed they must not, be involved in the operation of the business

- the role of those charged with governance is of a high level, supervisory nature, so that they too cannot become involved with monitoring the detail of how well the company is run.

Unfortunately, if no one considers how well the company is actually being run in practice, none of these mechanisms will have any impact.

There is therefore a need for a separate department within the company who can check that

- systems are operating effectively
- the procedures put in place to deliver good corporate governance really work.

In a large, public company, therefore there is a need for **internal audit**.

In a small, owner managed business there is unlikely to be a need for internal audit because the owners are able to exercise more direct control over operations, and are accountable to fewer stakeholders.

The need for internal audit, therefore will depend on:

- scale, diversity and complexity of activities
- number of employees
- cost/benefit considerations
- the desire of senior management to have assurance and advice on risk and control.

What do internal auditors do?

We have seen in chapter 1 that the function of auditors is to provide assurance, usually about financial information.

Internal auditors provide assurance to the company's management that:

- systems are operating effectively
- internal controls are effective
- laid down procedures are being followed
- financial and other information being produced is sound and reliable
- complying with the OECD.

Internal auditors do this by:

- carrying out assignments and

- producing reports of their findings.

If the internal audit department is to be effective in providing assurance it needs to be :

- sufficiently resourced in terms of budgets and people.

- well organised so that it has:
  - well developed work practices
  - competent staff who receive high quality training.

- independent and objective.

This last point needs some explanation. Because internal auditors:

- are employed by the company about which they are reporting (although see below about **outsourcing** the internal audit function).

- are often managed as part of the finance function

- will often have to report on the effectiveness of financial systems.

Care needs to be taken to ensure that their reports are independent and objective.

Expandable Text - Organised

How this is organised will depend on the scale of the organisation employing them, but usually it is necessary that:

- The head of internal audit has sufficient seniority within the organisation.

- Lines of communication ensure that internal audit reports, or at least a summary of them are reviewed by the audit committee or some other body which is independent of management.

- There should be 'whistleblowing' arrangements so that where circumstances demand, internal auditors can report directly to the company's chairman or the chair of the audit committee.

Expandable Text - Internal audit and corporate governance

Illustration – Internal audit and corporate governance

A local authority wants to assess whether it would be worthwhile to outsource the collection of garbage in its area. It asks its internal audit department to prepare a report summarising the full costs of its internally operated garbage collection service and to make a comparison with tenders from external contractors.

Consider the complexity of the task e.g.:

- assembling the data about:
    - staff costs
    - equipment costs (garbage trucks, etc.)
    - other external costs – use of sites to dump the garbage, etc.
- assessing the reliability of external contractors.
- making the cost comparison.

Then consider other factors.

- Internal auditors are assisting with a decision which could end in redundancy for some of their fellow employees.
- The local authority has a duty to obtain best value for local residents.

Expandable Text - Internal audit and corporate governance

Illustration - Internal audit and corporate governance

On a regular basis an internal audit team review the operation of the purchasing department of a manufacturing company to assess whether it is being conducted effectively. The team discovers that substantial contracts are regularly placed with suppliers in whom the plant manager and the local works accountant have an interest.

Clearly the internal audit team will need:

- work programmes not influenced by the plant manager or the local accountant, so that they are not diverted from finding the possible wrongdoing
- a communications channel, if there is any wrongdoing, so that their reports cannot be suppressed.

Limitations of the internal audit function

Reporting system

The chief internal auditor reports to the finance director. This limits the effectiveness of the internal audit reports as the finance director will also be responsible for some of the financial systems that the internal auditor is reporting on. Similarly, the chief internal auditor may soften or limit criticism in reports to avoid confrontation with the finance director.

To ensure independence, the internal audit should report to an audit committee.

Scope of work

The scope of work of internal audit is decided by the finance director in discussion with the chief internal auditor. This means that the finance director may try and influence the chief internal auditor regarding the areas that the internal audit department is auditing, possibly directing attention away from any contentious areas that the director does not want auditing.

To ensure independence, the scope of work of the internal audit department should be decided by the chief internal auditor, perhaps with the assistance of an audit committee.

Audit work

The chief internal auditor may audit their own work. This limits independence as the auditor is effectively auditing his own work, and may not therefore identify any mistakes.

To ensure independence, the chief internal auditor should not establish control systems in the company. However, where controls have already been established, another member of the internal audit should carry out the audit of that system to provide some limited independence.

Lengths of service of internal audit staff

All internal audit staff may have been employed for a long period of time. This may limit their effectiveness as they will be very familiar with the systems being reviewed and therefore may not be sufficiently objective to identify errors in those systems.

To ensure independence, the existing staff should be rotated into different areas of internal audit work and the chief internal auditor independently review the work carried out.

Appointment of chief internal auditor

The chief internal auditor is appointed by an executive director/CEO. Given that the CEO is responsible for the running of the company, it is possible that there will be bias in the appointment of the chief internal auditor; the CEO may appoint someone who he knows will not criticise his work or the company.

To ensure independence, the chief internal auditor should be appointed by an audit committee or at least the appointment agreed by the whole board.

- **Variation of standards** – not uniform across the profession.Compare this with external auditors who, on a global basis, have ISAs against which their performance can be measured.

- **Expectations gap** – problem of what the internal auditor's role is perceived to be.

- **Understanding of internal audit** – negative view by some – perhaps seen as 'checking up' on other employees on behalf of 'the bosses'.

Consideration of outsourcing the internal audit function

In common with other areas of a company's operations, the directors may consider that outsourcing the internal audit function represents better value than an in-house provision. Local government authorities are under particular pressure to ensure that all their services represent 'best value' and this may prompt them to decide to adopt a competitive tender approach.

Advantages

- Greater focus on cost and efficiency of the internal audit function.
- Staff may be drawn from a broader range of expertise.
- Risk of staff turnover is passed to the outsourcing firm.
- Specialist skills may be more readily available.
- Costs of employing permanent staff are avoided.
- May improve independence.
- Access to new market place technologies, e.g. audit methodology software without associated costs.
- Reduced management time in administering an in-house department.

Disadvantages

- Possible conflict of interest if provided by the external auditors (In some jurisdictions – e.g. the UK, the ethics rules specifically prohibit the external auditors from providing internal audit services).

- Pressure on the independence of the outsourced function due to, e.g. threat by management not to renew contract.

- Risk of lack of knowledge and understanding of the organisation's objectives, culture or business.

- The decision may be based on cost with the effectiveness of the function being reduced.

- Flexibility and availability may not be as high as with an in-house function.

- Lack of control over standard of service.

- Risk of blurring of roles between internal and external audit, losing credibility for both.

Minimising these risks

Some general procedures to minimise risks associated with outsourcing the internal audit function will include:

- Controls over acceptance of internal audit contracts to ensure no impact on independence or ethical issues.

- Regular reviews of the quality of audit work performed.

- Separate departments covering internal and external audit.

- Clearly agreed scope, responsibilities and reporting lines.

Performance measures, management information and risk reporting

- Procedure manuals for internal audit.

7 Internal audit assignments

We consider below examples of Internal Audit assignments.

In this section we look at generic types of assignment:

- Value for money/best value assignments.

- Assignments dealing with IT.

- Project auditing.
- Financial audit.

In the next section we will consider operational assignments – those which examine particular aspects of a business' operations.

Expandable Text - Value for money

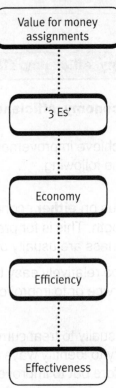

Value for money (VFM) is concerned with obtaining the best possible combination of services for the least resources. It is therefore the pursuit of 'Economy', 'Efficiency' and 'Effectiveness' – often referred to as the 3Es.

- **Economy** – least cost. Accomplishes objectives and goals at a cost commensurate with the risk.
- **Efficiency** – best use of resources. Accomplishes goals and objectives in an accurate and timely fashion with minimal use of resources.
- **Effectiveness** – best results. Providing assurance that the organisation objectives will be achieved.

Comparisons of value for money achieved by different organisations (or branches of the same organisation) are often made using performance indicators that provide a measure of economy, efficiency or effectiveness.

Examples of local government indicators are given below:

- Economy – cost of waste collection per local taxpayer.

- Efficiency – number of households (premises) covered per waste collector.

- Effectiveness – % of waste recycled measured against target for the year.

Expandable Text - Economy, efficiency, effectiveness

The tensions between economy, efficiency and effectiveness

It is not really possible to achieve improvements in these three aspects simultaneously. Consider the following:

- VFM audits tend to focus on **either** economy and efficiency **or** effectiveness, but not both. This is for practical reasons because economy and effectiveness are usually opposed to one another.

- For example, it would be relatively easy to reduce costs by providing a lower standard of service or to improve effectiveness by spending more.

- The solution to this is usually to treat current or target effectiveness levels as fixed and to try to identify ways of cutting costs or to aim to spend the same as before but to improve results in the process.

Measurement is also an issue:

- Audits frequently focus more on economy and efficiency. This is because it can be difficult to measure effectiveness.

- For example, measuring the effectiveness of a hospital department or a school might be difficult because there is no reliable measure of 'output'.

- Performance indicators such as the numbers of patients treated or the percentage of operations that are successful may be misleading.

- For example, one hospital might have a reputation for excellence in a particular area and have to treat the most seriously ill patients. Any statistical comparison with other hospitals might be affected by this.

- The push towards measuring and reporting performance has led to some unfortunate and unintended problems.

- For example, government targets to improve waiting times for hospital operations might mean that minor ailments are treated sooner than more serious ones, because the hospital managers may schedule treatments in the order that achieves the best statistics, rather than in order of clinical need.

Expandable Text - The 4Cs

- **Challenge** – review internally the different options for providing services and question the status quo.

- **Compare** – compare with other service providers to review options for improving performance.

- **Consult** – consult all users of services and those affected by services.

- **Compete** – demonstrate through performance management and continuous improvement that the most efficient and effective service is being provided.

Best value is a requirement for local authorities to demonstrate achievement of the '4C' principles, as well as demonstrating service delivery and meeting customer needs through effective performance management systems.

Expandable Text - Best value in the context of current trends

Best value in the context of current trends

- Reviewing best value is a major trend within local government, following an increasing focus on tendering for contracts and ensuring 'best value' through regulation and political pressures.

- Best value is changing the local government operating environment and affecting all services and activities. It cannot, therefore, be ignored by internal audit; in fact, auditors can play a major role in providing assurance on best value.

- These approaches differ in detail and emphasis but they share an important common theme – that of assisting the organisation to achieve its objectives by identifying and managing the risks to which it may be exposed. These risks may inhibit the achievement of objectives.

- The 4Cs apply equally to internal auditors, who must demonstrate best value in the provision of their own service, including appropriate consultations with customers and effective performance management information.

Expandable Text - Audit of information technology

In chapter 8 we consider the different strengths and weaknesses of manual and IT based systems.

We do this mainly from the external auditor's point of view, which is to ascertain whether or not the company's systems provide a reliable basis for the preparation of financial statements, and whether there are internal controls – mechanisms built into the systems – which are effective in reducing the risk of misstatement.

The internal audit approach to IT will cover all of this but with some additional objectives.

- Does the system represent value for money/best value.

- Were the controls over awarding contracts for IT installations effective?

Project auditing

Best value and IT assignments are really about looking at **processes** within the organisation and asking:

- were things done well?

- did the organisation achieve value for money?

Project auditing is about looking at a specific project:

- commissioning a new factory

- implementing new IT systems

KAPLAN PUBLISHING

and asking whether these were done well. So the focus is different and has more to do with:

- were the objectives achieved?
- was the project implemented efficiently?
- what lessons can be learned from any mistakes made?

A number of projects when taken together can become a programme.

Financial internal audit

Financial auditing was traditionally the main area of work for the internal audit department. It embraces

- the conventional tasks of examining records and evidence to support financial and management reporting in order to detect errors and prevent fraud
- analysing information, identifying trends and potentially significant variations from the norm.

8 Operational and internal audit assignments

Operational auditing covers:

- Examination and review of a business operation.
- The effectiveness of controls.
- Identification of areas for improvement in efficiency and performance including improving operational **economy**, **efficiency** and **effectiveness** – the **three Es** of value for money auditing.

We will now look at operational internal audit in practice, considering four of the main areas where such an approach is commonly used

- procurement
- marketing
- treasury
- human resources.

General approach

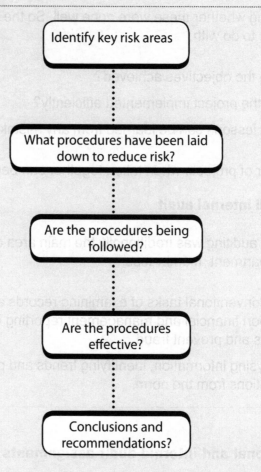

Identify key risk areas

What procedures have been laid down to reduce risk?

Are the procedures being followed?

Are the procedures effective?

Conclusions and recommendations?

In all cases, the audit work should be based on an approach which starts by identifying the objectives of the audit. These should focus on:

- the identification of the principal business risks involved which may prevent the organisation achieving its objectives
- the assessment of the extent to which controls are in place and are operating effectively in order to manage these risks.

The outcome of each assignment should be a report to management which appraises the control systems which are currently in place and which makes appropriate recommendations for improvement. This reporting aspect is dealt with later.

Expandable Text - Procurement

Procurement

Key question: Is the organisation achieving value for money in its purchases of goods and services?

Is it paying:

- the right people?
- the right amount?
- for the right goods and services?

This is one area where the interests of internal and external auditors are very similar and the detail of the work to be done and the issues to be considered will be dealt with in depth in chapter 8 on Systems and Controls, chapter 9 on Audit Evidence and chapter 10 on Audit Procedures.

Expandable Text - Marketing

Marketing

Definition

Marketing encompasses all aspects of the promotion and branding of an organisation, including branding and image management, product promotion and advertising and pricing.

Internal audit sometimes shies away from reviewing areas like marketing, because of the 'artistic' nature of the work carried out. However, there are significant risks associated with marketing that could damage the finances and/or reputation of the company or organisation.

For example, some major organisations have been significantly caught out by marketing campaigns offering free or reduced travel that have far outweighed the increased volume of sales. When organisations cannot meet the needs of such promotions, the damage to reputation can be enormous, as well as the impact on the bottom line.

An internal audit assignment into marketing activities will therefore consider:

- Did the campaign deliver on its objectives?

- Were the proper procedures followed in awarding any external contracts? (tenders, beauty parades etc).

- Possible breaches of regulatory requirements – this could be a particular risk in marketing campaigns that could result in fines or censure.

- Shareholder value lost or damage to reputation through poor brand image.

- Financial loss arising from poor cost control.

- Fraudulent practices.

- Excessive or inappropriate use of marketing entertainment.

The actual procedures to be undertaken will follow the usual pattern of planning and evidence gathering which are covered by later chapters.

Expandable Text - Treasury

Treasury

Treasury management: the process of managing cashflow and investments within an organisation to maximise the use of available finances.

Treasury is a high-risk area for many organisations but frequently an area where internal audit lacks specialist skills.

You are not expected to know the detail of treasury operations, but a simplified view of the possible risks would be to consider the organisation's exposure to:

- currency (forex) fluctuations

- interest rate fluctuations

- inflation (in some economies).

Treasury departments have ways of protecting against these risks – usually through a process known as **hedging**. Basically this means covering yourself so that if a particular currency or investment goes down in value you have an arrangement in place (usually through options to buy or sell currencies/investments) which will reduce your loss.

If these procedures are followed properly they should reduce the organisation's exposure to risk. If similar transactions are used speculatively, however, they can expose the organisation to additional, sometimes catastrophic risk.

Examples are:

- Barings Bank – the Nick Leeson 'Rogue Trader' case
- the Sumitomo copper trader case
- the Allied Irish Bank's North American forex operations.

You know that you are going to have to pay a supplier a large amount in a foreign currency in 6 month's time.

- If that currency weakens it would be sensible to wait until you need the currency before you buy it.
- If that currency strengthens, you would be better off buying it now.

What you can do, is buy the currency now and take an option to sell it in 6 month's time at a price, not too different from the price you pay now.

Then:

- If the currency falls you exercise your option and make a profit on the difference between the option price and the new cost of the currency in the open market.
- If the currency rises you simply do not exercise your option. – You will have lost the option, but if things have been done properly this will not be a great cost.

As with all things, risk cannot be eliminated altogether, but the organisation should have a 'rulebook' of laid down procedures and the internal audit team will need to check that these procedures have been followed.

Alternatively, Internal Audit may be asked to check whether the procedures were appropriate in the first place.

Expandable Text - Human Resources

Human resources

HR consists of a number of key areas:

- policy
- recruitment
- pay and benefits administration
- performance management
- training and development
- disciplinary and grievance
- leavers.

It is sometimes easy to focus on the financial areas such as payroll administration, but other areas of HR can be equally or more important to the future of the company.

Main areas of risk exposure:

- failure to identify and recruit the right skills
- setting up of 'ghost' employees
- inappropriate means of recruitment
- excessive reliance on consultants or contractors resulting in high costs and financial loss
- failure to document decision making on candidates for interview, resulting in vulnerability to challenge or legal action
- inaccurate or incomplete standing data on staff, resulting in failure to maximise potential of individuals
- failure to provide feedback to staff on performance
- over-reliance on small number of key staff or loss of key staff
- failure to provide training and development of staff
- inappropriate training and development
- incorrect or fraudulent payments to leavers
- leavers do not return company property on departure
- failure to understand reasons for leaving and address any underlying problems of staff morale
- inappropriate payments made to staff through fraud or error

KAPLAN PUBLISHING

- disciplinary procedures not carried out appropriately or in line with company or legal requirements – this could lead to an individual taking legal action resulting in damage to reputation and financial loss.

The pattern of work for HR assignments will follow that of other assignments:

- are the organisation's procedures being applied properly?

- are the procedures appropriate?

9 Internal audit reports

Key principles

Who is the report for?

With any report the most important person in the process is the reader **not** the writer.

- If the report does not address the objective of the assignment.

- If the recipient of the report cannot understand its recommendations and the reasoning behind them, then the report might as well never have been written.

The report should be customer focused, meeting organisational needs. The internal auditor should always be conscious of the organisational philosophy, management styles and reporting objectives.

Purpose and structure of the report

Although it is possible to set out a format for reports which represents good practice (see below), the purpose of any report is to summarise the results of the work undertaken, so that lessons can be learned and appropriate action taken.

The content of any report will be determined by the nature of the assignment (see the section on Internal Audit assignments above).

Short and sweet

Clear, concise, easy to read format will mean it is more likely to be read and understood.

Measurable/quantifiable outcomes

It is easy to recommend in a report that something should be improved, but without:

- clear recommendations about how this is to be done

- some way of measuring whether the recommendations have been successfully implemented

it is less likely that improvements will actually happen.

Prioritisation

The important content needs to be readily accessible, not buried in the back of an appendix somewhere.

Avoid surprises

Discuss with management as points arise. This will mean less argument over facts or detail when the draft report is issued and will allow management to take steps promptly.

Fairness

Balanced and constructive reporting will be welcomed by management and the organisation. For example, recognising where controls are good and how they could be used elsewhere within the organisation.

Ensure consistency across reports, particularly where 'ratings' are used. If management feel unfairly treated or criticised, they will respond negatively to the report.

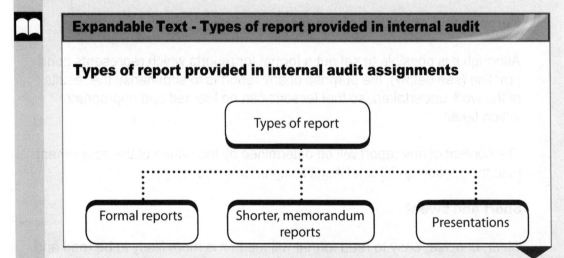

Expandable Text - Types of report provided in internal audit

Types of report provided in internal audit assignments

Formal reports

A formal written report is the traditional outcome from an internal audit assignment. A recommended structure for the report is set out in the following section.

Shorter memorandum reports

For:

- smaller scale assignments
- assignments where less depth is required
- assignments where results are required urgently
- a shorter, less formal report may be required.

Nevertheless, the same care needs to be taken with the contents of the report:

- **Addressees** – make sure it goes to the right people (especially reports delivered by email).
- **Subject matter** – make sure the purpose of the report is clear and that the objective is addressed by the content of the report.
- **Structure** – make sure the report is laid out well so that its message is communicated efficiently. Surprisingly, although this type of report is less formal, it still needs to be properly structured and lack of formality should not be taken as an excuse for sloppy drafting.

Presentations

- An oral presentation can have a greater impact than a written document.
- Usually, however, a presentation will be delivered as well as the main report and used to highlight the key findings.
- Although the delivery methods are clearly different, the structure of a presentation has much in common with the structure of a formal written report.

Expandable Text - Structure of a formal report

Structure of a formal report

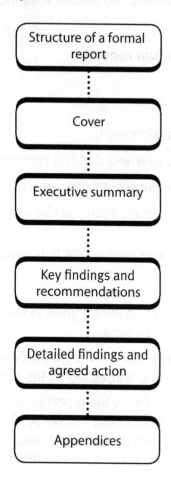

- Structure of a formal report
- Cover
- Executive summary
- Key findings and recommendations
- Detailed findings and agreed action
- Appendices

Cover of report

- Subject
- Distribution list
- Date of issue
- Any rating/evaluation.

The cover (or header for a shorter memorandum report) is surprisingly important:

- It makes sure the report goes to the right people.
- It can make the difference between the report being read or not – so the subject needs to be expressed carefully.

Executive Summary

The executive summary is like the whole report in miniature:

- It needs to grab the reader's attention to make sure they read the whole report.
- If the readers were only able to read the executive summary rather than all the detail of the whole report, they should still be able to come to the same conclusion and make the same decisions.

This is difficult in practice:

- Summarising is hard – how to get the essence of the whole report, without repeating everything.
- No one likes working through things twice – as the writer you have come to your conclusions and set them out in the report. To do it again, only shorter, is difficult, but it makes a fantastic difference to the reader.

In a memorandum report, because it should be quite short to start with, there will usually be a summary of findings rather than a full executive summary.

In a presentation, a very early slide should give the equivalent of the executive summary.

If a question is asking you to demonstrate how a report should be structured always mention the executive summary, but it will probably be sufficient to state that its content would be a summary of the rest of the report.

Key findings and recommendations

Summary of key findings and recommendations

Short, clear summaries of the key findings and recommendations from the review.

- The main problems found.
- Breaches in procedures.
- Ineffective procedures.

Detailed findings and agreed action

Setting out agreed actions, timescale for action and responsibilities for resolution will be the meat of the report for line management.

- Recommendations for solving the problem.
- Who is to carry out the necessary actions.
- Deadlines and timescales.

Assessment gradings or ratings

In some organisations, internal auditors provide 'ratings' of the area under review, indicating the extent of concern over control or the level of risk, or the standard of performance in the area being reviewed.

This can be in various forms:

- colours – red/amber/green
- numbers/letters – A, B, C or 1, 2, 3
- wording such as 'acceptable' or 'satisfactory' and 'unacceptable' or 'unsatisfactory'
- star ratings ×, ××, ×××.

Such ratings can help senior management:

- form an overall opinion of the organisation
- identify trends
- facilitate high level reporting.

However, they can also be seen negatively if they result in management responding defensively to a report on their area that will result in a poor rating.

The most important consideration for rating a report is the basis on which any evaluation or measure will be carried out. This needs to be consistent and clear to ensure credibility of the ratings. The rating may be against a formal control or risk model that drives out the decision or opinion.

Alternative formats

The report can be set out either in:

- Paragraph format
- Tabular format.

Paragraph format

- Identify issue.
- Summarise impact.
- Make recommendation.
- Action by and timescale.

Tabular format

Ref	Finding	Action:	Action by:	Date
1	Purchase invoices of 30 invoices reviewed, 10 had no evidence of being checked and had no supporting data to support payment. **Risk** Fraudulent payment. Payment may be made for goods or services not received. Damage to reputation.	All invoices will be supported by a corresponding purchase order and evidence of receipt of goods or service, with a check by the manager being evidenced prior to processing.	DCXX	By end of month

Appendices

- Explanations/further detail.
- Appropriate analysis to back up the matters referred to in the main body of the report.

Expandable Text - Process for producing an internal audit report

Process for producing an internal audit report

```
┌─────────────┐          ┌──────────────────────────┐
│             │          │ OBJECTIVES OF ASSIGNMENT │
│  PLANNING   │◄────────►│   TERMS OF REFERENCE     │
│             │          │  WHAT IS REQUIRED FOR THE│
└──────┬──────┘          │         REPORT           │
       │                 └──────────────────────────┘
       ▼                              ▲
┌─────────────┐                       │
│   GATHER    │                       │
│  EVIDENCE   │                       │
└──────┬──────┘                       │
       │                              │
       ▼                              │
┌─────────────┐                       │
│  SUMMARISE  │                       │
│ RESULTS OF  │                       │
│ WORK DONE   │                       │
└──────┬──────┘                       │
       │                              │
       ▼                              │
┌─────────────┐                       │
│    DRAW     │                       │
│ CONCLUSIONS │                       │
└──────┬──────┘                       │
       │                              │
       ▼                              │
┌─────────────┐                       │
│  FORMULATE  │                       │
│RECOMMENDATIONS│                     │
└──────┬──────┘                       │
       │                              │
       ▼                              │
┌─────────────┐          ┌──────────────┐
│    DRAFT    │◄────────►│  OBJECTIVES  │
│   REPORT    │          │  ACHIEVED?   │
└─────────────┘          └──────────────┘
```

As we have seen, the report is the culmination of the assignment and without the report the assignment might as well never have happened.

However, it is equally true to say that if the assignment was not properly planned and executed, there could be no report.

So the production process for the report begins with the planning of the assignment itself:

- At the planning stage ensure that the work to be done:
  - will fulfil the objective of the assignment
  - will dovetail with the requirements for the report.

After all the work has been done the report needs to be drafted:

- It needs to be well structured.

- It needs to be clear and concise.

- Wherever possible, discuss it with those who will be affected by it so that there are no surprises.

- Check back with the original objectives/terms of reference of the assignment to make sure that the report delivers what it was supposed to.

Test your understanding 2

(1) **What is the role of internal audit in maintaining standards of corporate governance?**

(5 marks)

(2) **List the types of activities normally carried out by internal audit departments.**

(6 marks)

(3) **List and explain the limitations of internal audit.**

(4 marks)

(4) **List two types of internal audit report.**

(1 mark)

10 Chapter summary

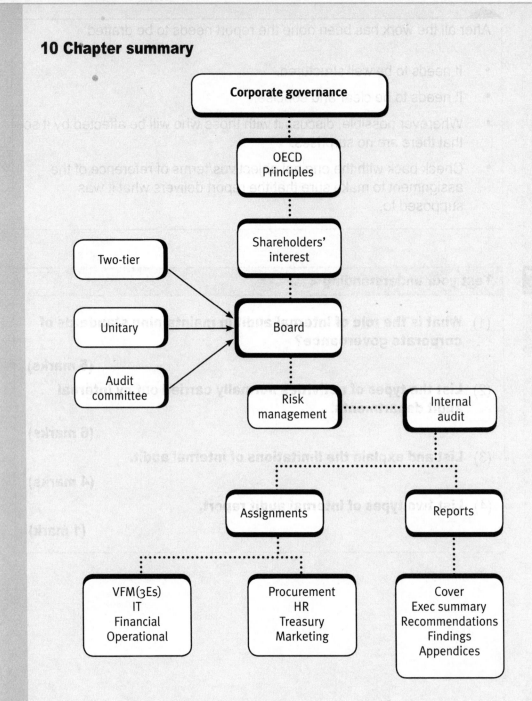

Test your understanding answers

Test your understanding 1

(1) What is meant by corporate governance?	The term corporate governance refers to the means by which a company is managed in the interests of all stakeholders. It will include consideration of:	
	(1) directors' responsibilities	1 mark
	(2) composition of the board of directors	1 mark
	(3) audit requirements (internal and external)	1 mark
(2) Why are the external auditors interested in corporate governance?	Corporate governance is the responsibility of the company's management and not its external auditors.	1 mark
	However, it is the responsibility of the external auditors to form an opinion on the truth and fairness of the company's financial statements.	1 mark
	If a company has good standards of corporate governance and is therefore managed well in the interests of all stakeholders, the auditors are likely to conclude that the risk of material misstatement in the financial statements is reduced.	1 mark
	As a result of this they may well be able to reduce the extent of the audit procedures they carry out.	1 mark

(3) What are the key things the OECD principles are intended to deliver?	A framework so that companies are governed well which should be beneficial to financial markets.	1 mark
	Fair treatment of all shareholders	1 mark
	Companies to be run in the interests of all stakeholders.	1 mark
	Transparency of disclosure about the company's performance and state of affairs.	1 mark
	The management of the company should carry out its role in the interest of all stakeholders.	1 mark
(4) Explain the difference between a unitary board of directors and a two-tier board?	**Unitary board** Single board of directors. Monitored by sub-committees and non-executive directors.	1 mark
	Two-tier board Two boards: Executive board (decision-makers) Monitored by supervisory board consisting of employees, investors etc.	1 mark
(5) Who should make up a typical audit committee?	The audit committee should be made up of non-executive directors and include someone with relevant financial experience.	1 mark
(6) What is the committee's role?	The audit committee provides a channel of communication between the internal workings of the company and the external auditor.	1 mark
	It also provides a channel of communication for employees who have concerns about the way the company is run.	1 mark

(7)	Why would a company need an audit committee if it has a good relationship with its external auditors?	A good relationship with external auditors is of immense help and support to an entity in complying with regulations, optimising controls and generally ensuring good corporate governance.	1 mark
		However, the existence of an audit committee will enhance the company's corporate governance profile by:	1 mark
		1 improving public confidence	1 mark
		2 providing further support to directors	
		3 strengthening the independence of the external auditor	1 mark
		4 improving internal procedures e.g. management accounting, & communication generally.	1 mark
			1 mark
(8)	A company has identified one of its major risks as loss of key staff. Explain • what they should do as a result of this? • how they might reduce or even eliminate the risk? • why the auditor is interested in this, given that it is not a direct financial risk?	The risk committee should discuss the issue and assess its seriousness in relation to its likelihood and potential impact. They should then decide what action is appropriate in order to manage the risk. This risk might be reduced by: • ensuring favourable employment packages for such individuals • ensuring training for other staff assists in case of succession issues • ensure key tasks are not carried out by just one person. The auditor must consider the possible impact of all significant risks as any of these could ultimately have financial consequences or going concern issues, hence impacting on the audit opinion.	1 mark 1 mark 1 mark 1 mark 1 mark

Test your understanding 2

(1) What is the role of internal audit in maintaining standards of corporate governance?	Internal audit is part of the organisational control of a business; it is one of the methods used by management to ensure the orderly and efficient running of the business as a whole and is part of the overall control environment.	1 mark
	A properly functioning internal audit department is part of good corporate governance, as recognised by national and international codes on corporate governance.	1 mark
	One of the objects of good corporate governance is to ensure that the needs of all stakeholders are met as far as possible and internal audit procedures meet the needs of the owners of the business, its employees, and the business community at large, as well as the needs of management. The main way in which internal audit exercises its functions is by enabling management to perform proper risk assessments in relation to corporate objectives by means of properly understanding the strengths and weaknesses in all of the control systems in the business.	2 marks
	The role of internal audit has expanded considerably in recent years and the scope of internal audit is no longer routine or low level; internal audit is involved at all levels of management and internal audit includes non-routine matters such as assisting in setting corporate objectives and assessing performance against them.	2 marks

(2)	List the types of activities normally carried out by internal audit departments.	The review of management, organisational, operational, accounting, internal control and other business systems.	1 mark
		Making recommendations in relation to the improvement of systems and monitoring the performance of systems against targets.	1 mark
		Performing value for money (economy, efficiency and effectiveness), best value and similar audits.	1 mark
		Compliance work involving the review of compliance with legislation, regulations and codes of practices.	1 mark
		The detailed examination of financial and operating data.	1 mark
		Special investigations, such as fraud investigations.	1 mark
(3)	List and explain the limitations of internal audit.	May not be independent.	1 mark
		There are no recognised standards for internal audit work.	1 mark
		There is an expectation gap in that internal audit cannot uncover every fraud or solve every problem, even though others in the organisation may wish it could.	1 mark
		Internal audit may be regarded as management's private police force, and as a result may not receive full co-operation from those whose work is being examined.	1 mark
(4)	List two types of internal audit report.	Formal report.	½ mark
		Shorter memorandum reports.	½ mark
		Presentations.	½ mark

4

Responsibilities

Chapter learning objectives

Upon completion of this chapter you will be able to:

- discuss the need for auditors to communicate with those charged with governance

- discuss the responsibilities of internal and external auditors for the prevention and detection of fraud and error

- compare and contrast the role of external and internal audit regarding audit planning and the collection of audit evidence

- compare and contrast the types of report provided by internal and external audit

- explain the importance of internal control and risk management.

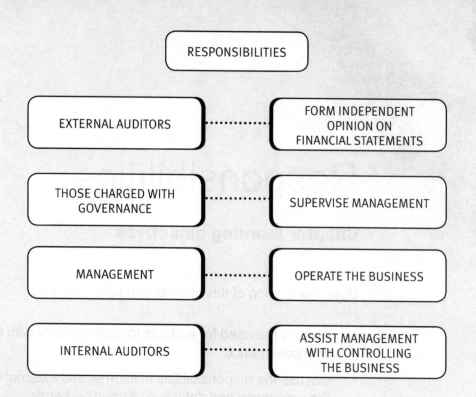

1 Introduction

The distinction between the responsibilities of a company's management and its external auditors is reasonably clear cut.

However, as we have seen in chapter 1, misconceptions, particularly about the role of audit, in the minds of the public, can lead to a phenomenon known as **the 'expectation gap'.**

2 Control structure within the organisation

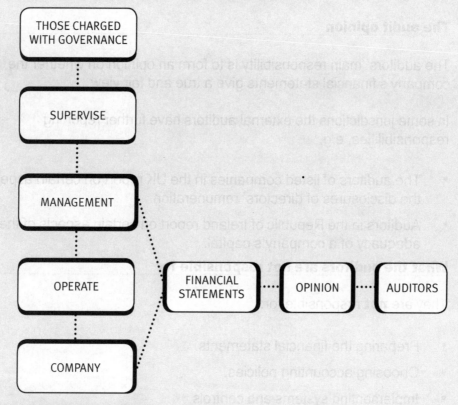

Corporate governance

As we have seen in chapter 3, a company's board of directors is responsible for operating the company in the interests of shareholders and other stakeholders.

To do this it needs to ensure that all the mechanisms for good corporate governance are in place.

Financial reporting

Management is responsible for preparing financial statements which give a true and fair view of the company's results for the period under review and its financial position at the year end.

In order to do this the directors are required to:

- Select suitable accounting policies and apply them consistently.

- Make judgements and estimates that are reasonable and prudent.

- Design and implement internal controls relevant to the preparation of financial statements and to prevent and detect fraud or error.

3 Responsibilities of the external auditors

The legal requirements for audit are set out in chapter 2.

The audit opinion

The auditors' main responsibility is to form an opinion on whether the company's financial statements give a true and fair view.

In some jurisdictions the external auditors have further reporting responsibilities, e.g.

- The auditors of listed companies in the UK report on certain aspects of the disclosures of directors' remuneration.

- Auditors in the Republic of Ireland report on certain aspects of the adequacy of a company's capital.

What the auditors are not responsible for

They are **not** responsible for:

- Preparing the financial statements.
- Choosing accounting policies.
- Implementing systems and controls.
- Establishing the mechanisms for ensuring that good standards of corporate governance are maintained.

Other responsibilities and consequences

As we shall see in the chapters which follow, the external auditors are responsible for:

- planning their work
- gathering sufficient appropriate audit evidence

so that the risk that they may come to the wrong conclusion is reduced to an appropriately low level.

As a consequence they are **interested** in:

- the quality of accounting systems from which the financial statements are produced
- the internal controls operated by the company to ensure that its financial information is as complete and accurate as possible
- the standards of corporate governance including the effectiveness of the internal audit function

because all of these factors will reduce the risk of misstatement in the financial statements.

But the establishment and maintenance of these things is the responsibility of the company and its management, **not** its auditors.

4 Communicating with those charged with governance

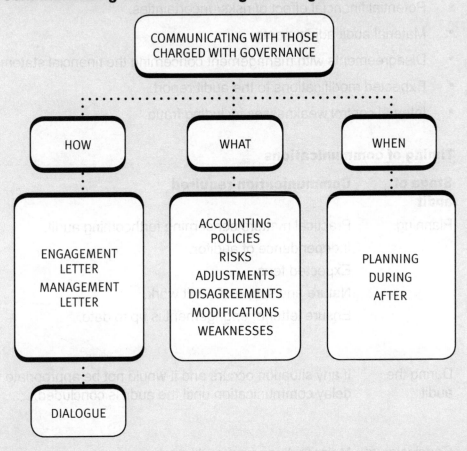

The ISAs and in particular ISA 260 Communication of audit matters with those charged with governance, places some further responsibilities on the external auditors.

The main forms of formal communication are:

- the letter of engagement (see chapter 5)
- the management letter – sent at the end of the audit.

There may also be ad hoc needs to communicate particular matters at other times.

Also, communication generally should be two-way and ongoing, with either party keeping the other informed about relevant matters throughout the year.

Summary of responsibilities

'Audit matters of governance' include:

- Effects of significant accounting policies.
- Potential financial effect of risks/uncertainties.
- Material audit adjustments.
- Disagreements with management concerning the financial statements.
- Expected modifications to the audit report.
- Internal control weaknesses including fraud.

Timing of communications

Stage of audit	Communication required
Planning	Practical matters concerning forthcoming audit. Independence of auditor. Expected fees. Nature and scope of audit work. Ensure letter of engagement is up to date.
During the audit	If any situation occurs and it would not be appropriate to delay communication until the audit is concluded.
Conclusion of audit	Major findings from audit work. Uncorrected misstatements. Qualitative aspects of accounting/reporting practices. Final draft of letter of representation. Expected modifications to audit report. Major internal control weaknesses.

5 Responsibilities of internal auditors

As we have seen in chapter 3, the internal auditors are either:

- employees of the organisation they are auditing; or
- contracted to provide internal audit services through an outsourcing arrangement.

It therefore follows that the precise responsibilities of internal auditors will be defined by whoever determines the objectives of the assignments they conduct.

ISA 610 Considering the work of Internal Audit gives the main activities of the internal audit function as:

- monitoring of internal control

- examination of financial and operating information

- review of the economy, efficiency and effectiveness of operations including non-financial controls of an entity

- review of compliance with laws, regulations and other external requirements and management policies and directives and other internal requirements

- special investigations into particular areas, for example, suspected fraud.

As assurance professionals, internal auditors are responsible for conducting their work bearing in mind the requirements for:

- independence

- objectivity

- compliance with the ethics rules of any professional body to which they belong.

6 Systems and controls

Directors need to **establish** suitable systems and controls to:

- safeguard the company's assets

- enable financial statements which give a true and fair view to be produced

- prevent and detect fraud.

External auditors need to **review** systems and controls to:

- assess whether the systems are such that the risk of material misstatement in the financial statements is reduced

- if they are to rely on the operation of controls in a system so that the extent of the procedures which they carry out will be reduced, they will need to test those controls and document their findings

- if the external auditors discover weaknesses in systems and controls, they will report their findings to those charged with governance in their management letter.

Internal auditors

* may be given an assignment to review systems and controls and to report to management about their effectiveness

* the nature of the work carried out by internal audit in these circumstances will be very similar to that performed by the external auditors and is covered in detail in chapter 8.

7 Fraud and error

What is fraud and error?

Major scandals that have affected the accounting profession in recent times have usually been as a result of fraud. Therefore, in order to maintain confidence in the profession it is important for the auditors and the directors to understand their role in the prevention and detection of fraud.

ISA 240 The Auditor's Responsibility to Consider Fraud in an Audit of Financial Statements gives the definition of:

Fraud – 'an intentional act involving the use of deception to obtain an unjust or illegal advantage'.

Error – 'an unintentional mistake' and could include accidental misapplication of accounting policies, oversights or misinterpretation of the facts.

Both affect the accuracy of the financial statements and as such are a concern for the external auditor.

Fraud can be further split into two types:

* fraudulent financial reporting – deliberately misstating the accounts to make the company look better/worse than it actually is

* misappropriation of assets – the theft of the company's assets such as cash or inventory.

The external auditor's responsibilities

As we have seen, the external auditor is responsible for identifying material misstatements in the financial statements in order to ensure that they give a true and fair view. By definition then, the external auditor is responsible for detecting any material fraud that may have occurred as this will lead to a material misstatement.

However, they have no specific responsibility with regard to immaterial fraud. As with immaterial errors, if they identify them they will be reported to those charged with governance, but there is no duty to identify them.

The auditor cannot guarantee that the financial statements are free of all fraud and error because of the inherent limitations of the audit, for example the use of sampling. The risks in respect of fraud are higher than those for error because of the possibility of concealment and collusion between staff.

In order to have a chance of detecting fraud the auditor must maintain an attitude of professional scepticism when performing their work which involves keeping an open mind to the possibility of fraud occurring (see chapter 6).

Under ISA 240, the auditors are required to consider the risks of material misstatement in the financial statements due to fraud when planning and performing their audit. If their work confirms that, or is unable to conclude whether, the financial statements are materially misstated as a result of fraud, the auditors need to consider the implications for their audit.

Reporting of fraud

The external auditor needs to be careful of their duty of confidentiality to their client, therefore before reporting to any external party, it is advisable to seek legal advice unless there is a legal requirement to report e.g. money laundering regulations.

If fraud is identified the auditor should report it to:

- the audit committee, if one exists, or
- to the highest level of management, or
- the shareholders if the fraud is being committed by the highest level of management and no audit committee is in place.

The directors' responsibilities

The **directors** have a primary responsibility for the prevention and detection of fraud.

As we have seen the directors are responsible for:

- safeguarding the company's assets and
- implementing an effective system of internal control.

If they have been effective in meeting these responsibilities fraud and error should not occur.

The directors should be aware of the potential for fraud and this should feature as an element of the risk assessment and corporate governance procedures. The audit committee should review these procedures to ensure that they are in place and working effectively. This will normally be done in conjunction with the internal auditors.

Internal auditors may be given an assignment:

* to assess the likelihood of fraud, or if a fraud has been discovered,
* to assess its consequences and
* to make recommendations for prevention in the future.

Expandable Text - Planning audit assignments

Planning audit assignments
External audit

The whole of chapter 6 is devoted to the planning of audit assignments.

As assurance practitioners, both external and internal auditors will need to plan their work so that they gather sufficient, appropriate audit evidence, in keeping with the objectives of the assignment.

However, because the focus of the external audit is on ensuring that the financial statements

* give a true and fair view
* are free from material misstatement
* are properly prepared in accordance with the relevant reporting framework

the planning of the external auditors work will be done with this in mind.

Internal audit

Internal auditors need to plan their work so that they achieve the objective of the assignment.

Whilst all statutory external audits conducted under ISAs are risk based in their approach, some internal audit assignments may be procedural in nature.

In other words, that the audit team will follow a series of predetermined procedures that are not flexed depending on the possible risk of errors occurring in the specific circumstances of the assignment.

Who does the planning?

As we know, external auditors are **independent** so they must be in control of planning their own work, in accordance with the objectives above.

Internal auditors' work may be programmed for them by management so that they focus on the areas thought to be most important by the board and those charged with governance.

However, it adds to the strength of corporate governance if the internal audit function has a degree of independence in the selection and objectives of its assignments.

Expandable Text - Evidence

Evidence

- The general rule for all assurance engagements is that the practitioner should gather sufficient appropriate evidence to support the opinion in the report which is the outcome of the assignment. chapters 9 and 10 look at audit evidence and audit procedures in detail.

- ISA 330 states that under ISAs the auditor gathers evidence which addresses the risk of misstatement as assessed during the planning process and in the light of evidence gathered subsequently.

The external auditor, therefore is always governed by this when deciding what evidence is appropriate.

As we have seen above, the internal auditor may have different objectives, depending on the nature of the assignment.

Expandable Text - Illustration - Evidence

Illustration – Evidence

Take the example of non current assets

- The **external auditor** is concerned with whether the figures for non current assets are materially misstated. So the auditor may check purchase prices against invoices, check depreciation is applied properly and physically inspect some assets, all on a test basis, and may therefore conclude that the figure for non current assets is materially correct.

- The **internal auditor** may have an assignment to ensure that the plant register at a particular factory is up to date, and so will need to check that every item recorded exists and that all machines on the factory floor are recorded. The auditor may or may not be concerned with values, depending on the nature of the assignment.

Expandable Text - Reporting

Reporting

We have seen in chapter 3 that the report produced by the internal auditor, is determined by the nature of the assignment (there is a bit of a theme developing here!).

The external auditor's report on financial statements is determined by statute and by ISAs and will be examined in depth in chapter 12. Basically, auditors can issue an unqualified – satisfactory – report or a qualified – unsatisfactory – report.

The external auditor may also in appropriate circumstances produce a management letter which we will look at in more detail in chapter 8.

KAPLAN PUBLISHING

Test your understanding 1

Whose responsibility are the following:

- **Preparation of accounts.**

  (½ mark)

- **Undertaking the risk assessment exercise.**

  (½ mark)

- **Detection of fraud.**

  (½ mark)

- **Reporting on controls.**

  (½ mark)

Test your understanding 2

List matters should be communicated to those charged with governance following the conclusion of the audit?

(3 marks)

8 Chapter summary

```
┌─────────────────┐   ┌─────────────────┐   ┌─────────────────┐
│   MANAGEMENT    │   │ INTERNAL AUDIT  │   │ EXTERNAL AUDIT  │
└─────────────────┘   └─────────────────┘   └─────────────────┘
         ┆                     ┆                     ┆
┌─────────────────┐   ┌─────────────────┐   ┌─────────────────┐
│ RESPONSIBLE FOR │   │ RESPONSIBLE FOR │   │ RESPONSIBLE FOR │
└─────────────────┘   └─────────────────┘   └─────────────────┘
         ┆                     ┆                     ┆
┌─────────────────┐   ┌─────────────────┐   ┌─────────────────┐
│   PREPARING     │   │                 │   │ FORMING OPINION │
│   FINANCIAL     │   │   ASSISTING     │   │  ON FINANCIAL   │
│   STATEMENTS    │   │  MANAGEMENT     │   │   STATEMENTS    │
└─────────────────┘   └─────────────────┘   └─────────────────┘
         ┆                     ┆                     ┆
┌─────────────────┐   ┌─────────────────┐   ┌─────────────────┐
│  IMPLEMENTING   │   │     DRIVES      │   │     DRIVES      │
│  SYSTEMS AND    │   └─────────────────┘   └─────────────────┘
│   CONTROLS      │            ┆                     ┆
└─────────────────┘       ┌──────────────────────────────┐
         ┆                │          PLANNING            │
┌─────────────────┐       └──────────────────────────────┘
│ PREVENTING FRAUD│            ┆                     ┆
│   AND ERROR     │       ┌──────────────────────────────┐
└─────────────────┘       │          EVIDENCE            │
                          └──────────────────────────────┘
                               ┆                     ┆
                          ┌──────────────────────────────┐
                          │         REPORTING            │
                          └──────────────────────────────┘
```

Test your understanding answers

Test your understanding 1

- Directors.   ½ mark
- Directors/management/outsourced/internal auditors.   ½ mark
- Directors.   ½ mark
- External/internal auditor.   ½ mark

Test your understanding 2

The auditor will include in his post-audit communication to those charged with governance:

- Significant audit findings.   ½ mark
- Whether the audit report is likely to be modified.   ½ mark
- Control weaknesses (with explanations of their potential impact).   ½ mark
- Uncorrected misstatements – unless trivial.   ½ mark
- His views on the qualitative aspects of the entity's accounting practices and financial reporting.   ½ mark
- Final draft of letter of representation.   ½ mark
- Any other matters of governance interest/issues required by other ISAs.   ½ mark

Ethics and acceptance of appointment

Chapter learning objectives

When you complete this chapter you will be able to:

- define and apply the fundamental principles of professional ethics of integrity, objectivity, professional competence and due care, confidentiality and professional behaviour

- define and apply the conceptual framework

- discuss the sources of, and enforcement mechanisms associated with, ACCA's Code of Ethics and Conduct

- discuss the requirements of professional ethics and other requirements in relation to the acceptance of new audit engagements

- discuss the process by which an auditor obtains an audit engagement

- explain the importance and state their contents of engagement letters.

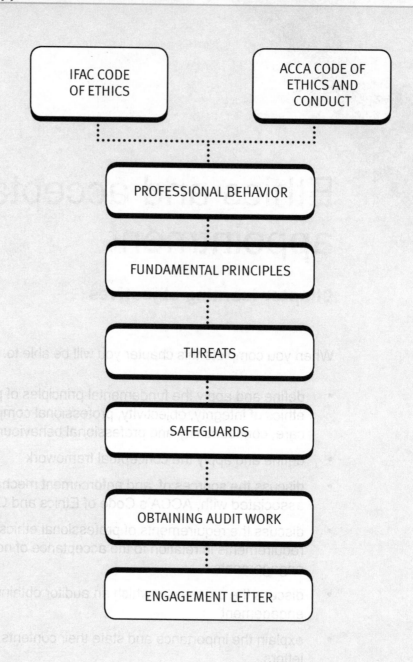

1 Introduction – the need for professional ethics

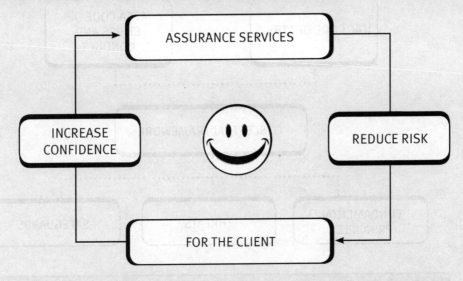

We have seen in chapter 1 that the purpose of assurance engagements is to increase the confidence of end users by reducing their level of risk.

It follows from this that the user needs to trust the professional.

In the light of the various corporate scandals which have occurred in the past decade – Enron, Worldcom etc. – but which have happened for decades, even centuries, there is a need for a basis for this level of trust.

*   The **user** needs to believe that assurance practitioners act in accordance with a code of ethics, and

*   the **practitioner** needs a code of ethics to make sure that he or she is worthy of that level of trust.

In order to be trusted the auditor needs to be **independent** of their client. Independence is defined in APB Ethical Standard 1 as 'freedom from situations and relationships which make it probable that a reasonable and informed third party would conclude that objectivity either is impaired or could be impaired.'

2 The IFAC and ACCA codes and the conceptual framework

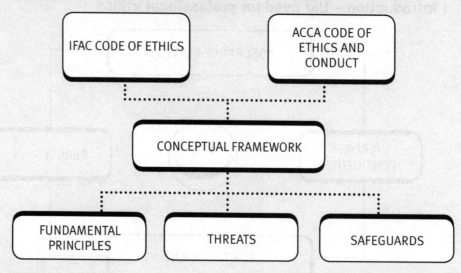

Expandable Text - IFAC

We have seen in chapter 2 that IFAC's membership consists of accountancy bodies throughout the world and that through the IAASB it is responsible for issuing ISAs and other standards for assurance engagements.

IFAC has also issued a code of ethics, as has the ACCA. The ACCA Code of Ethics is covered in this chapter however, both the IFAC and ACCA codes have the same roots and are, to all intents and purposes identical.

Both follow a conceptual framework which identifies:

* fundamental principles of ethical behaviour
* potential threats to ethical behaviour
* possible safeguards which can be implemented to counter the threats.

A conceptual framework relies on a principles rather than a rules based approach. That means that the spirit of the code is followed rather than a strict set of rules. It is guidance so the actual application will depend on the individual circumstances of a specific situation.

You should remember that sometimes the only viable safeguard is not to accept an assurance engagement, or to resign from it.

Giving the framework some teeth

The framework and principles would be of little use if they could not be enforced.

KAPLAN PUBLISHING

Professional bodies like the ACCA therefore reserve the right to discipline members who infringe the rules through a process of:

- Disciplinary hearings which can result in:
  - fines
  - suspension of membership
  - withdrawal of membership.

3 The fundamental principles

THE FUNDAMENTAL PRINCIPLES

Objectivity
Professional behaviour
Professional competence and due care
Integrity
Confidentiality

The formal definitions of the fundamental principles are as follows:

- **Objectivity**: Members should <u>not allow bias</u>, conflicts of interest or undue influence of others to override professional or business judgements.

- **Professional behaviour**: Members should comply with relevant laws and regulations and should avoid any action that <u>discredits</u> the profession.

- **Professional competence and due care**: Members have a <u>continuing duty</u> to maintain professional <u>knowledge</u> and skill at a level required to ensure that a client or employer <u>receives competent</u> professional <u>service</u> based on current developments in practice, legislation and techniques.

  Members should <u>act diligently</u> and in accordance with applicable technical and professional standards when providing professional services.

- **Integrity**: Members should be <u>straightforward</u> and <u>honest</u> in all professional and business relationships.

- **Confidentiality**: Members should respect the confidentiality of information acquired as a result of professional and business relationships and should <u>not disclose</u> any such information to third parties <u>without</u> proper and specific <u>authority</u> or unless there is a legal or professional right or duty to disclose. Confidential information acquired as a result of professional and business relationships should not be used for the personal advantage of members or third parties.

Illustration 1 – The fundamental principles

Some examples of the fundamental principles in action might be:

Objectivity

The owners of a private company have the opportunity to sell their shareholdings to a large listed company and have asked for your advice. It looks like an excellent deal, but which will almost certainly mean that your firm will lose the audit to a larger competitor. Your advice might not be impartial – you may be tempted to advise against the deal in order to keep the client.

Professional behaviour

This is possibly the most difficult principle to illustrate. Clearly you, as a professional, would not indulge in illegal behaviour. But does it matter what you do in the evenings or on your lunch break?

Professional competence and due care

A client is starting to expand into areas where there are complex tax issues. You have no direct experience of this area, but you know that a larger firm in the town does have a number of specialists in this field. You might be tempted to think that you can 'get yourself up to speed' quite quickly.

Integrity

You find out that one of your listed audit clients is shortly to be taken over, or has access to technological advances which will give it a fantastic competitive advantage. You might be tempted to buy some shares or encourage your friends to do so.

Confidentiality

You are tempted to share your knowledge of the takeover or technical advances mentioned above, or even of the level of directors' salaries, with your friends on a night out on the town.

4 Threats and safeguards

THE TREATS ⟶ TO OBJECTIVITY

1 SELF-INTEREST

2 SELF-REVIEW

3 ADVOCACY

4 FAMILIARITY

5 INTIMIDATION

Note: 6) Management – but this is an APB ethical standard.

Principles rather than rules based

Both the IFAC and ACCA codes have developed a 'principles approach' rather than a 'rules based' approach to ethical professional behaviour.

This has taken the form of identifying five potential threats to ethical behaviour and the suggestion of a number of safeguards which might be appropriate, including the possibility of ceasing to act for the client.

Throughout, the consideration is not simply the practitioner's view as to whether his or her integrity is under real threat, but how the situation might appear to a third party.

The practitioner needs to:

'behave **and be seen** to behave' in an ethical, professional manner.

Expandable text - Definitions of threats

Self Interest Threat

Financial or other interests of members or their close family. For example, if the auditor or a member of their family owns shares in a client they will want the client to do well in order for a dividend to be paid and for the share price to increase. Clearly the auditor cannot be objective in this situation. They will be reluctant to raise any issues that could adversely affect the performance of the client as this would result in personal financial loss.

Significant outstanding fees from a client may lead the auditor not to raise issues for fear that the fees will not be paid. This may be a particular problem if the client is suffering going concern problems.

Dependence on one client for a significant proportion of the firm's total fee income is a self interest threat. The firm may not raise issues with the client for fear of losing them.

The acceptance of gifts and hospitality is also an example of a self interest threat. The auditor should not accept gifts from the client unless 'modest', otherwise it may be seen as a bribe to keep quiet about issues in the financial statements.

In order to determine whether a gift is modest the auditor should refer to their firm's ethical guidance on acceptance of gifts from clients. Some firms have a complete ban regardless of the value of the gift to avoid any doubt. Another consideration is whether the gift is available to a wider group of people e.g. is it a staff discount scheme that the auditors are being offered or is it a benefit that is only being offered to the auditors? If the latter, it is more likely to constitute a bribe. At all times the auditor should consider how it would look to a third party. If it would be seen to jeopardise the objectivity of the auditor it should not be accepted.

All judgements made regarding the acceptance of gifts and hospitality should be documented on the audit file to show that due consideration was taken to the potential issues.

Self Review Threat

A self-review threat occurs when the auditor has to re-evaluate work completed by himself e.g. if the external auditor prepared the financial statements and then audited them, or if the external auditor advised on the implementation of the financial reporting system of the client.

Here there is a risk that the auditor does not identify the shortcomings in his own work because he does not review it thoroughly, assuming that it is up to standard because he did the work in the first instance. Alternatively, the auditor may identify shortcomings in his work but may not highlight them because it will imply that his work was not up to standard.

Advocacy Threat

This may occur when the auditor is asked to promote the client's position or represent them in some way. In this situation the auditor would have to be biased in favour of the client and therefore cannot be objective. This could happen if the client asked the auditor to promote their shares for a stock exchange listing or if the client asked the auditor to represent them in court.

Familiarity Threat

A familiarity threat occurs when the auditor is too sympathetic or trusting of the client because of a close relationship with them. This may be because a close friend or relative of the auditor works in a key financial role for the client. The auditor may trust their friend or relative to not make mistakes and therefore not review their work as thoroughly as they should and as a result allow material errors to go undetected in the financial statements.

Intimidation Threat

The client may harass or bully the auditor into giving an unqualified opinion when a qualified opinion is appropriate.

If the auditor is dependent on fees from a client the client may use this to their advantage and threaten to take their business elsewhere unless the auditor gives in to their demands.

The auditor should not give in to such pressure and may choose to resign from such a client.

Identifying the threats

In order to guard against the threats or perceived threats the firm needs procedures to enable it to:

- identify possible threats
- evaluate the risk arising from the threat
- evaluate whether the necessary safeguards are in place
- take corrective action if necessary.

Usually this will be done through the use of checklists and the issues need to be considered.

- On acceptance of a new client.

- At the planning stage of any audit.

- At the completion stage of any audit.

- Whenever additional, non audit services are provided to an audit client.

- If any event, or change in circumstances occurs which may mean that the firm's independence may be threatened.

The procedures operated by the firm will normally consist of the following.

- 'Fit and proper' or 'independence' forms to be completed by all staff on a regular, usually annual basis disclosing financial interests and other relevant factors.

- A checklist of procedures to be filled in when a new appointment is accepted covering such issues as:
    - proof of the client's identity
    - consideration of relationships with the firm, its staff, other clients etc.

    See the section below on accepting new appointments.

- Consideration of independence issues when files are reviewed as part of the firm's quality control process.

- Appointment of a senior partner with responsibility for ethical issues.

Possible safeguards

General safeguards

- **Safeguards created by the profession** (these might include education, training and experience requirements for entry into the profession, professional development requirements, corporate governance regulations, professional standards, monitoring, external review of work and reports).

- Also ACCA have the right to discipline through fines, suspension of membership or even withdrawal.

- **Safeguards in the work environment** (such as oversight structures, ethics and conduct programmes, good recruitment procedures, strong internal controls, disciplinary procedures, strong ethical leadership, policies and procedures to promote quality control, culture of strong ethics in the organisation).

- **Safeguards created by individuals** (complying with professional development requirements, keeping records of contentious issues, keeping a broader perspective, using a mentor, keeping in contact with professional bodies).

Specific threats to objectivity

Self-interest – this being interested in the client financially or personally

Threat	Why	Safeguard
Dependence on client	The auditor will have a fear of losing a lot of income therefore will appease the client	• Should not audit if the client provides a large proportion of regular/recurring income to the audit firm • Total gross recurring fees should be no more than: – Listed Co's – 10% of the Firms total fees (review at 5%) – Other Co's – 15% of the Firms total fees (review at 10%)
Lowballing	The auditor will keep the client happy to ensure further work. Therefore will not disagree with client	• Setting an audit fee low to try and get more lucrative work is frowned upon the fee must be based on pre-determined level of work required
Loans, guarantees and overdue fees	The auditor will have fear of not getting paid so will keep the client happy to ensure payment	• No loans or guarantees allowed to or from client, unless in normal course of business • Significant overdue fees are deemed a loan, hence not allowed
Hospitality or other benefits	This could be deemed a bribe and potentially the auditor may lose professional sceptism	• Benefits should not be accepted unless modest • Modest – means available to all the company's staff at same terms • The assurance firm should establish policies on gifts and hospitality and should be communicated

Threat	Why	Safeguard
Contingent fees	The auditor has an incentive, therefore may not be independent	• Assurance work should not be conducted on a contingent basis (i.e. where you receive a commission, or a % of fees is payable upon a specific event occurring) • No safeguard – fee must be based on pre-determined amount
Financial/business interest can also lead to intimidation threat	The auditor will want the greatest return from investment, therefore may cover anything that could devalue the interest	• Close business, family or personal relationship should be avoided between the client and the assurance firm • i.e. seeking to gain employment with an assurance client • i.e. entering a joint venture / arrangement with client

Financial interest in shares etc		• Anyone involved with assurance must NOT have direct or indirect interest in a client i.e. holding shares
		
		• Rules apply to
		  – Assurance firm
		  – Any partner in the firm
		  – Person in a position to influence engagement
		  – Immediate family member of above
		
		• Safeguards:
		  – Dispose of interest
		  – Remove individual from the team
		  – Independent partner review
		  – Internal QC procedures in place (i.e. prohibited shareholding list)

Threat	Why	Safeguard
Cross selling	The auditor has an incentive, therefore may not be independent	Assurance team should not be remunerated on their success in selling other services to the client

Self-review threats

Providing other services to the client and then also doing the Statutory Audit – the auditor will then be reviewing their own work.

Threat	Why	Safeguard
Accounting services	If the auditor reviews their own work they may miss errors, or be more relaxed about doing the work. Also if they do find any errors it's easier to cover them up and not disclose in the fear of looking incompetent	• Should not do for LISTED companies, unless it is an emergency • For non-listed clients – permitted as long as safeguards in place (applicable to all self-review threats) • No management decisions are made; client to prepare judgemental area • Seperate personnel / terms / partners • Independent partner review
IT		• Should not design, provide or implement IT systems which are important to a significant part of the accounting system or undertake the role of management
Valuation services		• Should not provide valuation services if they involve degree of judgement and have a material effect on the FS being audited
Tax services		• Should not be undertaken if audit firm seen to be taking on management role or if they are likely to have a material effect on the FS

Threat	Why	Safeguard
Corporate finance services		• Acceptable, as long as not making decisions • Allowed to assist client raising finance/developing corporate strategies
Internal Audit Services (Session 9)		• Should not be undertaken where significant reliance will be placed on the IA work by the auditors from same firm
Former employee of client joining assurance firm		• The employee cannot be involved with the audit until 2 years have elapsed

Familiarity

Where the auditor is familiar with the client

Threat	Why	Safeguard
Participation in client affairs/family and personal relationships	The auditor may lose professional sceptism, or have the fear of upsetting the client	• Cannot be director, employee or a business partner if you are going to audit a client • Must not take part in audit if have been officer / employee in that period, or in the last 2 yrs • If the director / employee or business partner is an immediate family member of someone on the audit team, that audit team member must be removed • May be extended to other close relationships within the firm (not just those on the team)

KAPLAN PUBLISHING

Threat	Why	Safeguard
Audit partners leaving to join the client		• Can join the client, but must sever all links with the assurance firm (e.g. pension) • Audit partner has to inform the audit firm immediately and is then removed from audit team as soon as decision to join client is made • If partner becomes director or key management and has worked as partner on the audit in prior 2 years the audit firm must resign as auditors • 2 year period must then elapse before the firm can be re-appointed as auditors
Acting for prolonged period		• Listed clients – Engagement partners can act for a maximum of 5 years, should then have a break of a minimum of 5 years before resuming role • Anyone who has acted as a key audit partner for a period of 7 years should have a break of 2 years • Senior staff on listed clients should also not act for longer than 7 years • Non-listed clients – No compulsary rotation, but firm carry out annual reviews to ensure objectivity not threatened, but is advised that partners act for no longer than 10 years

Advocacy

When the auditor promotes the client or represents them

Threat	Why	Safeguard
Legal services	When representing the client you automatically view the same views as the client therefore may lose independence	• Should not offer legal services to a client and defend them in dispute or litigation which is material to the FS
Corporate finance services		• Should not advise on debt restructuring as part of Corporate finance – don't enter negotiations with bank on clients' behalf
Contingent fees		• See SELF-INTEREST THREAT
Dealing in clients shares		• This could be seen as signal to other investors if dealing in clients shares

Intimidation

Being harassed or bullied

Threat	Why	Safeguard
Close business, family and personal relationships	The auditor has the fear of upsetting the client, therefore will agree with what they say	• Also see SELF-INTEREST
Litigation	The client may harass or bully the auditor into giving an unqualified report	• If there is actual or threatened litigation between client and assurance firm, the firm should not continue to act
Assurance staff move to join clients		• See SELF-REVIEW

Management

Taking on a management role.

Threat	Why	Safeguard
Undertaking any work which involves making judgements and taking decisions that are responsibility of management		• An engagement partner or employee of the assurance firm should not serve on the board of directors as they would be involved with decision making • Performing other services is also a management threat – See SELF-REVIEW • Safeguards; Informed management

Test your understanding 1

List and explain – the fundamental principles of the ACCA and IFAC Codes of Ethics?

(2 marks)

List the threats to objectivity.

(2 marks)

FIXED TEST 1 - JT & Co.

You are a manager in the audit firm of JT & Co; and this is your first time you have worked on one of the firm's established clients, Pink Co. The main activity of Pink Co is providing investment advice to individuals regarding saving for retirement, purchase of shares and securities and investing in tax efficient savings schemes. Pink is regulated by the relevant financial services authority.

You have been asked to start the audit planning for Pink Co, by Mrs Goodall, a partner in JT & Co. Mrs Goodall has been the engagement partner for Pink Co, for the previous six years and so has a sound knowledge of the client. Mrs Goodall has informed you that she would like her son Simon to be part of the audit team this year; Simon is currently studying for his first set of fundamentals papers for her ACCA qualification. Mrs Goodall also informs you that Mr Supper, the audit senior, received investment advice from Pink Co during the year and intends to do the same next year.

In an initial meeting with the finance director of Pink Co, you learn that the audit team will not be entertained on Pink Co's yacht this year as this could appear to be an attempt to influence the opinion of the audit. Instead, he has arranged a day at the horse races costing less than two fifth's of the expense of using the yacht and hopes this will be acceptable.

JT & Co have done some consultive work previously and the invoice is still outstanding.

Required:

(a)   (i)   Explain the ethical threats which may affect the auditor of Pink Co.

(6 marks)

        (ii)   For each ethical threat, discuss how the effect of the threat can be mitigated.

(6 marks)

(12 marks)

Expandable Text - Answer plan

You are a manager in the audit firm of JT & Co; and this is your first time you have worked on one of the firm's established clients, Pink Co. The main activity of Pink Co is providing investment advice to individuals regarding saving for retirement, purchase of shares and securities and investing in tax efficient savings schemes. Pink is regulated by the relevant financial services authority.

You have been asked to start the audit planning for Pink Co, by Mrs Goodall, a partner in JT & Co. Mrs Goodall has been the engagement partner for Pink Co, for the previous six years and so has a sound knowledge of the client. Mrs Goodall has informed you that she would like her son Simon to be part of the audit team this year; Simon is currently studying for his first set of fundamentals papers for her ACCA qualification. Mrs Goodall also informs you that Mr Supper, the audit senior, received investment advice from Pink Co during the year and intends to do the same next year.

In an initial meeting with the finance director of Pink Co, you learn that the audit team will not be entertained on Pink Co's yacht this year as this could appear to be an attempt to influence the opinion of the audit. Instead, he has arranged a day at the horse races costing less than two fifth's of the expense of using the yacht and hopes this will be acceptable.

JT & Co have done some consultive work previously and the invoice is still outstanding.

Required:

(a) (i) Explain the <u>ethical threats</u> which may affect the auditor of Pink Co.

(6 marks)

(ii) For each ethical threat, discuss how the effect of the threat can <u>be mitigated</u>.

(6 marks)

(12 marks)

Other proposals to improve independence

- Compulsory rotation of audit firms (already happens in some countries).
- A ban on the provision of certain (maybe all) other services.
- A State Auditing Board to audit all major companies.
- Government to appoint auditors of listed companies.

Other issues

Opinion Shopping

Whilst shareholders appoint auditors, the Directors typically seek out a potential firm for the shareholders to vote on. The Board might be tempted to interview several firms until it found one that accepted its accounting methods.

Any firm of auditors aware that a potential client is engaged in this process should not accept nomination.

Confidentiality

External auditors are in a unique position of having a legal right of access to all information about their clients. It goes without saying that the client must be able to trust the auditor not to disclose anything about their business to anyone as it could be detrimental to their operations. As a basic rule, members of an audit team should not disclose any information to those outside of the audit team, whether or not they work for the same firm. There is little point using different teams for different work assignments if staff from different teams are disclosing information to each other!

Information should only be disclosed under certain circumstances.

- If the client has given their consent.
- If there is an obligation to disclose, e.g. if the client is suspected of money laundering, terrorism, drug trafficking.
- If it is required by a regulatory body, e.g. financial services legislation.
- If a court order has been obtained.
- If a member has to defend himself in court or at a disciplinary hearing.
- If it is in the public interest.

This latter point is difficult to prove and the audit must proceed with caution if thinking of disclosing information for this reason. Such examples could include fraud, environmental pollution, or simply companies acting against the public good.

Legal advice should be sought beforehand to avoid the risk of being sued. Matters to consider before disclosing information in the public interest are whether that matter is likely to be repeated and how serious the effects of the client's actions are.

Where an auditor feels the need to disclose information, they should consider disclosing to the company's Audit Committee (or Board of Directors, if there is no Audit Committee).

In certain circumstances auditors may be required by law to disclose information. For example, where money laundering is suspected, UK auditors must disclose their suspicions to the Serious Organised Crime Agency (SOCA).

On some occasions, auditors may come under pressure to disclose information (e.g. to customers, suppliers, tax authorities). There is no duty for the auditor to disclose to these parties therefore should only do so if a court order has been obtained.

Conflicts of interest

Members should place their clients' interests before their own and should not accept or continue engagements which threaten to give rise to conflicts of interest between the firm and the client. Any advice given should be in the best interests of the client. Where clients' interests conflict (for example, clients in the same line of business), the firm's work should be arranged to avoid the interests of one being adversely affected by those of another.

The steps to be taken by the auditor are:

- once a conflict is noted, you should advise both clients of the situation

- reassure the client that adequate safeguards will be implemented, e.g. separate engagement leaders for each, separate teams, 'Chinese walls' to prevent the transfer of client information between teams and a second partner review

- suggest they seek additional independent advice

- if adequate safeguards can't be implemented, the auditor should resign.

Safeguards can help to avoid or manage a problem situation, but problems are often hard to foresee as the auditor may have no knowledge that two clients are related in some way until a problem comes to light.

5 Accepting new audit engagements

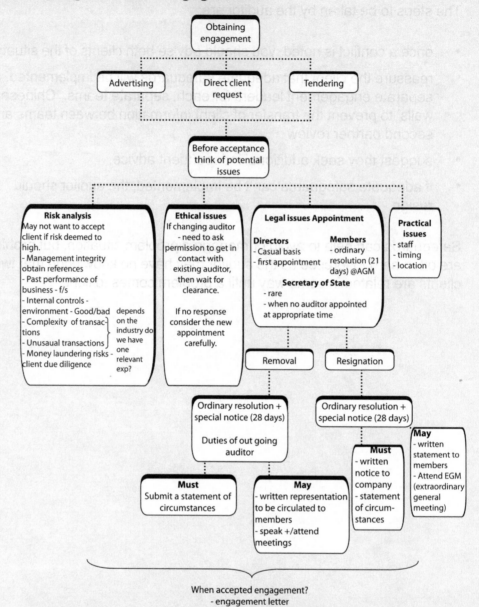

```
                        Obtaining
                        engagement

Advertising         Direct client         Tendering
                    request

                    Before acceptance
                    think of potential
                    issues
```

Risk analysis
May not want to accept client if risk deemed to high.
- Management integrity obtain references
- Past performance of business - f/s
- Internal controls - environment - Good/bad
- Complexity of transactions
- Unusaual transactions
- Money laundering risks - client due diligence

depends on the industry do we have one relevant exp?

Ethical issues
If changing auditor
- need to ask permission to get in contact with existing auditor, then wait for clearance.

If no response consider the new appointment carefully.

Legal issues Appointment

Directors
- Casual basis
- first appointment

Members
- ordinary resolution (21 days) @AGM

Secretary of State
- rare
- when no auditor appointed at appropriate time

Practical issues
- staff
- timing
- location

```
                Removal              Resignation
```

Ordinary resolution + special notice (28 days)

Duties of out going auditor

Ordinary resolution + special notice (28 days)

Must
Submit a statement of circumstances

May
- written representation to be circulated to members
- speak +/attend meetings

Must
- written notice to company
- statement of circumstances

May
- written statement to members
- Attend EGM (extraordinary general meeting)

When accepted engagement?
- engagement letter

Expandable Text - Procedures

Procedures

If offered an audit role, the auditor should:

- ask the client for permission to contact the outgoing auditor (reject role if client refuses)

- contact the outgoing auditor, asking for any professional reasons why they should not accept appointment (if the client has caused problems, you may wish to say no to the appointment). If a reply is not received, the prospective auditor should always try and contact the outgoing auditor by other means e.g. by telephone or in person. Even if there are professional reasons or if a reply is still not received, the prospective auditor may still choose to accept but must proceed with care and be alert to increased risk

- ensure that the legal requirements in relation to the removal of the previous auditors and the appointment of the firm have been met (these were covered in chapter 2)

- carry out checks to ensure the firm can be independent, is competent to do this audit and has the necessary resources

- assess whether this work is suitably low risk (a sound knowledge of the client will be required in order to make this assessment, see below)

- assess the integrity of the company's directors

- as a commercial organisation, the firm should also ensure that this client is one it wants (e.g. right industry, suitable profit margin available, etc)

- not accept the appointment, where it is known in advance a limitation will be placed on the scope of their audit (likewise, if a restriction is imposed during an audit, resignation should be considered). In general, the question of what constitutes a reason for not accepting nomination is one of judgement for the prospective auditor and will primarily depend on the level of risk willing to be accepted.

Expandable text - Know your client

Know your client

ISA 315 Obtaining an Understanding of the Entity and its Environment and Assessing the Risks of Material Misstatements, requires the auditors to obtain a knowledge of the business sufficient to enable them to identify and understand those issues that may have a significant impact on the financial statements.

Client screening procedures are designed to identify potentially high risk audit clients. A high risk client is one where total costs will exceed the benefits to the auditor.

Considerations which are relevant in deciding whether a client is high risk include the following.

- Evidence of client involvement in fraudulent or illegal activities.

- The state of the economic sector in which the client operates (a depressed sector may indicate risk).

- The nature of the industry and the client's product lines or services.

- The client's previous audit history (frequent changes of auditors, and/or qualified reports, are obviously bad news).

- The general abilities of the client management.

- Understanding, by the directors, of their own role and that of the auditor.

- Management permission or refusal to allow auditors to examine significant documents, such as the minutes of directors' meetings.

- Evidence of management intentionally failing to record a material transaction.

The review procedure is best carried out by means of a standard checklist. A client may exhibit some of the above risk factors and yet still be accepted due to the relatively high level of the proposed audit fee. It is very much a commercial decision to be made by the audit firm.

Auditors are required to adopt more rigorous client identification procedures as a result of the money laundering regulations.

Expandable text - Matters to consider with a new client

The audit firm Brice and Winterhouse has just been asked to tender for the audit of Telstar. There is a team of audit staff members assigned to putting the tender together, including an audit engagement partner, a tax partner and two other members of audit staff.

The first matter for the team to undertake is to determine whether Brice and Winterhouse would be capable of accepting the audit if the tender was successful, as there is little point in carrying out the tender exercise if not.

The team will consider the following matters.

- Ethical matters.

- Legal matters (although these will be limited at this stage).

- Practical and risk related matters.

Ethical matters

Important matters to consider are whether the firm has any connection with Telstar that might threaten the objectivity and independence of the audit. The tender team should:

- confirm with other departments in the firm whether they carry out any work for Telstar

- check that there are no personal connections between audit staff members and the company

- check that the firm (perhaps via its pension scheme) or staff members do not own shares in Telstar.

Legal matters

Before accepting the engagement, the firm would have to ensure that Telstar had dealt with the outgoing auditors and the incoming auditors correctly. At this stage, it is probably not possible to do this, particularly as the present auditors may still be incumbent – they may have been asked to submit a tender alongside Brice and Winterhouse.

Practical and risk related matters

- The team will need to assess Telstar itself, and consider the market it operates in, the nature of its business, the size of its business and how these things will affect the audit.

- It will be important to ensure that the firm has sufficient knowledge and experience of the sector to carry out the audit properly (the Telstar directors are unlikely to have asked them to tender if this did not appear to the be case).

- It will be important to assess when the audit work will be required, and whether the firm has the resources to meet the staffing needs in relation to that audit work.

- It will be important to assess the likely level of fee income (perhaps compare to the existing auditors' (if any) fees as disclosed in the financial statements) because if the fees are large, they might be proportionally too large for Brice and Winterhouse to accept under the ethical rules.

- It will be important to assess the likely risk of Telstar as a client – is it established and well-financed, with prudent accounting policies, or is it an overtrading start-up with dubious accounting policies and no experienced accounting staff, for example.

- In addition, any press coverage relating to Telstar could be considered, if there is any. Does the company appear to attract bad press, if so, why? Is it a high risk audit client that the firm would prefer not to be associated with?

- Lastly, the auditors should consider whether Telstar has any future plans that would change the assessments being made at the current time and introduce reasons why Brice and Winterhouse should not be the auditors of Telstar.

6 Obtaining new audit work

The most common way of obtaining an audit engagement is by recommendation. It is not uncommon for up to 90% of a firm's new business to come from its existing client base.

However, the second most common way of obtaining new work is by submitting a successful tender, after being invited to participate in what is frequently referred to as a 'beauty parade'.

'Tendering' is the process of quoting a fee for work before the work is carried out.

Risks associated with the tender process

In addition to the risk associated with any other new client the specific risks of being involved with the tender include:

- wasted time – if the audit tender is not accepted
- setting an uncommercially low fee in order to win the contract (lowballing, discussed above)
- making unrealistic claims or promises in order to win the contract.

Expandable Text - Before the tender

Before the tender

Prior to tendering, the auditor should establish:

- the specific needs of the prospective client
- an acceptable fee level.

The audit firm will want the following information before drawing up its proposal:

- precisely what does the company expect from the auditors?
- what timetable does the client expect, an interim audit followed by a final audit, or a longer final audit after the year end?

- by what date are the audited financial statements required?

- what are the company's future plans, e.g. public flotation, expansion, contraction, concentration on certain markets?

- what are the problems with the current auditors, if the company is seeking to replace them?

The contents of the proposal

The content of the proposal should include:

- the fee and how it has been calculated

- the nature, purpose and legal requirements of an audit (clients are often unclear about this)

- an assessment of the requirements of the client

- an outline of how the audit firm proposes to satisfy those requirements

- the assumptions made e.g. on geographical coverage, deadlines, work done by the client, availability of information etc.

- the proposed approach to the audit or audit methodology

- an outline of the firm and its personnel

- the ability of the firm to offer other services

The presentation will be in the format as required by the prospective client and should be dynamic and professional. Possible presentation requirements are:

- written

- oral presentation using visual aids, etc.

How will the proposal be judged?

After each of the prospective firms of auditors has made its presentation, the company must make its choice. Relevant criteria are likely to include:

- clarity

- relevance

- professionalism

- personal/standardised

- timeliness of delivery
- originality
- range of other services
- ability to deliver
- reputation.

7 Engagement letters

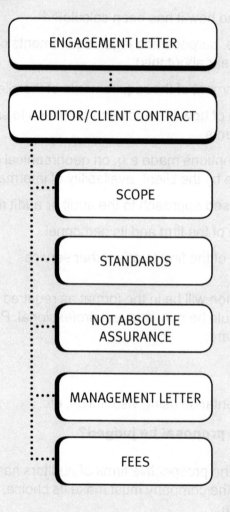

Engagement letters – main considerations

- The engagement letter will be sent before the audit.
- It specifies the nature of the contract between the audit firm and the client.
- It minimises the risk of any misunderstanding of the auditor's role.
- It should be reviewed every year to ensure that it is up to date but does not need to be reissued every year unless there are changes to the terms of the engagement.
- The auditor **must** issue a new engagement letter if the scope or context of the assignment changes after initial appointment.
- Many firms of auditors choose to send a new letter every year, to emphasise its importance to clients.

Expandable Text - Reasons for changes

Reasons for changes include:

- Changes to statutory duties … new legislation.
- Changes to professional duties … new ISAs.
- Changes to 'other services' … requested/provided.

Expandable Text - Contents of the engagement letter

The contents of the engagement letter

The contents of a letter of engagement for audit services will include the following.

- Objective of the audit.
- Management's responsibility for the financial statements.
- The scope of the audit including reference to legislation and professional standards.
- A description of audit procedures including their inherent limitations (e.g. for the discovery of fraud and irregularities)
- The form of reports to be issued.
- Use of the work of internal audit.
- Risk assessment matters.
- The auditor's use of specialists.
- Deadlines.
- Access to information.

- Communications between the auditor and the client (e.g. form of audit report, management representations, letter of weakness, etc.).
- A reference to other services (normally covered in a separate letter).
- The basis of fees.
- Complaints procedures and jurisdiction.
- The need for co-operation and agreement of terms.

Test your understanding 2

List 6 items you would see in an engagement letter.

(3 marks)

8 Chapter summary

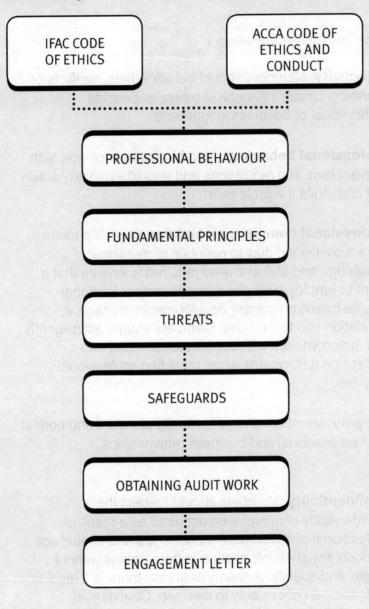

IFAC CODE
OF ETHICS

ACCA CODE OF
ETHICS AND
CONDUCT

PROFESSIONAL BEHAVIOUR

FUNDAMENTAL PRINCIPLES

THREATS

SAFEGUARDS

OBTAINING AUDIT WORK

ENGAGEMENT LETTER

Test your understanding answers

Test your understanding 1

Objectivity: Members should not allow bias, conflicts of interest or undue influence of others to override professional or business judgements.	½ mark ½ mark
Professional behaviour: Members should comply with relevant laws and regulations and should avoid any action that discredits the profession.	½ mark ½ mark
Professional competence and due care: Members have a continuing duty to maintain professional knowledge and skill at a level required to ensure that a client or employer receives competent professional service based on current developments in practice, legislation and techniques. Members should act diligently and in accordance with applicable technical and professional standards when providing professional services.	½ mark ½ mark
Integrity: Members should be straightforward and honest in all professional and business relationships.	½ mark ½ mark
Confidentiality: Members should respect the confidentiality of information acquired as a result of professional and business relationships and should not disclose any such information to third-parties without proper and specific authority or unless there is a legal or professional right or duty to disclose. Confidential information acquired as a result of professional and business relationships should not be used for the personal advantage of members or third parties.	½ mark ½ mark

FIXED TEST 1 - JT & Co.

THIS IS A FIXED TEST – Please answer the question in full (long form written). Then log on to en-gage at the following address: www.en-gage.co.uk. Follow the link to 'Fixed Test 1' and answer the questions based on your homework answer.

Once you have answered the questions on en-gage a model answer will be available for your reference.

Test your understanding 2

Objective of the audit.	½ mark
Management responsibilities.	½ mark
Fee's.	½ mark
Deadlines.	½ mark
Complaints procedures.	½ mark
Auditors responsibilities.	½ mark

6

Planning

Chapter learning objectives

When you have completed this chapter you will be able to:

- identify and explain the need for planning an audit
- identify and describe the contents of the overall audit strategy and the audit plan
- explain the difference between interim and final audit
- discuss the effect of fraud and misstatements on the audit strategy and extent of audit work
- explain and describe the relationship between the overall audit strategy and the audit plan
- explain how auditors obtain an initial understanding of the entity and knowledge of its business environment
- define and explain the concepts of materiality and tolerable error
- compute indicative materiality levels from financial information
- develop and document an audit plan
- describe and explain the nature and purpose of analytical procedures in planning.

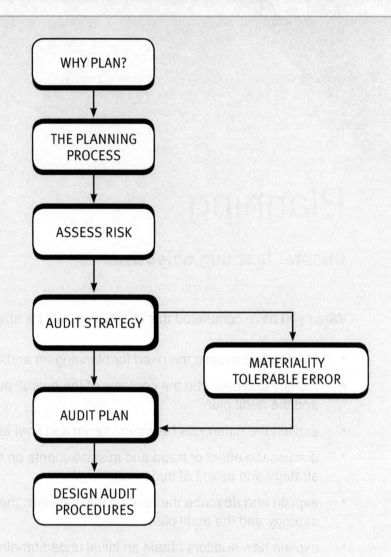

1 Why plan?

The auditor should plan the audit so that the engagement will be performed in an effective manner.

ISA 300 para 2

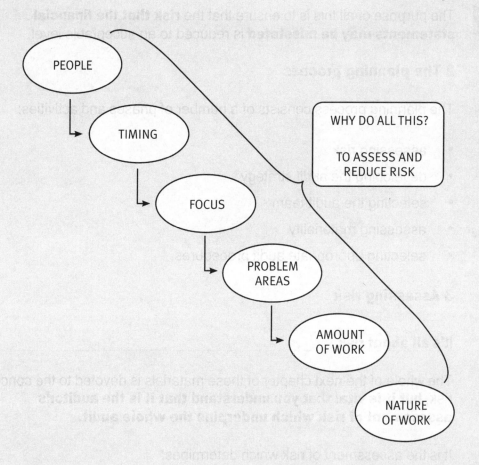

An audit is:

- an expensive process

- a potentially complex project which needs to be managed effectively.

Although it is tempting to assume that it is simply a question of following a tried and tested programme and that the important thing is to 'get busy', the extra time spent planning the engagement properly will repay itself by:

- Ensuring the right team is selected for the assignment.

- Ensuring that staff are employed effectively rather than simply 'given something to do'.

- Ensuring the work is properly focused on material areas of risk.

- Identifying potential problem areas.

- Ensuring that the nature and quantity of the work done addresses the risks and problem areas.

- Ensuring the work can be fully completed in time for the review process.

- Enabling deadlines to be met so that there is time for due consideration of the important issues.

 The purpose of all this is to ensure that the **risk that the financial statements may be misstated** is reduced to an acceptable level.

2 The planning process

The planning process consists of a number of phases and activities:

- assessing risk
- developing the audit strategy
- selecting the audit team
- assessing materiality
- selecting appropriate audit procedures.

3 Assessing risk

It's all about risk

The whole of the next chapter of these materials is devoted to the concept of risk, **but it is vital that you understand that it is the auditor's assessment of risk which underpins the whole audit.**

It is the assessment of risk which determines:

- the audit strategy
- who should be on the audit team
- the potential impact of fraud
- the nature of the procedures to be carried out
- how much evidence needs to be gathered.

so everything in the planning process is about the auditor's response to assessed risk.

How do you assess risk?

There are two sources of information from which it is possible to assess risk:

- Knowledge of the business (KOB) which we will consider later in this chapter.
- Analytical procedures which we will consider in the chapter on evidence.

Risk and materiality

It follows that there is a relationship between risk and materiality in that:

- the greater the risk of material misstatement
- the lower the level of materiality.

Expandable text - Materiality

Imagine two clients with similar levels of revenue, profitability and net assets.

Client No 1

- Is well established in a stable industry.
- Management has a strong sense of ethics which is communicated throughout the business.
- Management regards the accounting function highly, understands the accounts and insists on accounts and other reports being produced promptly and to a high standard.
- Accounting systems are strong.
- Staff are well trained, well motivated and carry out their work efficiently.
- Audit adjustments are rare and, when they occur, are put through promptly.

Client No 2

Is recently established in a cut-throat, volatile industry.

- Management is driven by 'doing the deal' and are not averse to 'cutting the odd corner'.
- Management's interest in the accounts is limited to a focus on top line sales numbers.

- Staff are underpaid, poorly motivated and expected to 'pick up the systems as they go along'.

- The auditors spend a huge amount of time trying to 'get things to agree', tend to find a large number of errors, and experience resistance to any adjustments, particularly those which reduce the level of reported profits.

It is not too hard to see that Client No 2 is more risky than Client No 1.

It is also true to say that, strictly speaking, the user of the financial statements of both clients would probably put the same value on a misstatement to be regarded as material in both companies.

From the auditor's point of view, however, it is highly likely that the level of materiality set for Client No 1 would be higher than for Client No 2, because the level of risk is lower.

4 The audit strategy

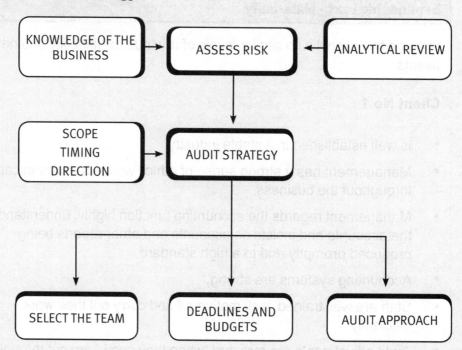

The audit strategy sets the overall approach of the audit and covers:

- the scope

- the timing

- the direction

of the audit.

Scope

What is the financial reporting framework for the financial statements?

- National GAAP?
- International Accounting standards?

Are there industry specific or other special reporting requirements?

- Listed companies.
- Charities.
- Other regulated businesses such as banks and insurance companies.

Are there other factors which influence the overall approach to the audit?

- Multiple locations.
- Group audits.

Timing

Deadlines for:

- final reporting
- any interim report
- reports to management
- reports to those charged with governance.

The timing of:

- interim; and
- final audit visits

to enable these deadlines to be met.

It is always good, when managing a project (even an audit) to start with the completion date and work backwards.

If there is to be an interim as well as a final audit the timing has to be:

- Early enough:
  - not to interfere with year-end procedures at the client and
  - to give adequate warning of specific problems.
- Late enough:
  - to enable sufficient work to be done to ease the pressure on the final audit.

Interim versus Final audits

The interim audit will normally focus on:

- documenting systems
- evaluating controls
- some tests of details – usually tests of income and expenditure and, perhaps, purchases and disposals of non current assets.

It may be possible to:

- attend an interim inventory count or
- carry out an interim receivables circularisation,

providing the results can be satisfactorily 'rolled forward' to the statement of financial position date. (A roll forward reconciles the movements between the date of the count or circularisation and the year end date.)

The final audit can then focus on:

- statement of financial position areas
- finalisation of the financial statements and the audit report.

For an interim audit to be justified the client normally needs to be of a sufficient size, although, if reporting deadlines are very tight it may be possible to audit up to 'Month 11' and then 'roll forward' to the statement of financial position date.

Direction

The 'direction' of the audit covers the overall approach and concerns such issues as:

- preliminary assessment of materiality

- preliminary identification of high risk areas
- preliminary identification of material components and account balances.

Component – A division, branch, subsidiary, joint venture, associated company or other entity whose financial information is included in financial statements audited by the principal auditor.

- Decisions about whether assurance is expected to be derived from reliance on controls or a fully substantive approach.
- The need for site visits and other logistical issues.
- The impact of recent developments at the client, in its industry, in regulatory or financial reporting requirements.

Small entities

In audit of small entities, the entire audit may be conducted by a very small audit team. Many audits of small entities involve the audit engagement partner (who may be a sole practitioner) working with one engagement team member (or without any engagement team members). With a smaller team, co-ordination and communication between team members are easier. Establishing the overall audit strategy for the audit of a small entity need not be a complex or time-consuming exercise; it varies according to the size of the entity and the complexity of the audit. For example, a brief memorandum prepared at the completion of the previous audit, based on a review of the working papers and highlighting issues identified in the audit just completed, updated and changed in the current period based on discussions with the owner-manager, can serve as the basis for planning the current audit engagement.

5 The impact of fraud on the audit strategy

Expandable Text - Preventing and detecting fraud

Responsibility for preventing and detecting fraud

We know that:

- It is not the auditors' job to prevent or detect fraud – this is the responsibility of management.

The auditor **is** concerned with fraud, however, because:

- Fraud may lead to a material misstatement in the financial statements.

If the auditor assesses that the risk of fraud is high, there is an increased probability of misstatement.

The impact on the audit strategy may be:

- A reduction in the materiality level set (see the section above on risk and materiality).
- An increased level of testing in the area(s) where fraud is suspected.
- A reduced reliance on evidence generated internally by the client.
- An increased focus on externally generated evidence.
- If senior management is suspected of involvement with the fraud, a reduced reliance on management representations.

Professional scepticism

We know that the auditor should **'maintain an attitude of professional scepticism throughout the audit'**

ISA 240 para 24

This means that the auditor needs to recognise the possibility that a material misstatement due to fraud could exist.

It involves:

- Having a questioning attitude.
- Supporting conclusions and opinions with appropriate relevant audit evidence.
- Safeguarding against threats to independence and objectivity (as explained in chapter 5).

This is particularly important with respect to fraud because, with fraud, there is **intent to deceive**, which is not the case with misstatements deriving from honest error.

6 Possible different strategies

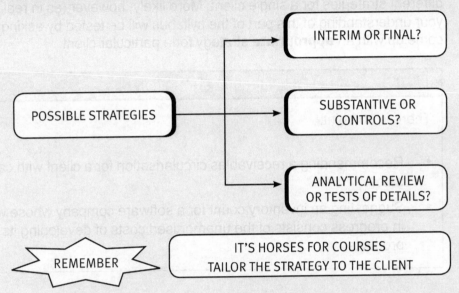

Illustration 1 – Possible different strategies

Possible different strategies could be:

- Final audit only.

- Interim and final.

- Reliance on controls with reduced reliance on substantive procedures.

- Reliance on substantive procedures rather than on internal controls.

- Heavy reliance on analytical procedures rather than tests of details.

The nature of the client's business and structure will have a huge impact on the appropriate strategy.

- Clients with multiple sites, such as retail chains or manufacturers with a number of factories, will require the planning of a programme of site visits, perhaps on a rotational basis.

- Finance companies where the confirmation of a bewildering number of bank balances is crucial to the audit.

- The need to use experts, e.g.
  - specialist inventory checkers in the restaurant and pub trade or for livestock
  - surveyors and valuers for property companies
  - actuaries for pension schemes.

NB. In the exam it is possible that you may be asked to come up with different strategies for a single client. More likely, however (as in real life) your understanding of this part of the syllabus will be tested by asking you to come up with an **appropriate** strategy for a particular client.

Illustration 2 – Possible different strategies

There is no point:

- Recommending a receivables circularisation for a client with cash sales.

- Suggesting an inventory count for a software company whose work in progress consists of the unamortised costs of developing its products.

7 The audit plan

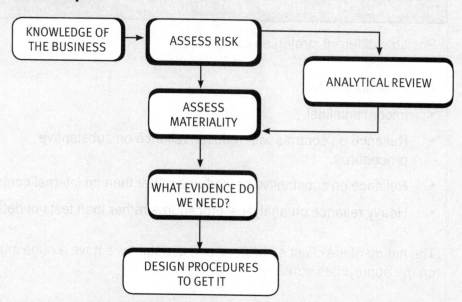

Once the audit strategy has been decided upon, the next stage is to decide how it is going to be carried out – we need the **audit plan.**

We also need to distinguish between:

- The plan itself – what needs to be done and how.
- Documenting the planning process (dealt with in the last section of this chapter).

The plan itself

Based on the assessed:

- risk
- materiality.

It is possible to decide:

- **what** audit procedures are to be carried out
- **who** should do them
- **how much** work should be done (sample sizes, etc)
- **when** the work should be done.

The relationship between the audit strategy and the audit plan

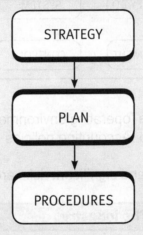

Whilst the strategy sets the overall approach to the audit, the plan fills in the operational details of how the strategy is to be achieved.

8 Knowledge of the business (KOB)

The need for KOB

If the audit strategy and the plan depend on the assessed level of risk, the auditor's ability to assess that risk will depend on an understanding of all aspects of the client's business:

- what the client does
- the environment in which it does it
- its management, systems and governance
- who it interacts with (key customers, suppliers, etc).

What KOB does the auditor need?

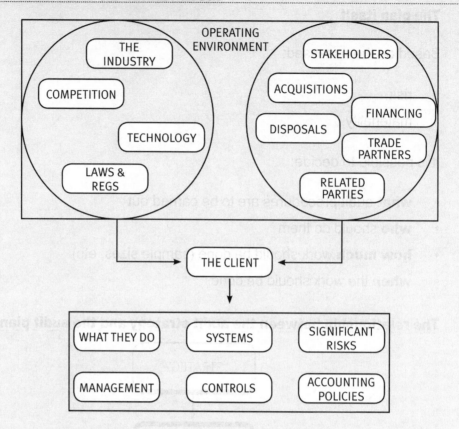

The subheadings in the 'operating environment' box as well as 'What they do', 'Management' and 'Accounting policies' are dealt with more fully below.

Systems and controls and significant risks are dealt with in other chapters.

Expandable Text - The industry

The industry

What's special about it?

Every client is different, but different clients in the same industry will have common characteristics.

- In the manufacturing sector, the auditor will need to understand something of standard costing, overhead absorption and variance analysis.

- A number of industries are affected by specific laws and regulations (see below).

- Pension schemes tend to own investments, which need valuing and earn dividends.

- For farmers there are the problems of valuing livestock and agricultural crops.

- Retailers may have multiple branches and may have specific problems with taking large amounts of cash, preventing credit card fraud etc.

Expandable Text - The competition

The competition

Consider:

- Who are the main competitors to the client?

- Are there alternative products/services to those offered by the client?

Knowledge of the competition is important because:

- They may represent a threat to the client leading to a deterioration in the client's business.

- If other businesses in the same industry are experiencing difficulties (or have opportunities for expansion and growth) it may indicate potential problems or opportunities ahead for the client.

Expandable Text - Technology

Technology

Consider:

- Could the client's products or services become obsolete?

- Could changes in technology have an impact on the client's processes?

Knowledge of the client's technological environment is important because:

- If the client is in a 'high tech' industry, changes in technology can be very rapid and, if the client is not investing enough and keeping up to date, the whole basis of the business could be undermined.

Consider the impact of downloads on the market for CDs, CD players and even car stereos.

- Even in more traditional industries technological change may change the way businesses operate, with serious consequences for those who do not adapt quickly enough.

Consider:

- IT developments have transformed the printing industry because many tasks, previously carried out by skilled and expensive operators have now been virtually eliminated through automation.

- In much engineering the use of digitally controlled equipment has meant that many manual, skilled tasks can be completed faster and with greater consistency and precision by machines.

Expandable Text - Laws and regulations

Laws and regulations

Is the client's business regulated in some way?

This is important because:

- Unexpected changes in regulation are factors which may have important consequences for the client, although the client has virtually no control over such changes.

- If a client fails to comply with applicable regulations it may find it is unable to trade.

Examples of industries which tend to be subject to such regulations are:

- investment services

- banking

- other financial services

- the preparation and selling of food products

- pharmaceuticals, drugs and medicines

KAPLAN PUBLISHING

- travel agents
- transport and haulage
- waste disposal
- betting and gambling
- charities and the not for profit sector.

Expandable Text - Stakeholders

Stakeholders

Consider:

- Who are the shareholders?
- Who controls the company?
- Are there groupings of shareholders who together can control the company?
- Is there the potential for deadlock between the shareholders?
- Are there particular stakeholders with specific demands? For example, Venture capital organisations.
- Are there other stakeholders who have influence comparable to shareholders? For example, Employee groups, regulatory authorities, providers of non-equity finance, significant trading partners, related parties.

This is important because:

- Stakeholders are those with significant influence over what the client does and how it is run.
- The demands of particular stakeholders could lead to parts of the business being discontinued or radically changed – which would invalidate all the knowledge of the business so carefully gathered.
- If there is deadlock between shareholders, the business may get bogged down in legal wrangling or may even cease to function altogether.
- There may be related party implications – see below.

Expandable Text - Acquisitions and disposals

Acquisitions and disposals

Consider:

- Is the client in the market to buy businesses?
- Might it dispose of a component?
- Might it be disposed of by its shareholders?

This is important because significant acquisitions and disposals:

- May radically affect the scale or nature of the client's operations.
- Lead to a change in stakeholders (see above)
- Invalidate current KOB.

Expandable Text - Financing

Financing

How is the client financed?

- Bank loans.
- Overdraft.
- Loans from holding company.
- Directors' loan/current accounts.

Are there any problems with financing?

- Overdraft limits might be breached.
- Other finance facility limits might be exceeded.
- Repayments due might not be met.
- Covenants might be breached.

This is important because:

- Access or lack of access to sources of finance can also have a huge impact on the scale or nature of the client's operations – access may enable the client to consider acquisitions, lack of finance may force the client to dispose of parts of the business (see acquisitions and disposals above).

- Insufficient financing will, sooner or later, cause the client to cease to be a going concern.

Expandable Text - Trading partners

Trading partners

Consider:

- Major customers.
- Major suppliers.

This is important because:

- Significant trading partners have significant influence over the client.

- Loss of a major customer will cause severe difficulties for the client as it will need to find new customers or change how it operates. (UK retailer Marks and Spencer switched many of its clothing suppliers from the UK to the Far East and several UK based clothing manufacturers closed down as a result).

- Customers who are in financial difficulties may become bad debts and cause the client cash flow problems.

- Major suppliers who fail, or who no longer supply the client with the required goods, or goods of the right quality, lead to the client being unable to supply **its** customers.

Expandable Text - Related parties

Related parties

Consideration of related parties is important for two reasons:

*   The need for related party disclosures required by IAS 24.
*   Related party relationships may affect the assessed level of risk (either favourably or unfavourably).

So we need to know:

*   who the shareholders are
*   who controls the entity
*   who manages the company
*   the names of partners, spouses etc of the above and the names of their children
*   companies and other entities in the same group as the client
*   companies and other entities under common control.

Expandable Text - What they do

What they do

It is only through an adequate understanding of what the client actually does, that sense can be made of all the KOB – the industry, technology, etc. – dealt with above.

When Enron collapsed, a journalist working for the business pages of *The Times* newspaper in the UK commented 'No one really understood what Enron did'.

There are particular problems for auditors with clients in 'High Tech' or specialised industries.

Expandable Text - Management

Management

The client's management is responsible for producing financial statements which give a true and fair view of its results and state of affairs.

The auditor therefore needs to form judgements about management's:

- competence
- reliability
- trustworthiness.

On a more practical level, the auditor needs to know who will supply information and respond to enquiries during the course of the audit.

Expandable Text - Accounting policies

Accounting policies

Knowledge of the client's accounting policies is vital to the auditor because:

- The use of inappropriate accounting policies, or inappropriate changes to accounting policies can lead to manipulation of the financial statements.
- Without an adequate understanding even of appropriate accounting policies, the auditor is unable to judge whether or not the financial statements give a true and fair view.

9 Sources of KOB

To get to know the client you would have to draw information from many sources of documents, it's always key to arrange a meeting with client. This enables you ask specific questions and go through the initial analytical procedures done.

Note: last years file is always a good resource, but only if its an existing client. So read the question carefully.

The sources

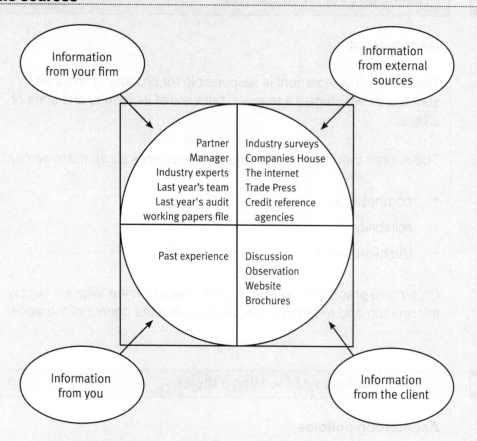

Discussion among the engagement team

'The members of the engagement team should discuss the susceptibility of the entity's financial statements to material misstatements.'

ISA 315 para 14

This discussion – effectively a planning meeting – is required by ISA 315.

In order to demonstrate that it has taken place and that the standard has been complied with, there will need to be evidence, usually in the form of minutes of the discussion meeting.

Expandable text - Risks

Topics to be covered will derive from all the aspects of KOB dealt with above, but particular care should be taken to address:

* Significant risks – particular issues which affect the client, e.g.
    - cash flow problems
    - an imminent takeover

>   –   major customers or suppliers in difficulties
>
>   –   quality or marketability issues with particular products.
>
> •   Risk of fraud – as required by ISA 240.

Analytical procedures

Analytical procedures are usually carried out at three stages of the audit process. They are mandatory at the planning and final review stages. At the substantive testing stage, they are one of several methods for obtaining evidence, so may not be appropriate in some circumstances.

Analytical procedures comprise the evaluation of financial information by studying the relationship between this information and other financial and non-financial data. They include comparison of financial information with prior periods, budgets and forecasts and similar industries.

At the planning stage, analytical procedures are used for two main reasons:

- to help understand the client's financial statements
- to help spot possible errors.

If errors look possible, the audit work will be directed towards those errors.

How this is done

Basic analytical procedures could involve simply looking at the client's trial balance or draft financial statements to see if they appear in line with the auditor's expectations. However, auditors will typically go further than this:

- monitoring statistical trends in key figures and ratios
- asking the client why certain balances appear out of line with expectations.

Computer programs are often used to select those balances that appear furthest from expectations.

Test your understanding 1

(a) With reference to ISA 520 *Analytical Procedures* explain

    (i)   what is meant by the term 'analytical procedures';

(2 marks)

    (ii) the different types of analytical procedures available to the auditor; and

(3 marks)

    (iii) the situations in the audit when analytical procedures can be used.

(3 marks)

Tribe Co sells bathrooms from 15 retail outlets. Sales are made to individuals, with income being in the form of cash and debit cards. All items purchased are delivered to the customer using Tribe's own delivery vans; most bathrooms are too big for individual's to transport in their own motor vehicles. The directors of Tribe indicate that the company has had a difficult year, but are pleased to present some acceptable results to the members.

The income statements for the last two financial years are shown below:

Income statement

	31 March 2009	31 March 2008
	$000	$000
Revenue	11,223	9,546
Cost of sales	(5,280)	(6,380)
	5,943	3,166
Operating expenses		
Administration	(1,853)	(1,980)
Selling and distribution	(1,472)	(1,034)
Interest payable	(152)	(158)
Investment income	218	–
	2,684	(6)

Financial statement extract

Cash and bank	380	(1,425)

Required:

(b) As part of your risk assessment procedures for Tribe Co, identify and provide a possible explanation for unusual changes in the income statement.

(9 marks)

(c) Confirmation of the end of year bank balances is an important audit procedure.

Required:

Explain the procedures necessary to obtain a bank confirmation letter from Tribe Co's bank.

(3 marks)

(20 marks)

10 Materiality

What is materiality?

We have already seen the definition of materiality:

'Information is material if its omission or misstatement could influence the economic decisions of users taken on the basis of the financial statements'

ISA 320 para 3

So what really is materiality?

* A big amount of money (material by size).

* An amount which although not big:
  - triggers a threshold
  - indicates future developments or other significant events
  - whose disclosure is compulsory

(material by nature).

Expandable text - Examples of material by nature

Examples of items which are material by nature include:

- The transaction which means the client makes a loss rather than a profit.

- A noteworthy threshold – $1bn profit.

- Transactions with directors e.g. salary and benefits, personal use of assets, etc.

- An accounting treatment which might be glossed over because the amount is small, but which, once the numbers get bigger, could be very serious indeed – during the Enron scandal, a technique which led to the omission of $21bn of debt from the statement of financial position, began with a desire to preserve the value of an immaterial investment.

Why is materiality important?

- If financial statements contain a material misstatement they cannot show a true and fair view.

- Auditors therefore must design their audit procedures to reduce the risk of material misstatement to an acceptable level.

- This means that auditors must decide on what they mean by 'material' before they design their procedures – hence its place in this chapter.

What are the implications for the work the auditors do?

Auditors will:

- Need to examine all items in the financial statements which are material

BUT

- they will also need to design tests to give assurance that material amounts have not been **omitted** from the financial statements

AND

- they will need to allow for the fact that a number of immaterial errors could together add up to a material misstatement.

Calculating materiality

Firms typically have a standard method for calculating a baseline materiality figure as part of the planning process.

Common measures are:

- ½ – 1% of turnover
- 5 – 10% of results
- 1 – 2% of assets

but these are up to the judgment of the auditor.

As a result, different firms use different measures.

Any calculation done is very flexible, and may have to be reassessed during the audit (if for example many large errors are found).

Expandable text - Example of materiality

Consider three companies, Red, Blue and Green in different industries.

Using the measures of materiality suggested above on the figures given below produces the following results:

Business	Red Limited	Green Limited	Blue Limited
	Manufacturing	Property Investment	Consultancy
	$000	$000	$000
Turnover	15,000	375	10,000
Gross profit	6,000	338	10,000
Profit before tax	1,500	38	2,000
Gross assets	20,000	7,500	5,000
Net assets	15,000	1,875	3,000
Materiality calculations			
Measures based on turnover			
½%	75	2	50
1%	150	4	100
Measures based on results			
5%	75	2	100
10%	150	4	200
Measures based on gross assets			
1%	200	75	50
2%	400	150	100

Notice the following things:

- Companies in different industries may well have very different profiles of profitability and return on capital employed.

- The property company generates comparatively lower levels of profit from its assets, has low direct costs and is more heavily geared.

- The consultancy business generates higher levels of profit from lower levels of assets because it makes its earnings from selling its employees' time. It has no direct costs.

- The manufacturer has less extreme differences between the figures in its income statement and its statement of financial position, has significant direct costs and is less heavily geared than the property company.

Possible levels of materiality for Red, Blue and Green

First a health warning!

- All three companies are fictitious – invented to illustrate the principles of calculating materiality.

- Every client has to be assessed on its merits.

- Assessing materiality is a matter of professional judgement and is not a mechanistic exercise.

BUT having said all that:

Materiality for all three companies might well be set at about $100,000. but note the following:

- Companies assessed as being higher risk would tend to have lower levels of materiality.

- For the manufacturer and consultancy businesses the figures derived from the income statement are likely to be weighted more heavily in the calculation than those derived from the statement of financial position, because that is where the bulk of their activity is focused.

- Conversely, the calculation for the property company is more likely to be focused on the statement of financial position figures.

Exam focus

Materiality is quite a difficult concept to explain.

Be familiar with the definition from ISA 320 quoted above remembering a phrase like **'influence the economic decisions of users'.**

Take some time to think about **why** materiality is important, as indicated above.

11 Tolerable error

What is tolerable error?

The maximum error in a population that the auditor is willing to accept.

ISA 530 para 12

This means that in the case of tests of control, the auditors will accept a certain number of instances of a failure to apply a control procedure and will still conclude that the procedure is operating properly.

Tolerable error is considered during the planning stage, and for substantive procedures, is related to the auditor's judgement about materiality.

The difference between materiality and tolerable error

- **Materiality** concerns the financial statements as a whole.
- **Tolerable error** only concerns the population being tested.

12 Documenting the planning process

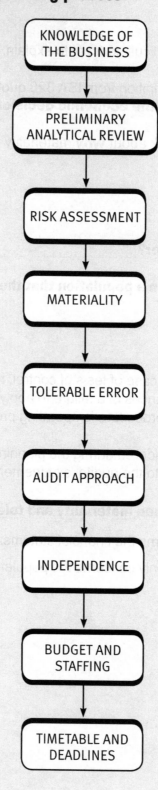

This chapter has considered all aspects of the planning process. ISAs require that all the elements of the audit should be documented, and so it is clearly necessary to produce a record of the audit strategy and plan, which can be referred to as the audit progresses and can be used in the completion stages to ensure that everything has been done which ought to have done.

Most firms will use 'audit packs' – pre-printed or computerised documents and checklists to ensure that the requirements of ISAs have been followed.

The stages of the plan

The plan usually consists of nine stages:

(1) **Gather/confirm knowledge of the business**

- Nature of the business

- Management

- Key staff

- Those charged with governance

- Accounting systems

- Internal controls

- KOB discussion

(2) **Preliminary analytical review**

(3) **Risk assessment**

- Overall

- By area

- Significant risks

(4) **Materiality calculation**

(5) **Tolerable error calculations for material areas**

(6) **The audit approach to be adopted for all areas**

(7) **Assessment of auditor's independence – See chapter 5 Ethics**

(8) **Budget and staffing**

(9) **Timetable and deadlines**

Variations on the theme

- For large audits much of the KOB information may be kept on a permanent file and the audit plan may contain a summary or simply cross refer to the permanent file.

- Increasingly KOB is being summarised in a planning memorandum which is updated each year.

- With computerised audit systems where all background documents may be scanned in, the distinction between current and permanent audit files is being eroded.

- For large audits, the planning may be so complex that it needs to be summarised in a separate memorandum.

- For small audits the summary may be all that is necessary.

 Permanent file – a file of information which is relevant for more than one year's audit, e.g.

- Names of management, those charged with governance, shareholders.
- Systems information.
- Background to the industry and the client's business.
- Title deeds.
- Directors' service agreements
- Copies of contract and agreements.

Current file – a file containing the documentation and evidence for the current audit.

Expandable text - Contents of a current file

Typically, there are sections as follows:

- planning
- completion
- one section for each major statement of financial position heading
- one section for each major income statement heading.

Planning

The main element of this section is likely to be the Audit Planning Memorandum.

This document is the written audit plan and will be read by all members of the audit team before work starts. Its contents are likely to include:

- background information about the client, including recent performance
- changes since last year's audit (for recurring clients)
- key accounting policies
- important laws and regulations affecting the company
- client's Trial Balance (or draft Financial Statements)
- preliminary Analytical Review
- key audit risks
- overall audit strategy
- materiality assessment
- timetable of procedures
- deadlines
- staffing and a budget (hours to be worked x charge-out rates)
- locations to be visited.

Completion

Mostly based around checklists, the completion (also known as Review) stage of an audit has a number of standard components:

- Going Concern review
- Subsequent Events review
- Final Analytical Review
- Accounting Standards Checklist
- Companies Act Checklist
- Letter of Representation
- Summary of adjustments made since Trial Balance produced
- Summary of Unadjusted Errors
- Draft final Financial Statements
- Draft Report to Those Charged With Governance (Management Letter).

Statement of financial position and income statement areas

For these final two areas, each section is likely to consist of:

- Lead Schedule – showing total figures, which agree to the Financial Statements
- Back-up Schedules – breakdowns of totals into relevant sub-totals

- Audit Work Programme – listing:
    - the objectives being tested
    - work completed
    - how sampled items selected
    - conclusions drawn
    - who did the work
    - date work completed
    - who reviewed it
- Audit Work – Descriptions of work carried out

Test your understanding 2

Amongst matters required to be considered by the auditor when planning the audit in accordance with the requirements of ISA 300 Planning an Audit of Financial Statements are those of 'materiality' and the 'direction, supervision and review' of the audit.

Materiality is further the subject of ISA 320 Audit Materiality. Direction, supervision and review are considered in more detail within other Auditing Standards.

Required:

(a) Explain the concept of materiality and how materiality is assessed when planning the audit. Your answer should include consideration of materiality at the overall financial statement level and in relation to individual account balances.

(12 marks)

(b) Explain the nature and significance of direction, supervision and review both in planning the audit and subsequently during the performance of the audit on a particular engagement.

(8 marks)

(Total: 20 marks)

Test your understanding 3

(1) Discuss issues to be considered as part of the planning process for an audit.

(6 marks)

(2) List 4 things which need to be done during the planning process.

(2 marks)

(3) List 2 sources of information which enable the auditor to assess risk.

(1 mark)

(4) What is the difference between the audit strategy and the audit plan?

(1 mark)

(5) Discuss aspects of the client's business which need to be explained in the audit plan.

(1 mark)

(6) List possible sources of knowledge of the business.

(4 marks)

(7) Define materiality.

(1 mark)

(8) Define tolerable error.

(1 mark)

(9) What is the difference between materiality and tolerable error?

(1 mark)

(10) List 8 stages of the audit plan.

(4 marks)

(11) Why is it important for the auditor to plan?

(5 marks)

13 Chapter summary

```
                        ┌──────────────┐
                        │  Why plan?   │
                        └──────┬───────┘
                               │                    ┌──────────────┐
                               │                    │     KOB      │
                        ┌──────┴───────┐            └──────────────┘
                        │ The planning │
                        │   process    │            ┌──────────────┐
                        └──────┬───────┘            │      AR      │
                               │                    └──────────────┘
    ┌──────────────┐    ┌──────┴───────┐
    │Impact of fraud│····│ Assess risk │            ┌──────────────┐
    └──────────────┘    └──────────────┘            │The audit team│
                                                    └──────────────┘

                        ┌──────────────┐            ┌──────────────┐
                        │The audit plan│············│ Materiality  │
                        └──────────────┘            └──────────────┘
    ┌──────────────┐
    │    Scope     │····                            ┌──────────────┐
    └──────────────┘    ┌──────────────┐            │Tolerable error│
                        │Audit strategy│            └──────────────┘
    ┌──────────────┐    └──────────────┘
    │    Timing    │····
    └──────────────┘                                ┌──────────────┐
                                                    │ Design audit │
    ┌──────────────┐                                │  procedures  │
    │  Direction   │····                            └──────────────┘
    └──────────────┘
```

Test your understanding answers

Test your understanding 1

(a) (i) Explanation of analytical procedures

Analytical procedures are used in obtaining an understanding of an entity and its environment and in the overall review at the end of the audit.   1 mark

'Analytical procedures' actually means the evaluation of financial and other information and the review of plausible relationships in that information. The review also includes identifying fluctuations and relationships that do not appear consistent with other relevant information or results.   1 mark

(ii) Types of analytical procedures

Analytical procedures can be used as:

– Comparison of comparable information to prior periods to identify unusual changes or fluctuations in amounts.   1 mark

– Comparison of actual or anticipated results of the entity with budgets and/or forecasts, or the expectations of the auditor in order to determine the potential accuracy of those results.   1 mark

– Comparison to industry information either for the industry as a whole or by comparison to entities of similar size to the client to determine whether receivable days, for example, are reasonable.   1 mark

(iii) Use of analytical procedures

Risk assessment procedures

Analytical procedures are used at the beginning of the audit to help the auditor obtain an understanding of the entity and assess the risk of material misstatement. Audit procedures can then be directed to these 'risky' areas.   1 mark

Analytical procedures are substantive procedures.

Analytical procedures can be used as substantive procedures in determining the risk of material misstatement at the assertion level during work on the income statement and statement of financial position (balance sheet).   1 mark

Analytical procedures in the overall review at the end of the audit.

Analytical procedures help the auditor at the end of the audit in forming an overall conclusion as to whether the financial statements as a whole are consistent with the auditor's understanding of the entity.   1 mark

(b) Net profit   ½ mark

Overall, Tribe's result has changed from a net loss to a net profit. Given that sales have only increased by 17% and that expenses, at least administration expenses, appear low, then there is the possibility that expenditure may be understated.   1 mark

Sales – increase 17%   ½ mark

According to the directors, Tribe has had a 'difficult year'. Reasons for the increase in sales income must be ascertained as the change does not conform to the directors' comments. it is possible that the industry as a whole, has been growing allowing Tribe to produce this good result.   1 mark

Cost of sales – fall 17%   ½ mark

A fall in cost of sales in unusual given that sales have increased significantly. This may have been caused by an incorrect inventory valuation and the use of different (cheaper) suppliers which may cause problems with faulty goods in the next year.   1 mark

Gross profit (GP) – increase 88%   ½ mark

This is significant increase with the GP% changing from 33% last year to 53% in 2008. Identifying reasons for this change will need to focus initially on the change in sales and cost of sales.   1 mark

Administration – fall 6%   ½ mark

A fall is unusual given that sales are increasing and so an increase in administration to support those sales would be expected. Expenditure may be understated, or there has been a decrease in the number of administration staff.   1 mark

Selling and distribution – increase 42%   ½ mark

This increase does not appear to be in line with the increase in sales – selling and distribution would be expected to increase in line with sales. There may be mis-allocation of expenses from administration or the age of Tribe's delivery vans is increasing resulting in additional service costs.   1 mark

Interest payable – small fall   ½ mark

Given that Tribe has a considerable cash surplus this year, continuing to pay interest is surprising. The amount may be overstated – reasons for lack of fall in interest payment e.g. loans that cannot be repaid early, must be determined.   1 mark

Investment income – new this year   ½ mark

This is expected given cash surplus on the year, although the amount is still very high indicating possible errors in the amount or other income generating assets not disclosed on the statement of financial position extract.   1 mark

(c) Obtaining a bank letter

- Review the need to obtain a bank letter from the information obtained from the preliminary risk assessment of Tribe.   1 mark

- Prepare a standard bank letter in the format agreed with banks in your jurisdiction.   1 mark

- Obtain authorisation on that letter from a director of Tribe for the bank to disclose information to the auditor.   1 mark

- Where Tribe has provided their bank with a standing authority to disclose information to the auditors, refer to this authority in the bank letter.   1 mark

- The auditor sends the letter directly to Tribe bank with a request to send the reply directly back to the auditors.   1 mark

Test your understanding 2

(a) Materiality

Financial statements are materially misstated when they contain errors or irregularities whose effect, individually or in the aggregate, is important enough to prevent the statements from being fairly presented. In this context, misstatements may result from misapplication of applicable Accounting Standards, departures from fact, or omissions of necessary information. ISA 320, Audit Materiality, requires auditors to consider materiality when determining the nature, timing and extent of audit procedures. In complying with this requirement ISA 320 recommends that auditors make preliminary judgements about materiality levels in planning the audit at the following two levels:

- The financial statement level (overall materiality), because the auditors' opinion on fair presentation extends to the financial statements taken as a whole.

- The account balance level (testing materiality), because the auditors verify account balances in reaching an overall conclusion that the financial statements are fairly presented.

The overall level of materiality and the nature of account balances enable auditors to determine which account balances to audit and how to evaluate the effects of misstatements in financial information as a whole. Materiality at the account balance level assists auditors in determining what items in a balance (or transactions class) to audit and what audit procedures to undertake; for example, whether to use sampling or analytical procedures.

Materiality at the overall financial statement level

There may be more than one level of materiality relating to the financial statements. For the income statement, materiality could be related to revenue or to profit (usually before tax). For the statement of financial position, materiality could be based on shareholders' equity, assets or liability class totals.

In making a preliminary judgement about materiality auditors initially determine the aggregate level of materiality for each financial statement. For example, it may be estimated that errors totalling $100,000 for the income statement and $200,000 for the statement of financial position would be material. For planning purposes, the auditors should use the smallest aggregate level of misstatement considered to be material to any one of the financial statements. This decision rule is appropriate because the financial statements are interrelated and many audit procedures pertain to more than one statement. For instance, the audit procedure to determine whether year-end credit sales are recorded in the proper period provides evidence about both accounts receivable (statement of financial position) and sales (income statement).

ISA 320 offers no guidance for determining this relationship but, where an item has an effect on profit, a widely used rule of thumb states that:

- an amount which is equal to or greater than 10% of profit is presumed to be material

- an amount which is equal to or less than 5% of profit may be presumed not to be material

- to determine whether an amount between 5% and 10% is material is a matter of judgement.

Other commonly used bases, and materiality thresholds expressed as a percentage of that base, are as follows.

	Materiality threshold (%)
Sales revenue	0.5
Gross profit	2.0
Total assets	0.5
Equity	1.0

Qualitative considerations

The emphasis in planning materiality is on quantitative considerations. ISA 320 acknowledges that in designing the audit plan, the auditor establishes an acceptable materiality level so as to detect quantitatively material misstatements. Since the errors are not yet known, their qualitative effect can be considered only during the testing phase of the audit, as evidence becomes available.

Qualitative considerations relate to the causes of misstatements or to misstatements that do not have a quantifiable effect. A misstatement that is quantitatively immaterial may be qualitatively material. This may occur for instance, when the misstatement is attributable to an irregularity or an illegal act by the entity. Discovery of either occurrence might cause the auditors to conclude there is a significant risk of additional similar misstatements. Although it is suggested that the auditors should be alert for misstatements that could be qualitatively material, it ordinarily is not practical to design procedures to detect them.

Materiality at the account balance or transaction class level

Account balance materiality – Tolerable error per ISA 530 – is the maximum misstatement that can exist in an account balance for it not to be considered materially misstated. In making judgements about materiality at the account balance level, the auditors must consider the relationship between it and financial statement materiality. This consideration should lead the auditors to plan the audit to detect misstatements that may be immaterial individually but that may be material to the financial statements taken as a whole when aggregated with misstatements in other account balances.

When the auditors' preliminary judgements about financial statement materiality are quantified, a preliminary estimate of materiality for each account may be obtained by allocating financial statement materiality to the individual accounts. The allocation may be made to both statement of financial position and income statement accounts. However because most income statement misstatements also affect the statement of financial position and because there are fewer statement of financial position accounts, many auditors make the allocation on the basis of the statement of financial position accounts.

Allocating overall materiality to accounts is heavily dependent on the subjective judgement of the auditors. The auditors' judgement may be influenced by qualitative considerations. Materiality in auditing cash balances may be set at a much lower level than materiality in auditing intangible assets. Cash is known to be capable of precise determination and is critical to the liquidity of the entity; intangible assets, on the other hand, are known to be incapable of precise valuation and users are unlikely to be misled by a relatively large misstatement in the reported amount.

(b) **Direction, supervision and review**

Direction

An important function in planning the audit is the generation of material necessary for the direction of staff assigned to the audit. Staff need to receive adequate guidance as to the nature of the business and, in particular as to any specific matters affecting the audit determined during the planning phase, such as recent or proposed changes in the nature of the business, its management or its financial structure. Assistants assigned to an audit must receive direction as to such matters to enable them to carry out the audit work delegated to them.

A principal purpose of planning is determining the mix of tests of controls and substantive procedures and the nature, timing and extent of those procedures. The results of the plan are documented in an audit program which specifies the individual procedures to be performed in sufficient detail relative to the experience of the staff assigned to the engagement.

Supervision

The assignment of staff to the audit as part of the planning process should ensure that they are subject to an appropriate level of supervision. The more junior or inexperienced the staff, the more supervision they will require. On small audits supervision is usually in the form of daily contact with the staff members at the client's premises by a supervisor, usually the audit manager; with regular visits to the clients' premises during the course of the audit.

On larger audits there will be a hierarchy of staff at different levels each with responsibility for supervising the work of assistants assigned to them. During the course of the audit supervisory staff should regularly monitor the work of assistants to ensure that:

- they understand the requirements of each procedure in the audit programme to which they are assigned
- they have the necessary skills and competence to perform their assigned tasks
- the work performed is in accordance with the requirements of the audit programme.

In addition, supervision should ensure that any important matters discovered during the audit are promptly dealt with and the audit programme modified as necessary. The supervisor should also monitor the time spent on each phase of the audit against time budgeted during the planning phase. Significant variances could indicate problems in the performance of the audit.

Review

Supervision also involves review of the work performed. All work must be reviewed to ensure that:

- the work has been performed in accordance with the programme
- the evidence has been properly documented
- all outstanding matters have been satisfactorily resolved
- conclusions drawn are consistent with the evidence and support the audit opinion.

KAPLAN PUBLISHING

In addition to the review of evidence obtained in accordance with the audit programme, there needs to be a review at a higher level of more significant audit decisions made. These include a review of:

- the audit plan and audit programme

- the assessment of inherent and control risk and the proposed audit strategy

- reviews of the working papers undertaken by staff at an appropriate level of responsibility

- the proposed audit opinion based on the overall results of the audit process.

On smaller engagements this review may be undertaken by the manager; with oversight by the engagement partner that the review has been properly conducted. On larger audits the final review will be carried out by the partner. On certain audits it is considered desirable for a second partner, not otherwise involved in the audit, to perform an additional review before issuing the auditors' report. This is sometimes referred to as a hot review.

Test your understanding 3

(1) Discuss issues to be considered as part of the planning process for an audit.	**People** – Who should make up the audit team?	1 mark
	Timing – What are the deadlines?	1 mark
	Focus – What are the key aspects of the audit?	1 mark
	Problem areas – What issues are likely to cause difficulties and how should they be addressed?	1 mark
	Nature of work – What audit approach should be used and what types of procedures are appropriate?	1 mark
	Amount of work – Sample sizes, number of tests etc. all driven by assessment of risk and materiality.	1 mark
(2) List five things which need to be done during the planning process.	Assess risk.	½ mark
	Develop the audit strategy.	½ mark
	Select the audit team.	½ mark
	Assess materiality.	½ mark
	Select appropriate audit procedures.	½ mark
(3) List two sources of information which enable the auditor to assess risk.	Knowledge of the business.	½ mark
	Analytical review.	½ mark
(4) What is the difference between the audit strategy and the audit plan?	Whilst the strategy sets the overall approach to the audit, the plan fills in the operational details of how the strategy is to be achieved.	1 mark

(5) Discuss eight aspects of the client's business which need to be explained in the audit plan.	Choose from: • The industry • The competition • Technology • Laws and regulations • Stakeholders • Acquisitions • Disposals • Financing • Trading partners • Related parties • What the client does • Management • Systems • Controls • Significant risks • Accounting policies.	1 mark per point
(6) List possible sources of knowledge of the business.	Choose from: • The engagement partner • The engagement manager • Your firm's industry experts • Last year's audit team • Industry surveys • The company's registry • The internet • Trade press • Credit reference agencies • Discussions with client's staff • Observation of events and processes at the client's premises • The client's website • Brochures and other publicity material.	½ mark per point

(7)	Define materiality.	'Information is material if its omission or misstatement could influence the economic decisions of users taken on the basis of the financial statements'.	1 mark
(8)	Define tolerable error.	'The maximum error in a population that the auditor is willing to accept.'	1 mark
(9)	What is the difference between Materiality and tolerable error?	**Materiality** concerns the financial statements as a whole. **Tolerable error** only concerns the population being tested.	1 mark
(10)	List 8 stages of the audit plan.	Knowledge of the business.	½ mark
		Preliminary analytical review.	½ mark
		Risk assessment.	½ mark
		Materiality.	½ mark
		Tolerable error.	½ mark
		Audit approach.	½ mark
		Independence.	½ mark
		Budget and staffing.	½ mark
		Timetable and deadlines.	½ mark
(11)	Why is it important for the auditor to plan?	To decide on the audit approach.	1 mark
		To decide how much work to do.	1 mark
		To decide what type of work to do.	1 mark
		To decide on the composition of the audit team.	1 mark
		To ensure that risk is reduced to an acceptable level.	1 mark

7

Risk

Chapter learning objectives

Upon completion of this chapter you will be able to:

- identify and describe the need to plan and perform audits with an attitude of professional scepticism

- compare and contrast risk-based, procedural and other approaches to audit work

- discuss the importance of risk analysis

- describe the use of information technology in risk analysis

- identify and describe engagement risks affecting the audit of an entity

- explain the components of audit risk.

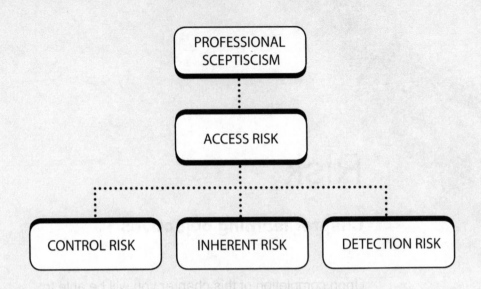

1 Risk-based and procedural approaches to auditing

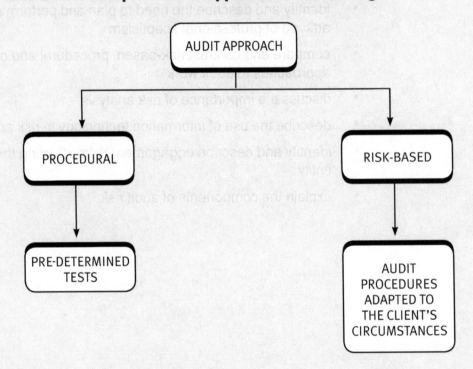

When doing an audit, auditors can take one of two basic approaches:

- procedural
- risk-based.

Procedural

The auditor carries out a set of standard procedures and tests regardless of the particular nature of the client.

Expandable Text - Risk based and procedural approaches

Illustration – Risk-based and procedural approaches

Possible examples are:

- the auditors execute pre-defined procedures to determine how shared costs should be determined and allocated between the owners of apartments in an apartment block

- procedures determined by legislation or regulation – e.g. in the UK auditors have to perform certain procedures to ensure that lawyers are dealing with client's money in accordance with the rules.

Risk-based

The auditor plans the audit around the risks that the client's financial statements may contain misstatements, whether as a result of fraud or not. As such, each audit will involve different priorities, different tests, and will take different lengths of time.

Traditionally, auditors have followed a risk-based approach, as this should minimise the chance of them giving the wrong opinion. It also helps to ensure that audit work is carried out as efficiently as possible, as assurance is obtained using the most effective tests.

2 Risk assessment as part of the audit process

If the auditor needs to conduct the audit with an attitude of professional scepticism, he or she needs to ask the question:

- **So what could go wrong?**

Professional scepticism – An attitude that includes a questioning mind and a critical assessment of evidence.

Expandable Text

Although approaches other than this risk-based approach to auditing are possible, since the introduction of ISAs and ISA 315 in particular, its use is compulsory for statutory audits.

We will see how audit risk breaks down into its three components:

- inherent risk
- control risk
- detection risk.

3 The importance of risk analysis

Risk analysis is the most important stage of the audit. If auditors assess risk properly, they will:

- Identify main areas where errors or misstatements are likely early in the audit.
- Plan audit work that addresses these possible mistakes.
- Discover errors as early as possible in the audit process.
- Carry out the most efficient (and hence profitable) audit possible.
- Minimise the chance of issuing an incorrect audit opinion.
- Reduce the chance of getting sued (and losing!).
- Have a good understanding of the risks of fraud, money laundering etc.
- Be in the best position to assess whether the client is a going concern.

Although the key to risk assessment is to do it as part of the planning process, it is important to understand that:

- Risk can be uncovered at any stage of the audit.
- In the light of the work done the level of risk may be reappraised.
- The review and completion phase of the audit has to confirm that the risk of material misstatement has been reduced to an acceptable level.

Expandable Text - The role of information technology

The role of information technology (IT)

IT can play an important part in risk analysis because it enables auditors to carry out analytical procedures (see the sessions on audit procedures) in a cost effective way to highlight:

- unusual relationships
- unusual trends

in the components of financial statements.

The use of IT also enables the auditor to process high volumes of data through computer-assisted audit techniques (CAATS), to screen for unusual relationships or unexpected repetition of data in a way which would be impossible without such technology. See chapter 10 Audit procedures for more on CAATS.

The impact of ISA 315

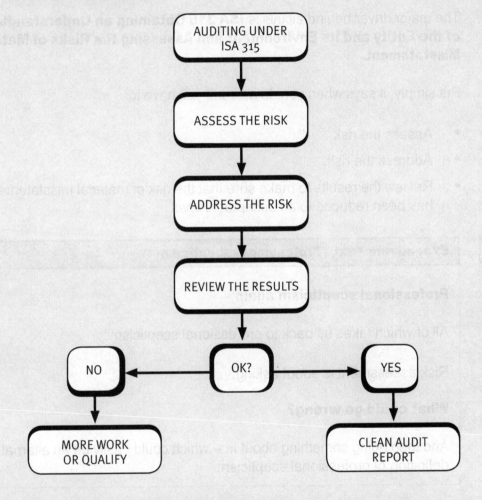

Audits conducted under ISAs **must** follow the risk-based approach

It is difficult to overstate how important this is. It affects:

- how audits are planned
- the sources of assurance
- the nature of audit evidence gathered by the auditor
- the nature of the procedures carried out by the auditor
- the amount of evidence gathered.

We consider all of these aspects in the chapters on planning, systems and controls, audit evidence and audit procedures.

Exam hint

It is also important for you and your approach to exam questions:

- Where there is a scenario given, you **must adapt** your answer to the facts of the scenario – the nature of the business, systems in operation, etc.

The major driver behind all this is **ISA 315 Obtaining an Understanding of the Entity and its Environment and Assessing the Risks of Material Misstatement.**

Put simply, it says when you do an audit you have to:

- Assess the risk.
- Address the risk.
- Review the results to make sure that the risk of material misstatement has been reduced to an acceptable level.

Expandable Text - Professional scepticism

Professional scepticism again

All of which takes us back to professional scepticism.

Risk assessment is about asking:

What could go wrong?

And then doing something about it. – which could easily be an alternative definition of professional scepticism.

Engagement risk

Expandable Text - Engagement risk

Before we look at the specifics of audit risk and its impact on the conduct of an audit, we need to consider other elements of risk which affect the engagement:

- ethical issues
- significant risks.

Expandable Text - Ethical issues

Ethical issues

We have looked at these in chapter 5 on professional ethics.

The auditor will need to consider potential ethical issues:

- on appointment
- on re appointment
- when planning the engagement
- when completing the engagement
- when accepting engagements to provide non-audit services.

The auditor will need to identify

- potential threats to independence and objectivity
- the safeguards in place.

Expandable Text - Significant risks

Significant risks

ISA 315 defines significant risks as:

'Risks which require special audit consideration.'

Expandable Text - Illustration - Engagement risk

Illustration – Engagement risk

These could be such things as:

- going concern problems
- imminent takeovers
- key staff leaving
- impact of laws and regulations

- limited availability of audit staff
- inexperienced audit staff
- tight deadlines.

4 Audit risk

Audit risk defined

Audit risk is defined as:

'The risk of that the auditor <u>expresses</u> an <u>inappropriate</u> audit <u>opinion</u> <u>when</u> the financial statements are <u>materially misstated</u>.'

(typically, stating that the financial statements are true and fair, when in fact they are not).

Audit risk is further defined by way of a formula:

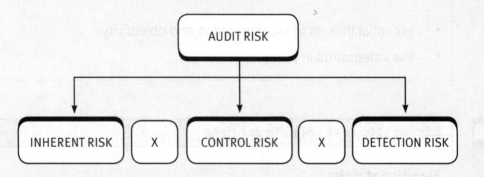

We will look at the components of audit risk below.

Inherent risk

The risk of <u>errors</u> or <u>misstatements</u> due to the <u>nature</u> of the company <u>and its transactions</u>.

Clearly this requires the audit team to have a good knowledge of how the client's activities are likely to affect its financial statements, and the audit team should discuss these matters in a **planning meeting** before deciding on the detailed approach and audit work to be used.

Such a meeting is compulsory under ISA 315 and must be documented.

At the account balance and assertion level

As well as considering the entity as a whole, the auditor needs to assess whether individual headings in the financial statements or assertions about those items, carry increased levels of inherent risk.

Management makes a number of **assertions** about items in the financial statements – whether they exist, their value, whether all are included, whether they are recognised in the correct accounting period etc. which we will consider in detail in the chapter on audit evidence.

Control risk

Control risk is the risk of errors or misstatements because the company's internal controls are not strong enough to prevent, detect and correct them.

We will consider internal control in depth in chapter 8 Systems and controls.

Control risk increases due to the lack of suitable procedures implemented by the client. The implementation of such procedures will have a cost, e.g.:

- the installation of new equipment
- the employment of extra staff
- the time taken by additional administrative procedures.

The client therefore needs to make a judgement about whether the benefits of the control outweigh the costs of implementing it.

- How much 'shrinkage' (jargon for theft of goods from a retail store) would there need to be to make it worthwhile employing a store detective or installing electronic tags and detectors?

Detection risk

This is the risk that the auditor's procedures do not pick up material misstatements.

Sampling risk

Detection risk includes sampling risk, which is defined as:

The risk which **'arises from the possibility that the auditor's conclusion, based on a sample may be different from the conclusion reached if the entire population were subjected to the same audit procedure'.**

ISA 530 Para 7

In other words it is the risk that the sample may not be representative.

Any other risks that the auditor may come to the wrong conclusion, e.g.:

- by misinterpreting the results of a test
- by using inappropriate procedures

- by failing to investigate a particular balance or transaction

- because a member of the client's staff misleads the auditor

is classified as **non-sampling risk.** Non-sampling risk is defined as arising from factors that cause the auditor to reach an erroneous conclusion for any reason not related to the size of the sample.

5 Assessing the risk

It can be seen that audit risk comprises three types of risk:

- inherent risk (IR)
- control risk (CR)
- detection risk (DR)

and that the formula mentioned below;

$$AR = IR \times CR \times DR$$

means that it is possible to 'score' the level of risk.

The assessment does not need to be a mathematical one – the equation helps us to understand how the risks interact – but many firms use a mathematical approach.

This involves the various risks being assessed (often using a checklist of relevant questions) and being issued a 'score', a process that may be carried out using software.

Inherent risk and control risk cannot be directly influenced by the auditor, as they relate to the nature of the entity and its systems. (Together these two risks are known as the **Entity risk.**)

The only risk that the auditor can change is detection risk.

Therefore, once inherent and control risk have been assessed, and with a maximum overall audit risk 'score' in mind, detection risk can be manipulated to make the audit risk an acceptable level.

Detection risk will be a major variable in determining the extent of audit procedures, e.g.sample sizes for audit tests.

If control risk and inherent risk are deemed low because the entity is not particularly risky and the its controls are effective, the auditor will place reliance on these factors. Detection risk can be allowed to be higher and still give an acceptably low level of audit risk. If detection risk needs to be low because the client is inherently risky or controls are not effective, the auditor will increase the sample size and/or use more experienced staff.

Factor/Identify	Audit risk	Work we need to perform/effect on the audit	Type of risk
Lack of physical controls • Valuable assets not being locked away. • No restricted access to sensitive areas. • No CCTV or other security measures for access to premises.	Employees are more likely to steal assets from the company or not look after them; therefore they get damaged and become impaired. Incorrect statement on Financial statements the asset position potentially over statement.	Physical checks of the assets required to determine completeness and value. Analytical review to see any unusual trends over excess ordering etc.....	Control risk
Lack of IT based controls • No passwords or lack of password protection (everyone knows each others passwords).	Computer systems can be changed or modified without suitable authorisation. Changes are not recorded and or notified to responsible individuals.	Analytical procedures to be performed to see if any unusual trends are happening. Review the integrity of the staff. Assess the systems to see how easy changes will go undetected.	Control risk

Factor/Identify	Audit risk	Work we need to perform/effect on the audit	Type of risk
Lack of authorisation controls.	Unnecessary expenditure incurred or even non business expenditure. Sales completed over the limits therefore potential for non payment. New staff employed without authorisation that may not be necessary.	Assess the systems to determine the likelihood of this happening. Review the old balances and credit limited and see what other controls the company have in place. Review the organisation chart for reasonableness and understand the roles within the company.	Control risk
Lack of segregation of duties.	Not identifying errors and fraud as only one person doing the job therefore concealment easier to perform.	Increase the substantive testing to ensure that the statements are true and fair.	Control risk
Account balances for example Research and development and warranty provisions.	Due to the natures of these transactions a high degree of judgement or estimation is involved and is therefore open to manipulation or error.	Get a understating of the criteria that needs to met and obtain sufficient evidence to support the calculations.	Inherent risk
Client operates in a high tech or fashion industry	Inventory may be obsolete Obsolete inventory may be overstated in the financial statements	Review events after the reporting period to determine the net realisable value of inventory Use an independent valuer to value inventory	Inherent risk

KAPLAN PUBLISHING

Factor/Identify	Audit risk	Work we need to perform/effect on the audit	Type of risk
Client is based in multiple locations	Inventory held at other locations may be omitted from year-end inventory Controls may be less effective	Attend inventory takes at all locations Review control procedures to ensure they are adequate Consider using a substantive approach	Control risk + Detection risk
Bank is relying on the financial statements or Directors are paid a bonus based on profits	Risk management bias	Pay more attention • accounting estimates • cut-off Obtain independent estimates re valuation of year-end inventory etc	Inherent risk
It is cash-based business	Cash may be misappropriated, causing turnover to be understated	Consider the adequacy of internal controls over sales (possible limitation in scope if we cannot verify the completeness of sales and internal controls are inadequate)	Inherent risk + Potentially control risk
The company trades overseas	Transactions in foreign currency may not be translated at the correct rate The company may make foreign exchange losses	Ensure foreign currency is correctly accounted for Review procedures to mitigate exchange loss risk, e.g. hedging	Inherent risk

Factor/Identify	Audit risk	Work we need to perform/effect on the audit	Type of risk
New computer system in the year	Errors in transferring the data from one system to another There may be inherent errors in the new system that have not yet been discovered	Review controls over the changeover: • parallel run • check opening balances transferred properly Use test data on the system to ensure it operates correctly	Control risk + Inherent
New audit client	Lack of cumulative audit knowledge and experience may lead to increased detection risk	Use an audit team that is experienced in the industry Gather knowledge of the company Check opening balances are correct	Detection risk
Tight audit deadline imposed by client	Staff working quickly to a tight deadline are more likely to make errors There is a shorter post statement of financial position period that we can use to help with our audit	Increase substantive testing Perform an interim visit to complete some audit work before the end of the year Agree a timetable re: • reporting deadline • client schedules to be available	Detection risk
Temporary staff used during the year	Errors more likely as staff are not familiar with the client's systems	Increase substantive testing	Control risk
A client in a specialised industry	Errors more likely or fraud more likely to be missed because of the complexity of the work	Ensure that the auditors understand the system, increase testing	Inherent risk

FIXED TEST 2

(a) Explain the term 'audit risk'.

(4 marks)

(b) You are the audit manager for Parker, a limited liability company which sells books, CDs, DVDs and similar items via two divisions: mail order and on-line ordering on the Internet. Parker is a new audit client. You are commencing the planning of the audit for the year-ended 31 May 20X5. An initial meeting with the directors has provided the information below.

The company's sales revenue is in excess of $85 million with net profits of $4 million. All profits are currently earned in the mail order division, although the Internet division is expected to return a small net profit next year. Sales revenue is growing at the rate of 20% p.a. net profit has remained almost the same for the last four years.

In the next year, the directors plan to expand the range of goods sold through the Internet division to include toys, garden furniture and fashion clothes. The directors believe that when one product has been sold on the Internet, then any other product can be as well.

The accounting system to record sales by the mail order division is relatively old. It relies on extensive manual input to transfer orders received in the post onto Parker's computer systems. Recently errors have been known to occur, in the input of orders, and in the invoicing of goods following despatch. The directors maintain that the accounting system produces materially correct figures and they cannot waste time in identifying relatively minor errors. The company accountant, who is not qualified and was appointed because he is a personal friend of the directors, agrees with this view.

The directors estimate that their expansion plans will require a bank loan of approximately $30 million, partly to finance the enhanced web site but also to provide working capital to increase inventory levels. A meeting with the bank has been scheduled for three months after the year end. The directors expect an unmodified auditor's report to be signed prior to this time.

Required:

(i) Identify and describe the matters that give rise to audit risks associated with Parker.

(10 marks)

(ii) Explain the enquiries you will make, and the audit procedures you will perform to assist you in making a decision regarding the going concern status of Parker in reaching your audit opinion on the financial statements.

(6 marks)

(Total: 20 marks)

6 Chapter summary

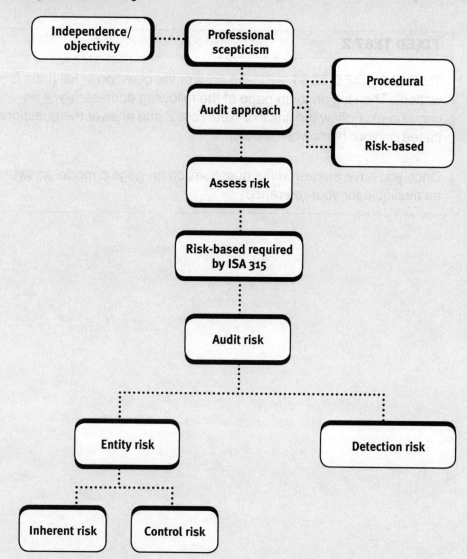

Test your understanding answers

FIXED TEST 2

THIS IS A FIXED TEST – Please answer the question in full (long form written). Then log on to en-gage at the following address: www.en-gage.co.uk. Follow the link to 'Fixed Test 2' and answer the questions based on your homework answer.

Once you have answered the questions on en-gage a model answer will be available for your reference.

Systems and controls

Chapter learning objectives

Upon completion of this chapter you will be able to:

- explain why an auditor needs to obtain an understanding of internal control activities relevant to the audit

- describe and explain the key components of an internal control system

- discuss the difference between tests of control and substantive procedures

- identify and describe the important elements of internal controls, including the control environment and management control activities

- explain the importance of internal controls to auditors

- explain how auditors identify weaknesses in internal control systems and how those weaknesses limit the extent of auditors' reliance on those systems

- explain and tabulate tests of control, suitable for inclusion in audit working papers, for
  - revenue
  - purchases
  - payrolls
  - revenue and capital expenditure
  - inventory
  - bank and cash

- provide examples of computer system controls and list examples of application controls and general IT controls

- analyse the limitations of internal control components in the context of fraud and error

- explain the need to modify the audit strategy and audit plan following the results of tests of control

- identify and explain management's risk assessment process with reference to internal control components
- discuss and provide examples of how the reporting of internal control weaknesses and recommendations to overcome those weaknesses are provided to management.

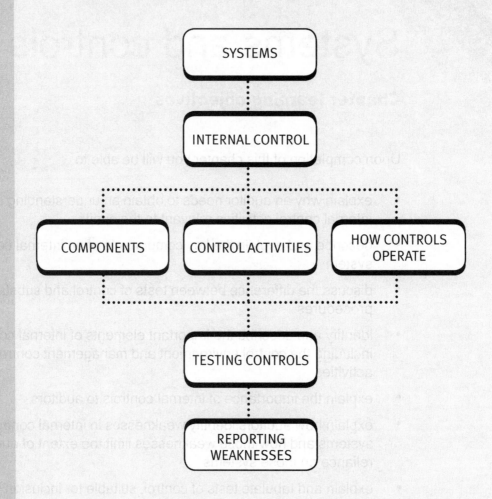

1 Client's systems

Auditors need to understand the client's systems so that they can:

- Assess their reliability for the preparation of financial statements.
- Design suitable audit procedures.

If the auditor is able to rely on the system it will be because it contains some of the components of internal control as set out in ISA 315.

This chapter takes you through:

- How a strong system operates.
- What internal control objectives are and how we meet control objectives.
- How auditors identify and test controls.
- Identify weaknesses and how we manage the weaknesses.

The above tend to be asked in Question 1 in the exam.

2 A word about systems

Why do companies have systems?

A company's management has a number of **obligations**:

- To manage the business effectively.
- To produce timely, and accurate financial statements and management information (both for management and statutory purposes).
- To safeguard the business' assets.
- To prevent and detect fraud.

The purpose of a system is to enable the business to:

- collect data
- summarise data
- produce financial statements and management information
- to aid the directors in complying with the above obligations.

Expandable Text - How do they do it?

How do they do it?

Manual systems

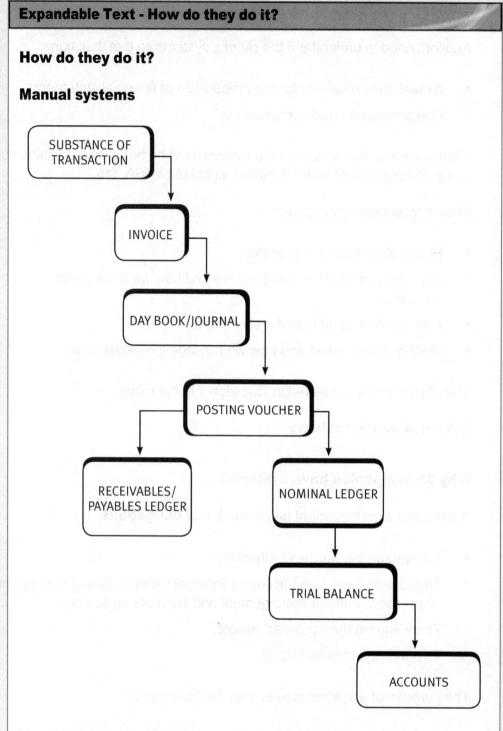

Manual systems are becoming quite rare because:

1   Large businesses have large volumes of data which means that
     manual processing is:

     –   too time-consuming

     –   too costly.

2   For smaller businesses:
  –   PCs are widespread
  –   PCs are cheap
  –   most staff either already have or can quickly learn the relevant IT skills
  –   accounting software is (relatively) cheap.

However:

- Manual bookkeeping still works!
- It can still be encountered in practice.
- It remains a good mechanism for understanding the ins and outs of double entry.

In practice a manual system may look a bit more like this:

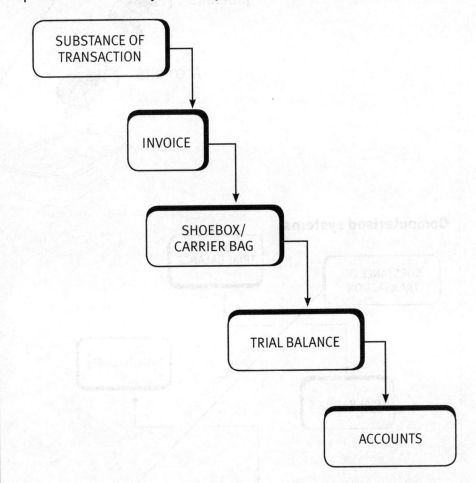

Manual systems are a bit like trying to fill a bath with a chain gang of people with buckets – there are plenty of opportunities for the water to get spilled, or for the information to become lost or corrupted.

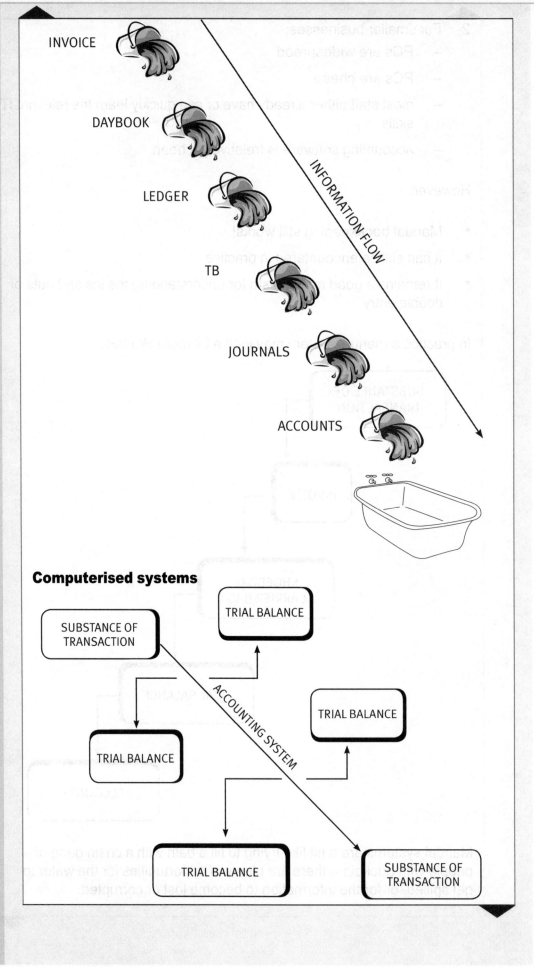

INVOICE

DAYBOOK

LEDGER

TB

JOURNALS

ACCOUNTS

INFORMATION FLOW

Computerised systems

SUBSTANCE OF
TRANSACTION

TRIAL BALANCE

TRIAL BALANCE

TRIAL BALANCE

TRIAL BALANCE

SUBSTANCE OF
TRANSACTION

ACCOUNTING SYSTEM

There are a number of things to understand about the impact of computerised accounting systems:

- The need to transfer information from one piece of paper to another is greatly reduced.

- The outputs from the system – the listings, trial balances, even the financial statements themselves – usually do not form part of a strict chronological sequence. So once an invoice is entered into the system, the TB, the ledger, the financial statements are all updated. There is no delay waiting for the purchase ledger clerk to 'do the postings'.

- Once a transaction is entered into the system it **will** be processed.

- Calculations **will** be accurate (unless someone has programmed them otherwise).

Computerised systems are more like filling the bath from a hosepipe – once the water (or information) enters the system, it is likely to get through.

3 What is internal control and how does it work?

Management's view

Logically, the more reliable a system is the more accurate its output will be as more reliable information will lead to better decision making.

What about the auditors?

The auditor's job is to form an opinion on the financial statements.

To do this the risk that the financial statements may be misstated, must be reduced to an acceptable level.

So, from the auditor's point of view:

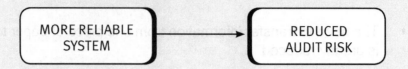

The next question must be, therefore, how to judge whether a system is more or less reliable. The answer will depend on the strengths or weakness of internal control.

It follows, therefore, that to form a view about the extent to which internal control can be relied upon, the auditor will need to:

(1) understand how the system works

(2) understand the controls within the system

(3) test whether or not the controls are effective.

We will look at all of this later in this chapter.

First, we need to consider the nature of internal control.

Internal control components

It is a **crime** not to have good internal controls, therefore to have good internal controls we would see:

ISA 315 states that there are **five** components of internal control:

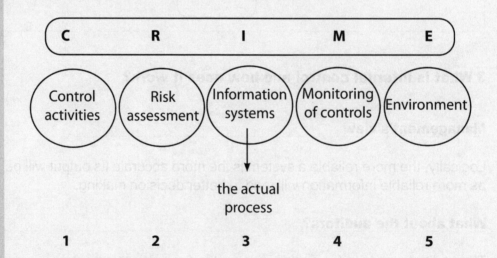

1 Control activities

A pproval – a senior employee like a manager to sign off an action. (Same as authorisation) e.g. an employee wants to do overtime, a manager should authorise this in advance.

C omputer controls – having passwords, backups, virus checks (see later).

C omparison – looking at budget versus actual and reviewing for variances, any variances should then be investigated.

A rithmetic controls – recalculating an employees work, sequence checking. (A check procedure.)

M aintain and review control accounts – like wages, PAYE, bank.

A ccount reconciliations.

P hysical controls – restricted access, either through locking doors, or code entry, CCTV, safes.

S egregation of duties – division of responsibilities to reduce the risk of fraud. E.g. one person dealing with ordering, processing purchase invoices and bank payments is a <u>lack of</u> segregation of duties, different people should process different stages of a system. Splitting the responsibility on a transaction stream.

In the exam the above will be your recommendations to a clients system.

2 Risk assessment process

If the client has robust procedures for assessing the business risks it faces, the risk of misstatement will be lower. There should be a monthly risk assessment done by the management.

3 The information system

We will examine the way controls operate for different transaction cycles later in this chapter. Here we need to stress that the consideration of systems is **not** optional.

ISA 315 states:

'The auditor should obtain an understanding of the information system, including the related business processes, relevant to financial reporting.'

NB – It says 'relevant to financial reporting' and we also know that the auditor is interested in whether or not there are material misstatements in the financial statements.

The standard therefore does **not** mean that:

- the auditor should look into every aspect of a client's systems, or that

- immaterial areas need to be considered.

Exam hint

Understanding the system is compulsory and in nearly every sitting of the predecessor paper over the last two years or so at least one and sometimes several questions have demanded an understanding of systems specific to the scenario client.

- Usually these systems are computerised.
- Often they involve use of the internet or some aspect of e-commerce.

Expandable text - The information system

The information system

The full relevant passage from ISA 315 para 81 is as follows:

'The auditor should obtain an understanding of the information system, including the related business processes, relevant to financial reporting, Including the following areas:

- **The classes of transactions in the entity's operations which are significant to the financial statements**

- **The procedures, within both IT and manual systems, by which those transactions are initiated, recorded, processed and reported in the financial statements.**

- **The related accounting records, whether electronic or manual, supporting information, and specific accounts in the financial statements, in respect of initiating, recording, processing and reporting transactions.**

- **How the information system captures events and conditions, other than classes of transactions, that are significant to the financial statements.**

- **The financial reporting process used to prepare the entity's financial statements, including significant accounting estimates and disclosures.'**

ISA 315 assumes that the vast majority of systems are IT based – see below about application controls and general controls in IT systems.

Expandable text

In the days of mainly manual systems, segregation of duties was the most common and cost-effective type of control. In fact, apart from physical controls, it was more or less the only kind of control an auditor could rely on.

It worked in one of two possible ways:

- The same person would not be allowed to have access to both an asset and the record of that asset.

So the warehouseman would not write up the inventory records.

The person with access to cash receipts would not also be allowed to write up the receivables ledger

or

- No one person would have responsibility for a complete transaction from initiation to final recording.

So the salesman will not be solely responsible for the recording of a sales transaction – usually someone else will need to be informed before goods are released to the customer.

In the 'Rogue Trader' collapse of Barings Bank, Nick Leeson was in a position to initiate trades in the futures markets, and, as the person in charge of the 'back office' function, he was also responsible for recording the trades and was able to hide losses as receivables.

It is interesting that segregation of duties is the last on the list of control activities included in ISA 315. This is probably due to the impact of computers on accounting systems which has meant a reduction in staffing levels as well as the possibility to build IT-based controls into the systems themselves.

4 Monitoring of controls

Clearly if:

- a control is either ineffective, or

- simply does not function,

it might as well not be there.

Management must therefore monitor controls to be sure that they are effective.

Expandable text - Manual and IT based systems

Manual and IT-based systems

Control implications of manual systems – weaknesses

The 'Bad News' about manual systems is:

- Manual systems are operated by people and are therefore more prone to simple errors and mistakes.

- Information is transferred from document to document leading to misposting or other transcription errors.

- Controls can be more easily bypassed, ignored or overridden.

Control implications of manual systems – strengths

The 'Good News' about manual systems is that they are better at:

- dealing with 'one off' transactions

- where the exercise of judgement is important.

The negative assumption

With manual systems because:

- information is transferred from one document to another

- people make mistakes

the auditor has to assume that things **will** go wrong **unless** controls such as segregation of duties are in place. As we shall see, the use of computers may have changed this way of thinking.

Control implications of computerised systems – strengths:

The strengths of computer-based systems are:

- consistent processing
- accurate calculation
- capacity to handle high volumes.

Control implications of computerised systems – weaknesses

The weaknesses of computer-based systems are:

- little exercise of judgement
- access to system = access to controls
- widespread impact of errors in:
  - installation
  - programming
  - override.

The positive assumption

Because of the nature of computer systems, in particular because:

- computers do calculations really well
- computers are consistent – once set up to process a transaction in a particular way, they will continue to do so

it is therefore possible to make a more positive assumption, that things **will** be done **right.**

UNLESS

- there is a threat of some kind.

Threats could be:

- Incompetence – the person doing the processing is unable to do their work reliably.
- Lack of training.
- Deliberate subversion, possibly by senior management.

5 The control environment

The control environment is defined in ISA 315 as being made up of:

The management should have the right <u>attitude</u>.

- communication and enforcement of ethical values
- commitment to competence
- participation by those charged with governance
- management's philosophy and operating style
- management need to have <u>awareness</u> and <u>action</u> in place
- organisational structure
- assignment of responsibility
- human resource policies and practices – staff training, recruitment procedures etc.

Controls in IT systems

Computer based controls are normally divided into two categories:

- Application controls.
- General controls.

Application controls

Application controls are controls that are built into the system, e.g.

- arithmetic checks
- range checks
- validation checks
- Quickbooks, the small business accounting package, for example, will not let you enter a sale until you have set up an 'item', which means you have to allocate the sale to a revenue account, set up the customer as a receivable, decide on VAT treatment, etc.
- some systems will not let you reverse or delete entries so that all errors have to be corrected through the use of journals. This may be seen as a strength, because all entries must leave an 'audit trail', although the system can be so cumbersome to operate and correcting journals become so difficult to follow, that the operational difficulties created outweigh the benefits of the control.

General controls

General IT – controls are policies and procedures that relate to many applications and support the effective functioning of application controls by helping to ensure the continued proper operation of information systems, e.g. controls over:

- data centre and network operations
- system software acquisition
- change and maintenance
- access security – passwords, door locks, swipe cards
- backup procedures.

We gave the example above of an application control that will not allow errors to be corrected by simply deleting the offending entry and replacing it with a correct one. In the absence of a control such as this, there will need to be general controls which ensure that staff are properly trained, so that errors are minimised and that the deletion of entries only happens in appropriate circumstances and with proper authorisation.

Expandable text - A changing world

A changing world

The rapid developments in IT have brought with them implications for systems and controls. For example:

Automated transactions
- Inventory re-ordering triggered by predetermined minimum inventory levels.
- Utilities bills issued to households on a regular basis, with estimated amounts.
- 'Programme trading' where purchases and sales of shares and bonds are triggered by predetermined price levels.

If the criteria that trigger the transaction are not set properly, things can go badly wrong, as the individual pieces of documentation – invoices, purchase orders, etc. – are not scrutinised.

High transaction volumes
- The huge volumes of goods shipped into large supermarkets, simply could not happen without the barcodes, scanners and automated warehousing which mean that the transactions can be processed and actioned sufficiently quickly.

All of this depends on:

- the correct barcodes being allocated
- the correct prices being held centrally
- the links between the various parts of the system not breaking down.

E-Commerce

E-Commerce has blurred the divide between buyer and seller

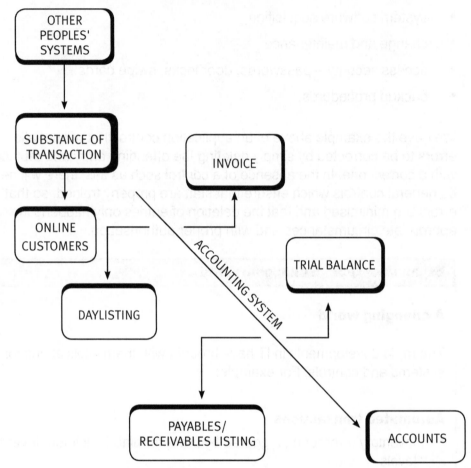

- The customer places the order directly into the supplier's system:
  - online supermarkets
  - online books and music
  - one business' systems communicate directly with another.

- Retail organisation and it's delivery company.

E.g. Bodyshop and Lane Distribution where:

- order from a store
- triggers supply from factory/warehouse
- automatically schedules the delivery with the distribution company
- automatically triggers invoice from the distribution company

- automatically triggers bonus/penalties for early/late delivery
- automatically triggers payment by online transfer in line with agreed payment schedule.

This is an example where there is a virtually seamless interface between the two companies' systems, which requires a good deal of openness and trust between the two organisations concerned.

- The business is actually conducted over the internet:
  - eBay
  - Online gambling
  - Online money transfer businesses
  - MySpace
  - YouTube.

4 What should the auditor do about internal control?

Test the internal controls

The internal controls produce the financial statements and the external auditor is giving an opinion on those financial statements on their truth and fairness.

The only way the external auditor will know if they are true and fair is by testing the financial statements.

If the systems produce the financial statements then we can test the systems because that is ultimately testing the financial statements.

If the internal controls are strong then we can have the confidence the financial statements are accurate.

From an audit point of view the systems can be tested and if the tests confirm the system is being complied with, then the auditor can assume the financial statements are accurate. The size of the transaction is irrelevant.

This is known as a test of control or compliance testing.

For example, if, when auditing the 'bank and cash' figure, an auditor is told that the client performs bank reconciliations at the end of every month and the auditor looks for evidence that this reconciliation is indeed taking place every month, and is done properly, a test of control has been performed.

This is one possible source of assurance that the financial statements are not materially misstated.

The other source of testing is known as substantive procedures.

With a **Substantive procedure**, the auditor is trying to gain assurance directly about the accuracy of a figure in the Financial Statements.

For example agree the bank balance on the financial statements to the bank statement.

5 The auditor and the system

We have already seen that the auditor needs to understand the system:

- To assess its reliability as a basis for preparing financial statements.
- To assess the effectiveness of controls.
- To design suitable audit procedures.

It is also compulsory as stated in ISA 315:

'The auditor should obtain an understanding of the information systems, including the related business processes, relevant to financial reporting.'

ISA 315 para 81

Establishing the system

Information about the system comes from:

- previous knowledge/experience
- client's staff
- client's system manuals
- walk-through tests (where transactions are traced through system to confirm our understanding).

Documenting the system

Possible ways of documenting the system and controls are:

- narrative notes (which can prove bulky if system is large or complex)
- flowcharts (which can make a complex system easier to follow)
- organisation charts – showing roles, responsibilities, and reporting lines
- Internal Control Questionnaire (**ICQ**)
- Internal Control Evaluation Questionnaire (**ICE**).

A word on questionnaires (ICQs)

ICQs

- An **ICQ** is a list of all possible controls for each area of the Financial Statements. The client's staff are asked questions and systems documentation reviewed, to establish which controls exist.

- The system is then appraised – but this can be difficult. Different combinations of controls could achieve the same result.

ICEs

- **ICE (sometimes referred to as ICEQ)** does not attempt to record ALL controls like an ICQ.

- Instead, for each control objective, it asks for the controls which achieve that objective.

- As such, an ICE may not record the entire system – but it is far more use as an evaluation tool for the auditor, as its focus is on whether IC Objectives are being met.

The examiner has stated this will not be tested directly, awareness only.

6 The limitations of internal control

Good, but not that good

We have seen that where internal control is strong, it may reduce the amount of evidence the auditor needs to gain from other sources.

Nevertheless ISA 315 insists that for material areas some substantive testing needs to be carried out.

The reason for this is that there are limitations to the reliance that can be placed on internal control because of:

- human error in the use of judgement
- simple processing errors and mistakes
- collusion of staff in circumventing controls
- responsible people abusing that responsibility to override controls.

Expandable Text - Problems with fraud

The problem with fraud is that it is specifically designed to mislead people. Consider a couple of relatively simple examples:

- A company only deals with suppliers on an authorised list. Payments to suppliers are made after the person in the accounts department has identified the payments to be made, but the cheques cannot be released until they have been signed by the Finance Director, who checks all the supporting documentation, and countersigned by the Managing Director, who does not check things in detail, but who has a good knowledge of the business done with the company's suppliers.

  A perfectly sensible combination of authorisation controls and segregation of duties.

  However what if one of the suppliers is actually controlled by the Finance Director, regularly overcharges and the person in the accounts department receives lavish Christmas gifts and foreign holidays from the supplier concerned? The auditor's reliance on the controls would be misplaced and the fraud would only be uncovered by detailed examination of transactions with the supplier concerned.

- Consider a project-based business where each project is headed up by a project leader and performance is monitored by management by comparing costs and revenues on any given project with the budget set at the start of the project.

  This may sound unusual, but think about the process operated in practising firms to monitor performance on audits and other assignments. ISA 315 calls the internal controls operating here 'performance review'.

  Usually this is an effective system of control, however, if a project leader and the person who prepares the detail of the budgets were to collude and inflate the budgets for that leader's projects, it would be possible to extract funds fraudulently from the business with minimal risk of detection.

7 What if the controls don't work?

The possibilities

As we have seen, the auditor draws assurance from a number of sources, including internal controls.

The chart below shows the decisions to be taken which depend on the effectiveness of controls and the impact on the audit plan if they are found not to be effective.

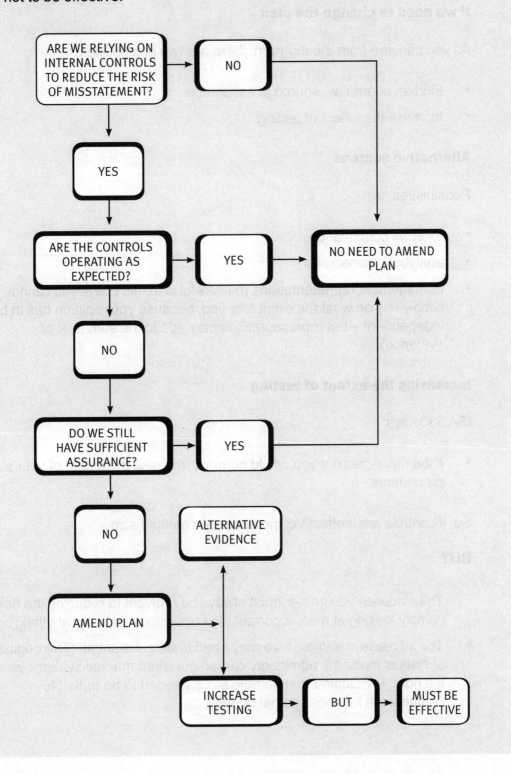

- It may be more efficient and cost effective not to rely on controls at all as a source of assurance (but we need sufficient assurance from other sources).

- It is possible that, even though the controls are not as effective as we would like, and the risk of misstatement may be increased, it may still be at an acceptable level.

- If we do need to amend the plan, it is not simply a matter of increasing the number of items we test.

If we need to change the plan

As you can see from the diagram, there are two possibilities:

- Find an alternative source of assurance.
- Increase the extent of testing.

Alternative sources

Possibilities are:

- external confirmation
- analytical procedures
- management representations (be careful with this one – you cannot simply rely on what the client tells you, because your opinion has to be independent – but representations may add to the sum total of evidence).

Increasing the extent of testing

ISA 330 says:

- If the risk increases you would normally increase the extent of your audit procedures.

So, if controls are ineffective, increase your sample size.

BUT

- The evidence you gather must always be relevant to reducing the risk (simply looking at more incorrect invoices will not achieve anything).

- The increase in sample size may need to be substantial. (The original statistical studies – admittedly carried out when manual systems were the norm – indicated that sample sizes needed to be tripled to compensate for poor internal control.)

ISA 330 states:

'Extent includes the quantity of a specific audit procedure to be performed, for example, a sample size or the number of observations of a control activity. The extent of an audit procedure is determined by the judgment of the auditor after considering the materiality, the assessed risk, and the degree of assurance the auditor plans to obtain.

In particular, the auditor ordinarily increases the extent of audit procedures as the risk of material misstatement increases. However, increasing the extent of an audit procedure is effective only if the audit procedure itself is relevant to the specific risk; therefore, the nature of the audit procedure is the most important consideration.'

ISA 330 Para 18

8 The 'nitty gritty' of controls

Each major accounting system should have control objectives and control procedures. The auditor can then perform tests of control to ensure the controls are working.

- Control objectives – what objectives are the internal controls seeking to achieve
- Control procedures – the procedures that should be in place to ensure that the control objectives are achieved
- Tests of control – audit work performed to generate evidence as to whether the controls are operating

Sales cycle

Objectives of controls

The objectives of controls in the revenue cycle are to <u>ensure</u> that:

- sales are made to valid customers
- sales are recorded accurately
- all sales are recorded
- cash is collected within a reasonable period.

This is a summary of the sales cycle, showing the possible problems and the related controls:

Stage	Risks	Control Objective	Control procedures
Receive an Order	Orders may not be recorded accurately.	To ensure that order is raised accurately	Confirm order back to customer (or) get all orders in writing
	Orders may be taken from customers that are unable to pay or unlikely to pay for a long time = financial loss	To ensure that the customer is creditworthy	All new customers subject to credit check
		To ensure that the order does not take customer over credit limit	Perform regular credit checks on existing customers
	Orders cannot be fulfilled and therefore customer goodwill is lost (and possibly the customer)		Credit limit check before order is accepted
		To ensure that the customer's order can be fulfilled correctly (items are in inventory)	Check inventory system before issuing order
			Automatic re-ordering system linked to customer order system
Goods are despatched to customer	Goods may not be despatched for orders made	To ensure that all orders are sent to warehouse	Use sequentially numbered customer order pads. Send a copy to the warehouse where they are filed numerically and sequence is checked to ensure that all are there (none missing)
	Incorrect goods may be sent to customers leading to loss of goodwill or goods may not be in inventory	To ensure that the right goods are in inventory	
		To ensure that the goods are sent to the right customer	Pick goods using a copy of the customer's order
			Get the copy signed by the picker as correct
			When GDN is raised check it matches with the customer order (staple together and file)
			Get the customer to sign a copy of the GDN and return to the company
			Use sequentially numbered GDNs, file a copy numerically and check that they are all there

Invoice is raised	Invoices may be missed, incorrectly raised or sent to the wrong customer	To ensure invoice is raised for every delivery	Copy of sequentially numbered GDN sent to invoicing dept, stapled to copy of the invoice, checked all GDNs are there and having invoice to match
		To ensure that the invoice is raised for the correct amount	
	Credit notes may be raised incorrectly, missed or to cover cash being mis-appropriated	To ensure that credit notes are raised correctly and are valid	On copy of the invoice sign as agreed to original order and GDN, signed as agreed to customer price list, signed as agreed it adds up properly
			Credit notes to be allocated to invoice it relates
			Authorised by manager sequence check done on a regular basis
Sale is recorded	Invoiced sales may be inaccurately recorded, missed or recorded for the wrong customer	To ensure that all sales are recorded	Review receivables ledger for credit balances (paid for goods but no debtor recorded)
		To ensure that the sale is recorded at the correct amount	Perform a receivables ledger reconciliation (check info in individual ledger matches that in nominal)
		To ensure that the sale is recorded in the right debtor's ledger	Computer controls
			Double check back to invoice
			Perform receivables ledger control account reconciliation
			Customer statements sent out (customers let you know if error)

Cash received	Incorrect amounts may be received	To ensure that the customer pays the correct amount	Agree cash receipt back to the invoice
	Customer may not pay for goods	To ensure that the customer does pay	Review receivables ledger for credit balances (customer overpaid)
			Review aged debt listing and investigate (customer underpaid)
			Review aged debt listing regularly, phone when overdue by 30 days, another letter at 45 days final letter threatening legal action at 60 days
			Refer receivable to solicitor
Cash recorded	Cash maybe incorrectly recorded or recorded against the wrong customer account	To ensure that all cash receipts are recorded	Customer statements
		To ensure that cash is recorded at the correct amount	Perform a bank reconciliation
	Cash received may be stolen		Customer statements
		To ensure that the cash is recorded in the right debtor ledger	Regular banking/physical security over cash (i.e. a safe)
			Reconiciliation of banking to cash receipts records
		To ensure all money received is banked promptly	Segregation of duties

Examples of control tests/(also known as compliance testing)

Tests of control should be designed to check that the control procedures are being applied and that objectives are being achieved. Tests may be appropriate under the following broad headings.

- Carry out sequence tests checks on invoices, credit notes, despatch notes and orders. Ensure that all items are included and that there are no omissions or duplications.

- Review the existence of evidence for authorisation in respect of:
  - Obtain goods despatch notes and ensure each note is signed by the warehouse foreman to confirm despatch of goods listed on the GDN to the customer.
  - Obtain a sample of credit notes and ensure each document is signed by the accounts clerk to confirm the arithmetical accuracy of the note has been checked.
  - Obtain a sample of despatch notes and goods returned notes; ensure that they are signed by a responsible official to confirm that details have been agreed with the relevant sales invoices and credit notes.

- This is often done by means of a "grid stamp" containing several signatures on the face of the document. Ensure that the control has been applied by checking the accuracy of such invoices and credit notes.

- Observe that control account reconciliations have been performed and reviewed. By reviewing the work done by the client or through observation.

In all cases, test should be performed on a sample basis. Aspects of sampling are dealt with in chapter 9.

Test your understanding 1

Rhapsody Co supplies a wide range of garden and agricultural products to trade and domestic customers. The company has 11 divisions, with each division specialising in the sale of specific products, for example, seeds, garden furniture, agricultural fertilizers. The company has an internal audit department which provides audit reports to the audit committee on each division on a rotational basis.

Products in the seed division are offered for sale to domestic customers via an Internet site. Customers review the product list on the Internet and place orders for packets of seeds using specific product codes, along with their credit card details, onto Rhapsody Co's secure server. Order quantities are normally between one and three packets for each type of seed. Order details are transferred manually onto the company's internal inventory control and sales system and a two part packing list is printed in the seed warehouse. Each order and packing list is given in a random alphabetical code based on the name of the employee inputting the order, the date and the products being ordered.

In the seed warehouse, the packets of seeds for each order are taken from specific bins and despatched to the customer with one copy of the packing list. The second copy of the packing list is sent to the accounts department where the inventory and sales computer is updated to show that the order has been despatched. The customer's credit card is then charged by the inventory control and sales computer. Bad debts in Rhapsody are currently 3% of the total sales.

Finally, the computer system checks that for each charge made to a customer's credit card account, the order details are on file to prove that the charge was made correctly. The order file is marked as completed confirming that the order has been despatched and payment obtained.

Required:

In respect of sales in the seeds division of Rhapsody Co, prepare a report to be sent to the audit committee of Rhapsody Co which:

(i)   identifies and explains FOUR weaknesses in that sales system;

(ii) explains the possible effect of each weakness; and

(iii) provides a recommendation to alleviate each weakness.

Note: Up to 2 marks will be awarded to presentation.

(14 marks)

Purchases cycle

Objectives of controls

The objectives of controls in the purchases cycle are to ensure that:

- purchases are only made when there is a genuine need
- value for money is achieved
- goods/services delivered are what was ordered
- quality of goods/services delivered is satisfactory
- liabilities are recorded completely and accurately
- only valid liabilities are paid
- liabilities are paid in a sensible, commercial timescale.

This is a summary of the purchases cycle, showing the possible problems and the related controls:

The table shows the various stages of the purchases 'cycle', together with:

- the **risks** (what could go wrong)

- **control procedures** (so that things **don't** go wrong!).

Stage	Risks	Control objective	Control procedures
Requisition raised	Unauthorised purchases may be made (i.e. for own personal use/fake suppliers entered onto payables ledger)	To ensure that requisition is for a valid business reason To ensure that it is cost effective To ensure items are actually needed	All requisitions authorised by department manager Central purchasing dept Preferred suppliers/agreed price lists/terms Check inventory levels first
Order is placed	Invalid or incorrect orders made or recorded The most favourable terms not obtained	To ensure that order is raised for all requisitions To ensure orders are accurately recorded by supplier To ensure items are correctly costed	Have sequentially numbered requisition pads, copies filed numerically with copy of order stapled to it. Periodically check that all are there Ask them to repeat the order back to you (on the phone) (or) send/confirm all orders in writing Check quoted price against supplier price list (discounts to contract)

Goods received	Goods may be misappropriated for own use or not received at all	To ensure goods received for all orders	Have one delivery area kept secure)
	Goods may be accepted that have not been ordered/wrong quantity/inferior quality	To ensure that the goods received are as ordered + correct quality	Inventory records updated on a timely basis
			Copy of Purchase order sent to warehouse, sequentially numbered, filed, matched to GRN stapled, checked all there
			Raise GRN and grid stamp it, signed as goods checked to PO and checked for quality
Invoice received	Invoices may not be recorded resulting in non-payment and loss of supplier goodwill	To ensure that an invoice is received for all goods received	Copy of sequentially numbered GRNs sent to invoicing department, filed and matched to copy of invoice (stapled), checked to see if all there.
	Invoices may be logged for goods not received	To ensure that do not get invoices for things we have not received, and valid business purchases	As above – if no GRN ask supplier for proof of delivery + match to PO (authorised as mentioned above)
	Invoices may contain errors	To ensure invoices are for right items, right price adds up	Grid stamp invoice signed as checked items to PO, GRN, agree price to supplier's price list
			Check invoice calculations

Purchase recorded	Some purchases may be missed or recorded incorrectly leading to loss of supplier goodwill	To ensure that all purchases are recorded	Batch controls on input
		To ensure that all invoices are recorded at the correct amount	Stamp the invoice to indicate recorded, check all filed invoices are stamped
		To ensure recorded in right supplier ledger	Suppliers send in monthly statements, reconcile these to suppliers ledger account (may need to consider cash/goods in transit)
			Grid stamp – signed
			Supplier statement reconciliation
Cash paid	Invoices may not be paid/the incorrect amount paid or may be paid twice	To ensure all invoices paid (and only once)	Stamp invoices when paid check all invoices stamped
		To ensure paid correct amount	Keep paid invoices separately from unpaid ones
		To ensure valid business expense	Cheque signatory to check to invoice when signing cheque/authorising BACS
			Have relevant bank authorised signatories (level $)
			Get invoices signed as authorised by relevant manager

Examples of control tests

As already noted, tests of control should be designed to check that the control procedures are being applied and that objectives are being achieved. One suggested way to design tests of control for a particular situation is to list the documents in a transaction cycle and generate appropriate tests of control for each document. This approach is illustrated here in connection with the purchases cycle – note that a similar technique could be applied to other transaction cycles.

- Obtain the ledger recording purchase orders; ensure each page has been signed by a responsible official to confirm all orders have been recorded and there are no gaps in the sequence of orders.

- Obtain a sample of purchase invoices; ensure each invoice has been signed by a responsible official to confirm checks on the invoice have been completed and the invoice is passed for payment.

- Obtain a sample of credit notes; ensure each credit note is signed by a responsible official to confirm credit note details (goods description and quantity) have been agreed to the relevant goods returned note.

- Review the purchase order for the relevant signature for approval.

- Review purchase invoice for evidence that the invoice has been reviewed and checked.

- Review purchase invoice for initialling of the grid stamp.

- Review/observe the supplier reconciliation note to ensure the control has been complied with.

Test your understanding 2

You are carrying out the audit of the purchases system of Spondon Furniture. The company has a turnover of about $10 million and all the shares are owned by Mr and Mrs Fisher, who are non-executive directors and are not involved in the day-to-day running of the company.

The bookkeeper maintains all the accounting records and prepares the annual financial statements.

The company uses a standard computerised accounting package.

You have determined that the purchases system operates as follows:

- When materials are required for production, the production manager sends a handwritten note to the buying manager. For orders of other items, the department manager or managing director sends handwritten notes to the buying manager. The buying manager finds a suitable supplier and raises a purchase order. The purchase order is signed by the managing director. Purchase orders are not issued for all goods and services received by the company.

- Materials for production are received by the goods received department, who issue a goods received note (GRN), and send a copy to the bookkeeper. There is no system for recording receipt of other goods and services.

- The bookkeeper receives the purchase invoice and matches it with the goods received note and purchase order (if available). The managing director authorises the invoice for posting to the purchase ledger.

- The bookkeeper analyses the invoice into relevant nominal ledger account codes and then posts it.

- At the end of each month, the bookkeeper prepares a list of payables to be paid. This is approved by the managing director.

- The bookkeeper prepares the cheques and remittances and posts the cheques to the purchase ledger and cashbook.

- The managing director signs the cheques and the bookkeeper sends the cheques and remittances to the payables.

Mr and Mrs Fisher are aware that there may be weaknesses in the above system and have asked for advice.

Identify the weaknesses in controls in Spondon's purchases system, explain what the impact is and suggest improvements.

(12 marks)

Payroll

Objectives of controls

The objectives of controls for the payroll cycle are to ensure that the company will:

- pay the right people
- at the right rate
- for valid work done.

And

- deal correctly with taxes and other deductions.

This is a summary of the payrolls cycle, showing the possible problems and the related controls:

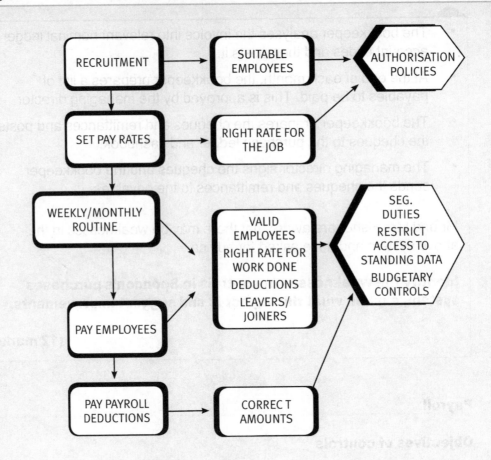

The table shows the various stages of the payroll 'cycle', together with:

- The **risks** (what could go wrong).

- **Control procedures** (so that things **don't** go wrong!).

Stage	Risks	Control objectives	Control procedures
Clock cards / timesheets submitted	Cards may be missed, bogus employees paid or employees paid for hours not worked	To ensure all cards received	Check number of cards to number of employees
		To ensure that no bogus clock cards submitted	Keep all spare cards locked in cupboard
		To ensure the hours noted have actually been worked	Get departmental managers to sign clock cards as authorised hours (and especially any overtime)

Clock cards input into computer	Cards may not be recorded accurately	To ensure all clock cards entered	Batch total or hash total checks
		To ensure details input correctly	Range checks inputter signs clock card to say double checked details to screen
		To ensure inputter doesn't input data twice/input bogus employees	Programme only allows input for each person once, can only input for employees held within standing data
			Hierarchical password control to payroll system
			Different person should be responsible for updating standing data, to those responsible for the monthly processing (segregation of duties)
Standing data input	Standing data could be compromised. Unprocessed updates may mean employees who have left are paid or joiners are missed	To ensure leavers are not paid after they have left/joiners are paid when they start	Managers should complete a leavers/joiners form noting date of departure/arrival and send promptly to Payroll dept
		To ensure standing data input is accurate	Standing data files regularly printed out and sent to department managers for them to sign and return confirming all staff there
			Inputter to sign joiner/leaver form /wage rise form to say checked to input
			Monthly print of any changes to go to senior management for review, they should sign print as authorised

Processing of data	Inaccurate processing of data could lead to wages and taxes being incorrectly calculated	To ensure correct wage is calculated	Sample of wages recalculated manually, print out signed as checked
		To ensure correct tax is calculated	Exception report produced automatically for anyone paid over $xxx, or paid under $xxx
			Sample of deductions (PAYE, NIC) recalculated manually print out signed as checked
Recording of payroll	Recorded payroll may not match actual payroll	To ensure correct wages, NIC, PAYE recorded	Nominal ledger clerk signs payroll print out to confirm entries double-checked to print
			Senior management review wages expenses for reasonableness
Staff paid	Staff may not be paid	To ensure all staff are paid (employees will complain if not!!!)	Have two people present where cash wages are paid. (See controls above over standing data)
	Bogus staff could be paid	To ensure no bogus employees are paid	Responsible individual should review any BACS payroll summary prior to paying staff – sign to confirm reviewed

Examples of control tests

A suggested programme of tests of control is set out below. This would, of course, be modified to suit the particular circumstances of the client.

- Test a sample of timesheets, clock cards or other records, for approval by a responsible official. Pay particular attention to the approval of overtime there relevant.

- Observe wages distribution for adherence to procedures ensuring employees sign for wages, that unclaimed wages are rebanked, etc.

- Test authorisation for payroll amendments by reference to personnel records.

- Test controls over payroll amendments by reviewing changes and seeing whether they have been authorised. You could print off an exception report highlighting changes and follow those through. You could also do a dummy transaction to see how the system handles change.

- Obtain the payment sheet for casual labour payments and ensure this has been signed by the chief accountant to authorise the payments made.

- Obtain the weekly payroll and ensure this have been signed by a responsible official to approval those payments.

- Examine evidence of independent checks of payrolls (e.g. by internal audit).

- Inspect payroll reconciliations done regularly, clearing wage control account, tying the PAYE liability up to the Inland Revenue records. Review the client working papers or observe the reconciliation process happening.

- Examine explanations for payroll expense variances.

- Test authorisation for payroll deductions by reviewing the employees records, looking at who is authorised to place through amendments, and observe the process.

- Test controls over unclaimed wages. You could do a dummy transaction to see how the system works, what happens to the wages unclaimed, are they place in a safe, if so tick the clients working to the amount in the safe.

Test your understanding 3

Bassoon Ltd runs a chain of shops selling electrical goods all of which are located within the same country.

It has a head office that deals with purchasing, distribution and administration. The payroll for the whole company is administered at head office.

There are 20 staff at head office and 200 staff in the company's 20 shops located in high streets and shopping malls all over the country.

Head office staff (including directors) are all salaried and paid by direct transfer to their bank accounts.

The majority of the staff at the company's shops are also paid through the central salary system, monthly in arrears. However, some students and part time staff are paid cash out of the till.

Recruitment of head office staff is initiated by the department needing the staff who generally conduct interviews and agree terms and conditions of employment. Bassoon has an HR manager who liaises with recruitment agencies, places job adverts and maintains staff files with contracts of employment, etc.

Shop managers recruit their own staff.

Shop staff receive a basic salary based on the hours worked and commission based on sales made.

The company has a fairly sophisticated EPOS (electronic point of sale) till system at all shops that communicates directly with the head office accounting system.

All staff when making a sale have to log on with a swipe card which identifies them to the system, and means that the sales for which they are responsible are analysed by the system and commissions calculated.

Store managers have a few 'guest cards' for temporary and part time staff, who generally do not receive commissions.

Store managers and regional supervisors are paid commissions based on the performance of their store or region. Directors and other head office staff usually receive a bonus at Christmas, depending on the company's performance. This is decided on by the board in consultation with departmental manages and put through the system by the payroll manager.

The payroll manager is responsible for adding joiners to the payroll and deleting leavers as well as for implementing changes in pay rates, tax coding and other deductions and for making sure that the list of monthly transfers is communicated to the bank.

The computerised payroll system is a standard proprietary system which is sophisticated enough to incorporate the commission calculations mentioned above which are fed in directly from the EPOS system.

The company employs an IT manager who is responsible for the maintenance of all IT systems and installing new hardware and software.

Comment on the strengths and weaknesses of the payroll system at Bassoon Ltd and recommend any changes which you think are appropriate.

(10 marks)

Inventory

Objectives of controls

The objectives of controls in the inventory cycle are to ensure that:

- inventory levels are in keeping with the needs of:
    - production (raw materials and bought in components)
    - customer demand (finished goods)
- inventory levels are not:
    - excessive
    - too low ('stockouts')
- value for money is achieved
- goods/services delivered are what was ordered
- quality of goods/services delivered is satisfactory
- liabilities are recorded completely and accurately
- only valid liabilities are paid
- liabilities are paid in a sensible, commercial timescale.

The table shows the various stages of the inventory 'cycle', together with:

- the **risks** (what could go wrong)
- **control procedures** (so that things **don't** go wrong!).

Process	Risks	Possible control procedures
Inventory arrives because it has been purchased, or a sale has been returned	Inventory stolen on arrival.	All goods inward received at set locations and signed for/logged in by stores manager.
	New purchases mixed up with returns.	
	Poor quality inventory accepted.	All returns sent to a returns department for checking.
	Inventory accepted that was never ordered.	See purchase cycle.
	No record is made of its arrival.	

Inventory is stored until it is needed	Poor storage conditions lead to damaged inventory.	Storage areas fitted with sprinklers, fire alarms, temperature monitors.
	Inventory items not used before their useful life ends.	Inventory 'rotated' to ensure FIFO usage where relevant.
	Inventory stolen from storage areas.	Valuable inventories locked away and inventory areas limited to a single exit (security guard?).
Raw materials leave stores, to be used in production	Materials over-ordered to enable theft.	All requisitions from stores to have signed authorisation from production manager.
		Use of standard quantity requirements.
Finished goods leave because they have been sold	Wrong goods sent.	See sales cycle.
	Goods being stolen (no real sale).	
	Poor quality sent.	
	Records not updated.	
Goods leave because they are being returned to suppliers	Returned goods actually being stolen.	See purchase returns.

An inventory count is performed (may be annual, or more regular)	Counting lacks accuracy.	All counted areas to be marked as completed.
	Staff lie about amounts counted to cover up their theft.	Managers to check by doing random second counts.
	Inventory records lost during count.	Staff do not count areas that they are usually responsible for.
	Inventory wrongly counted because it is moved during count.	Counting done in pairs.
		Inventory sheets sequenced and counters sign out (and in) the count sheets.
		All inventory movements during count authorised by management.
		Closure during inventory accounts to avoid problems.

Examples of control tests

- Observe physical security of inventories and environment in which they are held.

- Obtain inventory records. Where quantity of inventory has been changed without reference to GDN and GRN, ensure that amendment is signed by a responsible official to authorise that change.

- In the client's warehouse, observe client staff ensuring that where a movement in inventory occurs, that movement is recorded on the appropriate GDN or GRN.

- Test for evidence of authorisation to write off or scrapping of inventories (existence of signature).

- Observe controls over recording of movements of inventory belonging to third parties.

- Observe the procedures for authorisation for inventory movements i.e. the use made of authorised goods received and despatch notes.

- Inspect reconciliations of inventory counts to inventory records (this gives overall comfort on the adequacy of controls over the recording of inventory).
- Test for evidence of sequences checks of despatch and goods received notes for completeness.
- Assess adequacy of inventory counting procedures and attend the count to ensure that procedures are complied with.

Capital and revenue expenditure

This area looks at expenditure on items other than purchases. However, the controls are virtually identical to controls over purchases as seen above.

Some controls may vary, such as:

- Capital expenditure is often for substantial amounts. As such, most companies would require such items to be included in an annual budget and authorised by very senior level management.
- Regular revenue expense items may be monitored by simple variance analysis (i.e. actual versus budget) on a monthly basis.
- Capital items are likely to be stored on an asset register, which records details of supplier, price, insurance details, current location, responsible employee, etc.
- Just as inventories are counted, assets are likely to be checked against the register on a regular basis.
- When assets are sold second-hand, the items will be checked against similar items or price guides to ensure the company receives fair value.
- Ownership documents (title deeds, vehicle registration documents) will be safely stored.

Bank and cash

Objectives of controls

The objectives of controls over bank and cash are to ensure that:

- cash balances are safeguarded
- cash balances are kept to a minimum
- money can only be extracted from bank accounts for authorised purposes.

Possible controls

Objective	Possible control procedures
Cash balances are safeguarded.	Safes/strongroom/locked cashbox with restricted access. Security locks. Swipe card access. Key access to tills. Night safes. Imprest system. Use of security services for large cash movements. People making bankings vary routes and timings.
Cash balances are kept to a minimum.	Tills emptied regularly. Frequent bankings of cash and cheques received.
Money can only be extracted from bank accounts for authorised purposes.	Restricted list of cheque signatories. Dual signatures for large amounts. Similar controls over bank transfers and online banking, e.g. secure passwords and pin numbers. Cheque books and cheque stationery locked away. Regular bank reconciliations reviewed by person with suitable level of authority.

Examples of control tests

Cash receipts:

- observe that mail is opened by two staff to minimise the possibility of fraud (cash being stolen on receipt)
- test independent check of cash receipts to bank lodgements
- test for evidence of a sequence check on any pre-numbered receipts for cash

- test authorisation of cash receipts
- test for evidence of arithmetical check on cash received records.

Cash payments:

- inspect current cheque books for:
    - sequential use of cheques
    - controlled custody of unused cheques
    - any signatures on blank cheques
- test (to avoid double payment) to ensure that paid invoices are marked "paid"
- test for evidence of arithmetical checks on cash payments records, including cashbook
- obtain the file of direct debit payments – ensure each payment is authorised.

Bank reconciliations:

- examine evidence of regular bank reconciliations, at least once per month, but in larger organisations this should be done daily or weekly
- examine evidence of independent checks of bank reconciliations (e.g. a signature)
- examine evidence of follow up of outstanding items on the bank reconciliation. Pay particular attention to old outstanding reconciling items that should be written back such as old, unpresented cheques.

Petty cash:

- Test petty cash vouchers for appropriate authorisation.
- Test cancellation of paid petty cash vouchers.
- Test for evidence of arithmetical checks on petty cash records.
- Test for evidence of independent checks on the petty cash balance.
- Perform a surprise petty cash count and reconcile to petty cash records.

Expandable Text - Writing up the tests

Writing up the tests

There are three vitally important rules to remember for all working papers.

- **Rule 1** If you don't do the work, you can't write it up.
- **Rule 2** If you don't write it up, you might as well not have done the work.
- **Rule 3** If the person reviewing your work can't understand what you've done, you might as well not have done it in the first place.

These rules are the same for all audit work – so you need to:

- say what you did
- say why you did it
- say what your conclusions were. We will look at this in more detail in chapter 10.

Expandable Text - Control weaknesses and what to do about

Control weaknesses and what to do about them

Management's role

As we have seen, any business faces risks of various types and it is management's responsibility to implement procedures to mitigate those risks.

The risk assessment process will depend to a large extent on:

- the nature
- the size
- the complexity

of the business. However, for larger businesses it will normally consist of:

- agreed programmes of work for the internal audit department to regularly review the company's financial systems for internal control weaknesses
- supervision of the process by, and reports to, the audit committee
- liaison with the external auditors.

The external auditor's role

We know that the external auditor is not responsible for implementing or maintaining internal controls. The auditor needs to:

- assess internal controls as a source of assurance
- report material weaknesses in internal controls to those charged with governance.

9 Reporting to those charged with governance

Auditors should communicate material weaknesses in internal control in writing to 'those charged with governance' – the audit committee (if one exists) or management in general.

The form, timing and addressees of this communication should be agreed at the start of the audit, as part of the terms of the engagement.

This report has traditionally been known as a **management letter** or **report to management** and is usually sent at the end of the audit process.

In the exam you could be asked to write a management letter.

Recent revision of audit standards has added other matters that should be communicated.

- For listed companies, a report on audit independence.
- A report at the planning stage, identifying key audit risks and the work to be performed.
- At the end of the audit, a report covering:
  - expected audit report
  - unadjusted errors and misstatements

- comments on accounting practices and policies in use by the company any

- other relevant matters.

However, this section of the Notes will concentrate on internal control issues.

Reporting on controls

Where the auditor is reporting weaknesses, it should be made clear that:

- the report is not a comprehensive list of weaknesses, but only those that have come to light during normal audit procedures

- the report is for the sole use of the company

- no disclosure should be made to a third party the without written agreement of the auditor

- no responsibility is assumed to any other parties.

The usual structure of the report is:

- covering letter (which will include the above list of points)

- appendix, noting the weaknesses, consequences, and recommendations (often with a space left for management to respond with their planned action).

In the exam, an internal control question may require you to analyse controls and report weaknesses in the form of a management letter. If so, it is the appendix (see below) that you need to produce. A covering letter would be specifically requested by your examiner.

The best structure is:

Weakness — Clear description of what is wrong.

Consequence — What could happen if the weakness is not corrected. Focus on what matters to the client – the risk of lost profits, stolen assets, extra costs, errors in the accounts.

Recommendation This must deal with the specific weakness you have observed! It must also provide greater benefits than the cost of implementation.

Try to suggest who should carry out the control procedures, and when.

Illustration

(A table format is the best format, it keeps you structured and the markers find it easier to mark.)

Weakness	Consequence	Recommendation
There appear to be purchase invoices missing from the sequentially numbered invoice file.	There is a possibility that purchases and liabilities are not completely recorded. Also, it would be difficult to provide proof of purchase where the invoice is missing. This may make it difficult to obtain refunds for faulty goods, leading to increased costs. As such, the accounts could be incomplete and items may have been purchased without control over quality, price, etc.	All invoices should be sequentially filed on receipt by the Accounts Department. Regular checks should be made to ensure a complete record, with any missing items investigated (and copies requested if necessary).

10 Chapter summary

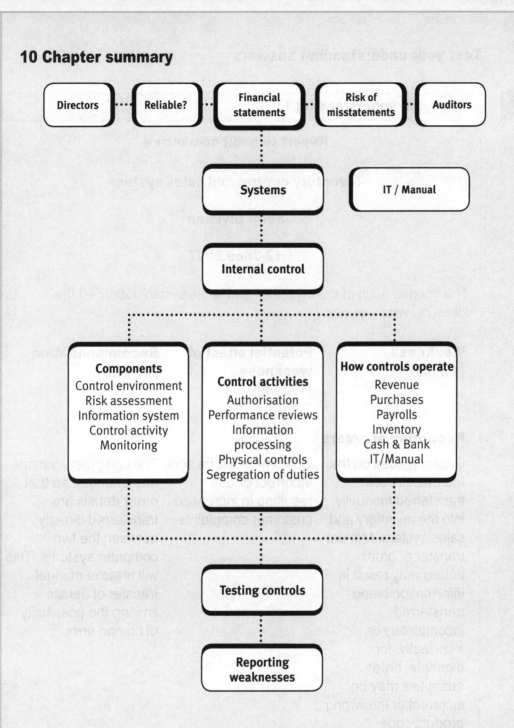

Directors ···· Reliable? ···· Financial statements ··· Risk of misstatements ··· Auditors

Systems

IT / Manual

Internal control

Components
Control environment
Risk assessment
Information system
Control activity
Monitoring

Control activities
Authorisation
Performance reviews
Information processing
Physical controls
Segregation of duties

How controls operate
Revenue
Purchases
Payrolls
Inventory
Cash & Bank
IT/Manual

Testing controls

Reporting weaknesses

Test your understanding answers

Test your understanding 1

Report to audit committee

Inventory control and sales system

Seed Division

12 June 2007

The internal audit of the inventory and sales system identified the following weaknesses:

Weakness (1 mark)	Potential effect of weakness (1 mark)	Recommendation (1 mark)
Recording of orders		
Orders placed on the Internet site are transferred manually into the inventory and sales system. Manual transfer of order details may result in information being transferred incompletely or incorrectly, for example, order quantities may be incorrect or the wrong product code recorded.	Customers will be sent incorrect goods resulting in increased customer complaints.	The computer systems are amended so that order details are transferred directly between the two computer systems. This will remove manual transfer of details limiting the possibility of human error.

Weakness (1 mark)	Potential effect of weakness (1 mark)	Recommendation (1 mark)
Control over orders and packing lists		
Each order / packing list is given a random alphabetical code. While this is useful, using this type of code makes it difficult to check completeness of orders at any stage in the despatch and invoicing process.	Packing lists can be lost resulting either in goods not being despatched to the customer (if the list is lost prior to goods being despatched) or the customer's credit card not being charged (if lost after goods despatched but prior to the list being received in the accounts department).	Orders/packing lists are controlled with a numeric sequence. At the end of each day, gaps in the sequence of packing lists returned to accounts are investigated.
Obtaining payment		
The customer's credit card is charged after despatch of goods to the customer, meaning that goods are already sent to the customer before payment is authorised.	Rhapsody Co will not be paid for the goods despatched where the credit company rejects the payment request. Given that customers are unlikely to return seeds, Rhapsody Co will automatically incur a bad debt.	Authorisation to charge the customer's credit card is obtained prior to despatch of goods to ensure Rhapsody Co is paid for all goods despatched.
Completeness of orders		
The computer system correctly ensures that order details are available for all charges to customer credit cards. However, there is no overall check that all orders recorded on the inventory and sales system have actually been invoiced.	Entire orders may be overlooked and consequently sales and profit understated.	The computer is programmed to review the order file and orders where there is no corresponding invoice for an order, these should be flagged for subsequent investigation.

Summary

We look forward to arranging a meeting to discuss these weaknesses with you in more detail.

Note to candidates: the marking scheme shows other valid points.

Test your understanding 2

Weakness *(1 mark)*	Effect *(1 mark)*	Recommendation *(1 mark)*
(1) Hand written orders are done (with no numbering).	Orders for goods not required and a potential orders being missed for action. Therefore over spending or potential shock outs due to orders not being processed.	Have prenumber orders which are authorised by a manager.
(2) Purchase orders are not issued for all goods and services.	Goods/services being purchased that are not legitimate or required.	Purchase orders required for all goods, for services a budget should be set and quotes obtained.
(3) No system for recording receipt of other goods and services.	Goods received that are of poor quality or incorrect amounts.	Count goods in before they are signed.
(4) It doesn't state that the GRN are checked to anything.	Goods received that are of poor quality or incorrect amounts.	Agree GRN back to the purchase order.
(5) There is no review done of the bookkeeper posting the invoices into the nominal ledger.	Errors could go undetected, therefore pay suppliers the incorrect amount.	A review by a manager should be done on a regular basis.

Weakness *(1 mark)*	Effect *(1 mark)*	Recommendation *(1 mark)*
(6) A list of payables is given to the managing director.	The managing director will not know if payables are valid or correct therefore could be paying incorrect amounts.	The managing director should also review source documents before signing the list.
(7) Lack of segregations The managing director authorises invoices, approves payment and signs cheques.	It is easy to place through a purchase invoice to pay himself and this would go undetected.	Segregate duties by sharing the responsibility with another manager.

Test your understanding 3

Strength	Weaknesses	Recommendation
Salaries are paid by direct transfer to the employees bank accounts (less chance of mis-appropriation of cash).		
	Cash paid to part time staff (easier to misappropriate cash).	Apply the payroll system to all employees.
	No control over the appointment of head office staff the HR Manager deals with (may recruit unnecessary staff).	Head office staff should be approved by the board.

Strength	Weaknesses	Recommendation
	No control over shop staff, the shop manager recruits own staff.	Should be approved by head office.
Having a sophisticated EPOS till system (unlikely for errors to occur).		
Individual swipe cards linked to commission (you know who is doing the transaction and because they receive a commission it encourages the staff to recognise the sale).		
	Guest cards, could be anybody and they could steal a card to access till at a later date to steal money.	A control system to monitor guest cards so management know who has a specific card.
	Lack of segregation of duties, the payroll manager is responsible for all processing.	Split the responsibilities up, maybe get a manager to review the payroll managers work.
	In the question it states the IT manager is responsible for systems, but doesn't state there is restricted access.	Place passwords on the system and change them on a regular basis.

9

Audit evidence

Chapter learning objectives

When you have completed this chapter you will be able to:

- explain the assertions contained in the financial statements

- explain the use of assertions in obtaining audit evidence

- explain the principles and objectives of testing transactions, account balances and disclosures

- discuss the sources and relative merits of the different types of evidence available

- define audit sampling and explain the need for sampling

- identify and discuss the differences between statistical and non-statistical sampling

- discuss and provide relevant examples of, the application of the basic principles of statistical sampling and other selective testing procedures

- discuss the results of statistical sampling, including consideration of whether additional testing is required

- describe why smaller entities may have different control environments

- describe the types of evidence likely to be available in smaller entities

- discuss the quality of evidence obtained

- explain the need for and the importance of audit documentation

- explain the procedures to ensure safe custody and retention of working papers

- describe and prepare working papers and supporting documentation.

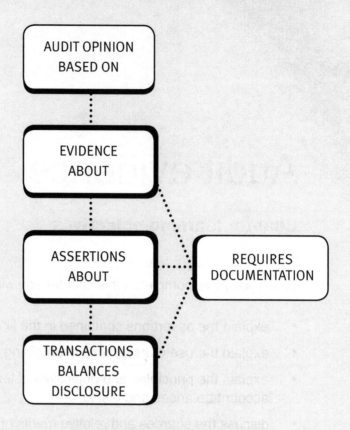

1 Why does the auditor need evidence?

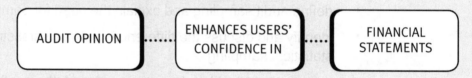

If the auditors are to:

- form an opinion which is worth something
- be paid good money for it

they will need to base their opinion on valid evidence.

2 Evidence about what exactly?

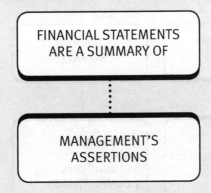

Financial statements are complex documents

They consist of:

- income statement
- statement of financial position
- cash flow statement
- notes.

Each of which contains numbers of headings:

- revenue
- expenditure
- non-current assets
- inventories
- receivables
- payables, etc.

Management is responsible for the preparation of financial statements that give a true and fair view, but what does this really mean?

For each item in the financial statements, management is making **assertions**.

Assertions like:

- This factory is owned by the company.
- The receivables really do owe us this money and will pay fairly soon.
- The payroll expense was for the company's genuine employees working on the company's business.

The auditors therefore need evidence that these assertions are valid.

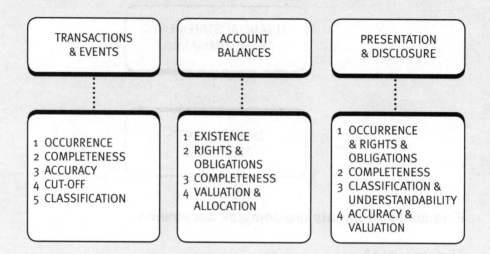

3 Financial statement assertions

Occurrence – did the transaction actually take place?

Completeness – are all transactions or balances that should be included in the financial statements, actually included?

Accuracy – are the amounts correct?

Cut-off – are transactions accounted for in the correct period?

Classification – are transactions recorded in the proper accounts?

Existence – do the assets or liabilities actually exist?

Rights and obligations – does the client own or have other rights over the assets and have a genuine obligation to pay liabilities?

Valuation – are assets or liabilities included at appropriate amounts?

Allocation – are account balances included in appropriate accounts?

Classification and understandability – are items in the financial statements disclosed under appropriate headings and in such a way that they can be readily understood by readers?

Accuracy – are the amounts disclosed in the financial statements appropriate?

Expandable Text - Transactions and events

Transactions and events

So, for a transaction such as the purchase of raw materials, the directors are asserting in the financial statements that:

Occurrence

- The purchase really did take place.

Completeness

- All purchase transactions are included in the financial statements.

Accuracy

- The quantities and prices are correctly stated.

Cut-off

- The transaction is dealt with in the correct accounting period.

Classification

- It really is a purchase of raw materials, not a payroll cost or a motor vehicle and it has been accounted for accordingly.

Account balances at the year end

For account balances at the year end, the assertions are slightly different, because the things about which the assertions are made are different:

Existence

- Are these motor vehicles, factory machines, land and buildings, inventories real? Do they exist?

- Are these trade receivables real? Have we sold them something for which they owe us the money?

- Have we bought something from these trade payables and therefore really owe them some money?

Rights and obligations

- Do we own the factory? The car? The computer?

- If we do not actually own the asset, do we have other rights over it, such as a lease, which means it should be included in the financial statements?

- The trade receivables may exist, but have we factored them or otherwise transferred our rights to them?

- For trade payables, if we have bought something it is usually certain to be our obligation to pay, but if we make an accrual or a provision for something less clear cut – warranty claims or the outcome of a court case – is it really our responsibility to pay? How certain are the amounts involved?

Valuation

- Has depreciation been calculated correctly on the non-current assets?

- Are the trade receivables actually going to pay us?

- Is the inventory damaged, slow moving or obsolete?

Formal definitions of assertions from ISA 500 Audit evidence

The illustrations above should give you a feel for what the assertions mean. Below are the formal explanations from ISA 500.

These are included because:

- A genuine understanding of assertions is vital if you are to understand the concepts underlying audit evidence.

- You will need to be able to apply your understanding of assertions in any exam question about planning audit procedures, gathering audit evidence or reviewing the results of audit tests.

- While it is **not** necessary for you to learn the formal wording it does give you the 'official view' of what these terms mean.

Assertions about classes of transactions and events for the period under audit

- **Occurrence** – transactions and events that have been recorded have occurred and pertain to the entity.

- **Completeness** – all transactions and events that should have been recorded have been recorded.

- **Accuracy** – amounts and other data relating to recorded transactions and events have been recorded appropriately.

- **Cut-off** – transactions and events have been recorded in the correct accounting period.

- **Classification** – transactions and events have been recorded in the proper accounts.

Assertions about account balances at the period end

- **Existence** – assets, liabilities and equity interests exist.

- **Rights and obligations** – the entity holds or controls the rights to assets, and liabilities are the obligations of the entity.

- **Completeness** – all assets, liabilities and equity interests that should have been recorded have been recorded.

- **Valuation and allocation** – assets, liabilities and equity interests are included in the financial statements at appropriate amounts and any resulting valuation or allocation adjustments are appropriately recorded.

Assertions about presentation and disclosure

- **Occurrence and rights and obligations** – disclosed events, transactions and other matters have occurred and pertain to the entity.

- **Completeness** – all disclosures that should have been included in the financial statements have been included.

- **Classification and understandability** – financial information is appropriately presented and described, and disclosures are clearly expressed.

- **Accuracy and valuation** – financial and other information are disclosed fairly and at appropriate amounts.

The assertions are **important** because they have an impact on how the auditor gathers evidence.

There are 13 different types of assertion across the three headings although some of them repeat each other and this may seem to be rather daunting to remember.

Remember that the audit evidence required depends on both:

- the nature of the item being tested

AND

- the assertion being tested

and it can all be simplified down to four key questions that the auditor needs to answer.

(1) Should it be in the accounts at all?

    – Occurrence.

    – Existence.

    – Rights and obligations.

    – Cut-off.

(2) Is it included at the right value?

    – Accuracy.

    – Valuation.

(3) Are there any more?

    – Completeness.

(4) Is it disclosed properly?

    – Classification.

    – Allocation.

    – Understandability.

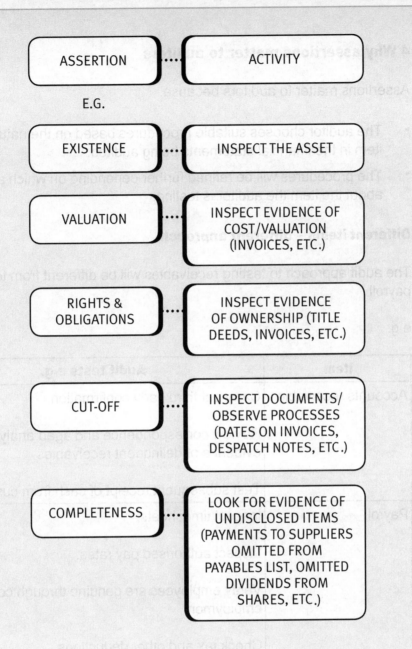

4 Why assertions matter to auditors

Assertions matter to auditors because:

- The auditor chooses suitable procedures based on the nature of the item in the financial statements being audited.

- The procedures will be refined further depending on which assertion about the item the auditor is testing.

Different items – different approach

The audit approach to testing receivables will be different from testing payroll.

e.g.

Item	Audit tests e.g.
Accounts receivable	Carry out third party confirmation.
	Review correspondence and aged analysis for evidence of delinquent receivables.
	Test subsequent receipt of cash from customers.
Payroll	Inspect timesheets.
	Inspect authorised pay rates.
	Verify employees are genuine through contracts of employment.
	Check tax and other deductions.

Different assertions – different approaches

For a single item in the financial statements – e.g. freehold property, the auditor may need to use different approaches for different assertions

Assertion	Audit tests e.g.
Existence	Inspect the property concerned.
Valuation	Agree cost to purchase contract or subsequent revaluation to valuer's report. Re-perform depreciation calculation.
Rights and obligations	Inspect title deeds.
Cut-off	Inspect purchase contract to verify date of purchase.
Completeness	Review repairs account, correspondence with lawyers and property consultants for evidence that there are no additional properties.

Note. The completeness assertion tends to be the most difficult assertion to test. It is usually easier to verify items we know about than to think about what should be there, but is not.

Test your understanding 1

(1) **List five assertions associated with transactions.**

(2 marks)

(2) **List four assertions associated with account balances.**

(2 marks)

(3) **List four assertions associated with disclosures in financial statements.**

(2 marks)

5 How does the auditor test things?

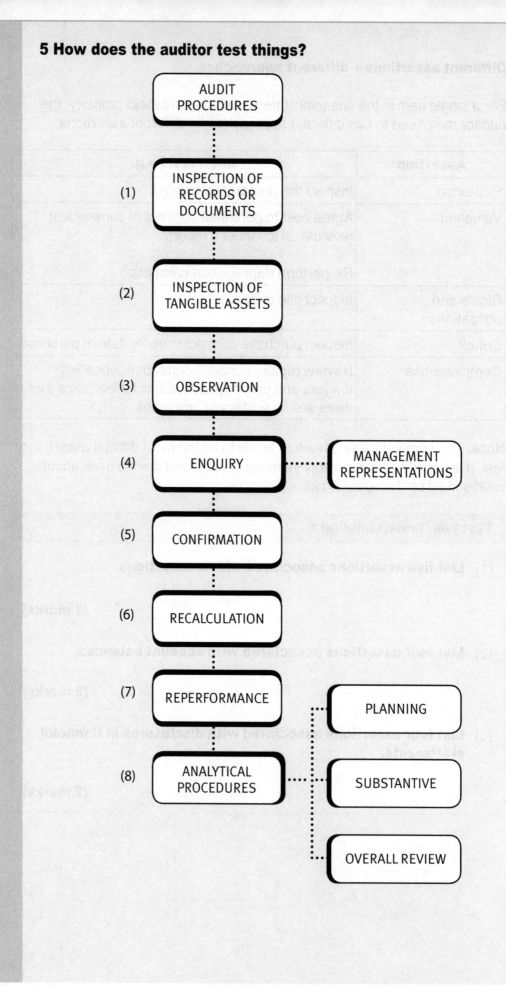

Audit procedures

We have seen above, that:

- the nature of the transaction or balance being audited and
- the assertion being tested

demand different approaches from the auditor.

ISA 500 identifies eight types of procedures that the auditor can adopt to obtain audit evidence:

In chapter 10 'Audit procedures' we will look in detail at how these procedures are applied in specific circumstances as well as at some of the more detailed requirements of ISAs.

ISA 500 identifies eight procedures that the auditor can adopt to obtain audit evidence:

5.1 Inspection of records or documents

> **Expandable Text - Examples of inspection of documents**
>
> - May give direct evidence of the existence of an asset, e.g. a share certificate.
>
> - May give evidence of ownership (rights and obligations), e.g. title deeds, but may be persuasive rather than conclusive, e.g. an invoice will usually provide evidence that goods or services are valid expenses or assets of the company, but they may have been ordered for someone's private use, and invoices addressed to a director **may** be for valid business purposes.
>
> - May give evidence that a control is operating, e.g. invoices stamped paid or authorised for payment by an appropriate signature.
>
> - May give evidence about cut-off, e.g. the dates on invoices, despatch notes, etc.
>
> **Note**. Records and documents are not just bits of paper, but include records held electronically and other media as well.

5.2 Inspection of tangible assets

- Will usually give pretty conclusive evidence of existence!

- May give evidence of valuation, e.g. obvious evidence of impairment of inventory or non-current assets.

- Unlikely to give evidence of rights and obligations, e.g. a vehicle may be leased, inventory held on behalf of a third party, etc.

5.3 Observation

- Involves looking at a process or procedure.

- May well provide evidence that a control is being operated, e.g. double staffing or a cheque signatory examining supporting documentation.

> **Expandable Text - Explanation of observation**
>
> - You need to remember that this is only evidence that the control was operating properly at the time of the observation, and the auditor's presence may have had an influence on the client's staff's behaviour.
>
> - Observation of a one-off event, e.g. an inventory count, may well give good evidence that the procedure was carried out effectively.

5.4 Enquiry

- Enquiry is a major source of audit evidence, however the results of enquiries will usually need to be corroborated in some way through other audit procedures.

- The answers to enquiries may themselves be corroborative evidence.

Management representations

Management representations are a sub-set of Enquiry.

The auditor obtains written representations from management to confirm oral enquiries where:

- the issue is material or

- where other sources of evidence cannot reasonably be expected to exist or

- where other evidence is of lower quality.

Expandable Text - Management representations

Management representations have a whole ISA – ISA 580 – to themselves and will be looked at in more detail in chapter 11. ISA 580 and a number of other ISAs specify issues about which the auditor should obtain written representations from management.

However, this is a tricky area because:

- the auditor forms an **independent** opinion but

- by their nature, management representations cannot provide independent evidence.

Representations, therefore, are usually considered to be corroborative evidence. If they are the best or perhaps the only evidence available it becomes a matter of professional judgement as to whether the auditor considers it to be sufficient.

5.5 Confirmation

- A specific form of enquiry
- Examples of use:
    - circularisation of receivables
    - confirmation of bank balances
    - confirmation from legal advisers of actual or contingent liabilities arising from legal proceedings
    - confirmation of inventories held by third parties
    - confirmation of investment portfolios by investment managers.

Expandable Text - Examples of confirmation

- May give good evidence of existence, e.g. receivables confirmation.
- May not necessarily give evidence of valuation, e.g. the customer may accept the debt but may be unable to pay.

5.6 Recalculation

- Checking the arithmetical accuracy of the client's calculations.

5.7 Reperformance

- May be something relatively simple, e.g. test checking inventory counts.
- May be more sophisticated, e.g. using IT tools to check a receivables ageing.

5.8 Analytical procedures

- The consideration of the relationships between figures in the financial statements or between financial and non-financial information.

Expandable Text - Overall picture of analytical procedures

Analytical procedures must be used:

- As part of the planning process to help identify areas of risk or which otherwise need particular attention.
- At the final review stage.

Analytical procedures may be used:

- As substantive procedures, e.g.

The consideration of changes in the gross margin as an indicator that either sales or cost of sales may be misstated (relationships within financial information).

For different outlets in a restaurant or retail chain, the relationship between floor space and revenue might be a guide to the reliability of the figure for revenue and might also be used as a measure of the performance of staff at the branch concerned (relationship between financial and non-financial information).

Testing disclosures

There is one group of assertions that we have not yet dealt with

– assertions about presentation and disclosure.

This is because:

- if the auditor considers the classification and allocation of transactions and account balances, this will clearly have implications for how items are disclosed in the financial statements

- the correct disclosure of items in the financial statements will normally be ensured by the use of disclosure checklists and financial reporting software which will be considered in the chapter dealing with completion and review.

Test your understanding 2

(1) **List the eight types of audit procedure?**

(4 marks)

(2) **Why does the auditor need to obtain management representations?**

(2 marks)

(3) **List three examples where an auditor might use confirmations.**

(3 marks)

6 How much evidence does the auditor need?

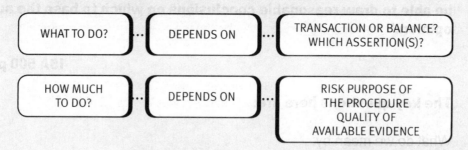

We have seen that the types of audit procedure the auditor can carry out:

- are quite limited – inspection, observation, enquiry, etc.

- are driven by the nature of the transaction or balance being audited and the assertion being tested.

We now need to consider how much evidence the auditor needs.

This is driven by:

- the risk of material misstatement
- the quality of the evidence obtained
- the purpose of the procedure (test of controls or substantive test).

These three factors – risk, purpose and quality – have a complex relationship, as we shall see. Although risk is the most important factor, as everything the auditor does on an audit is in response to the assessed level of risk, we will consider it after we have dealt with the quality and the purpose of audit evidence.

7 The quality of evidence – 'Sufficient appropriate evidence'

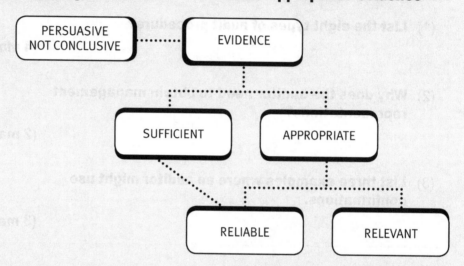

'**The auditor should obtain sufficient appropriate audit evidence to be able to draw reasonable conclusions on which to base the audit opinion.**'

ISA 500 para 2

The key questions here are:

What do we mean by:

- sufficient?
- appropriate?

'Appropriate' breaks down into two qualities:

- reliable
- relevant

and 'sufficient', 'reliable' and 'relevant' are all interlinked.

Sufficient

There needs to be 'enough' evidence, and what is 'enough' is a matter of professional judgement.

Example 1

For the client's bank balance, one confirmation letter from the bank (if the client has only one bank account) will be enough, and indeed is all there is available.

The bank letter will not, however, give the auditor all the information required. There will need to be consideration of the bank reconciliation as well.

So, 2 sources of evidence combining to be sufficient.

Example 2

To test purchases for a manufacturing client where there are literally thousands of transactions a year, the auditor may well decide to extract a statistical sample of purchase transactions to test to purchase orders, invoices, delivery notes, etc. But how many items should there be in the sample? Statistical sampling theory will give some help here – see below – but ultimately it is a question for the auditor's professional judgement.

Reliable

Reliable is deemed credible, trustworthy and dependable evidence therefore the following is deemed more or less reliable.

More reliable	Less reliable
Independent external evidence.	Internally generated evidence.
Internal evidence subject to effective controls.	Internal evidence not subject to such controls.
Evidence obtained directly by the auditor.	Evidence obtained indirectly or by inference.
Documentary.	Oral.
Original documents.	Photocopies or facsimiles.

ISA 500 gives the above guidance.

The link between sufficient and reliable

Broadly speaking, the more reliable the evidence the less of it the auditor will need.

However, the relationship is quite subtle:

If the evidence is found to be unreliable, looking at a greater quantity of such evidence will never be sufficient.

Expandable Text - Example

If a company's sales invoices tend to be made out to the wrong customer and for wrong amounts, simply looking at more, equally inaccurate invoices will do nothing to reduce the risk that the revenue figure in the income statement may be misstated.

Instead, the auditor may need to reconcile the revenue figure to the amounts paid in to the bank, carry out additional testing to ensure that opening and closing accounts receivable are fairly stated and test inventory movements and margins.

Relevant

As we have seen above the nature of the evidence the auditor wants depends on:

- the nature of the transaction or balance being tested

and

- the assertion being tested.

Persuasive not conclusive

Consider:

- The auditor gives an opinion about the financial statements **not** a certificate that the financial statements are correct.
- The audit report gives reasonable **not** absolute assurance about the financial statements.
- Audit procedures are designed to reduce the risk that the financial statements contain **material** misstatements **not** to eliminate all possibility of error.

The reason for all this lack of absolute, definitive certainty is the nature of audit evidence which is gathered by human beings in real live organisations.

- The auditor gathers evidence on a test basis (the sample may or may not be representative).
- People make mistakes (both client and auditor).
- Documents could be forged (increasingly easy with digital technology).
- The client's personnel may not always tell the truth.

As a result, we have to say that audit evidence is persuasive rather than conclusive in nature.

This also means that the auditor will need to gather evidence from a variety of sources.

The purpose of the test

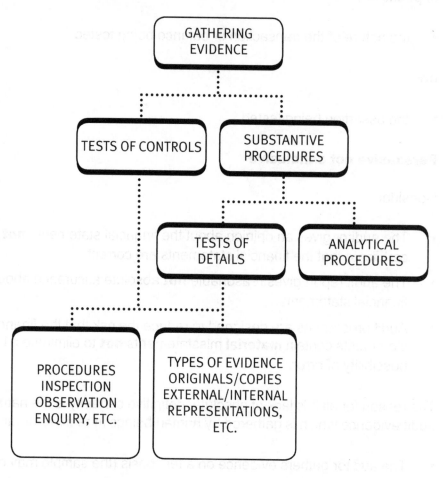

There is a subtle linkage between all of the factors affecting audit evidence that we have examined above:

*   Different items in the financial statements.

*   Different assertions about those items.

*   Sufficient evidence.

*   Relevant evidence.

*   Reliable evidence.

Thrown into the mix is the question about what we are trying to achieve by gathering the evidence:

*   Tests of controls.

*   Substantive procedures.

The auditor has to consider all of these points when deciding what evidence is relevant.

As we have seen in the chapter on systems and controls (chapter 8) there are two sources of assurance on which the audit opinion is based:

- controls
- substantive procedures.

We know that:

- the greater the assurance from controls
- the less is required from substantive procedures.

Substantive procedures are either:

- analytical procedures or
- tests of details.

We have also seen in this chapter that the audit procedures – inspection, observation, enquiry, etc. – may be used as both tests of controls and substantive procedures.

Testing controls

If the purpose of the test is to test controls, the auditor is aiming to establish that the control was operating effectively throughout the period under review.

It follows from this that the number of items tested could be very small if:

- there is no evidence that the systems have changed
- there is no evidence that the effectiveness of the people concerned may vary, e.g.
  - when staff leave
  - when duties are reassigned
  - during sickness or holidays.

Substantive testing

If the test is substantive the amount of evidence required will depend on three things:

- inherent risk

- control risk

- the nature of the appropriate procedure.

Consider:

- If **analytical procedures** are used as substantive evidence, the results of the analysis will either support the assertion, or not. If it does it will need to be backed up by a relatively small amount of corroborative evidence, e.g. reference to invoices, price lists, pay scales, etc.

- If **proof in total** is used (an extension of analytical procedures), e.g. number of pupils multiplied by fees charged to assess the turnover at a private school – the evidence will consist of a single, possibly quite complex, calculation with supporting notes.

- If the account balance or transaction stream consists of relatively few, high-value items, testing those items (providing the untested items do not amount to more than the figure for tolerable error for that population) should provide sufficient evidence. In some circumstances it may be appropriate to test all the items in the population.

- If the population to be tested consists of a large number of smaller items the auditor needs to consider **sampling** – see below.

8 Sampling

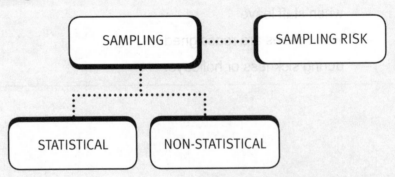

KAPLAN PUBLISHING

The need for sampling

It will usually be impossible to test every item in any accounting population because of the costs involved – remember the audit gives reasonable **not** absolute assurance. The audit evidence gathered, therefore, will be on a test basis – hence the need for the auditor to understand the implications and effective use of **sampling**.

However, it is important to understand that:

- there is no **requirement** to use sampling laid down in the ISAs

- 100% testing may be appropriate in certain circumstances – particularly where there is a small population of high-value items

- the use of analytical procedures – see section 7 above and the more detailed coverage in chapter 10 – and a variation on analytical procedures 'proof in total', may be a more effective and efficient method of gathering audit evidence

- because analytical procedures **are** a requirement of ISA 520 at the planning and overall review stages of the audit, it is sensible to make best use of the work done.

In other circumstances some form of sampling will be used.

Definition

The definition of sampling set out in ISA 530 Audit sampling and other means of testing is:

'Audit sampling' (sampling) involves the application of audit procedures to less than 100% of items within a class of transactions or account balance such that all sampling units have a chance of selection. This will enable the auditor to obtain and evaluate audit evidence about some characteristic of the items selected in order to form or assist in forming a conclusion concerning the population from which the sample is drawn. Audit sampling can use either a statistical or a non-statistical approach.

ISA 530

Statistical or non-statistical sampling

'Statistical sampling' means any approach to sampling that has the following characteristics:

- random selection of a sample, and

- use of probability theory to evaluate sample results, including measurement of sampling risk.

A sampling approach that does not have both these characteristics is considered non-statistical sampling.

ISA 530

Statistical sampling requires the following:

- **Random selection**, e.g. generating a random number to determine which item or $ in the population is the first in the sample and using a sampling interval, usually based on tolerable error, to select subsequent items.

  Judgmental or haphazard sampling – picking say two invoices from each month, or focusing on a particular period do not usually count as statistical sampling because of the risk of bias in selecting the sample.

- **Evaluation of results** using probability theory, e.g. if a sample with a total value of $100,000 contains errors of $1,000, it may be possible to extrapolate and say that there may be an error of 1% in the population as a whole, i.e $30,000 in a population of $3m or $100,000 in a population of $10m.

  Clearly this will depend on how representative the sample is and the margin of error according to probability theory.

  To be representative, a sample needs to be of sufficient size

  – usually at least 30 items – and the larger the sample size, the greater the precision it will give.

  If the results of the sample reveal potential errors which might be material, the auditor has to resolve the problem:

  - by considering whether there were special circumstances surrounding the errors, e.g. the absence of a key member of the client's staff and carrying out additional testing on items or the period likely to be affected

  - by deciding whether, because the risk of misstatement has clearly increased, which will lead to an increase in the level of materiality, the new level of materiality is too high. If it is, it will be necessary to increase the level of testing. However, care needs to be taken over this – see the section on risk revisited below.

Expandable Text - Risk revisited

Risk revisited

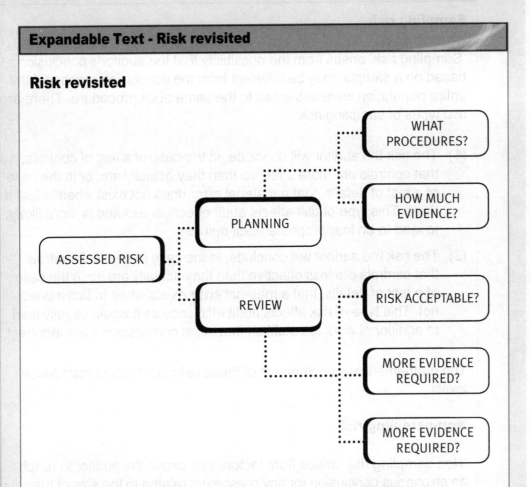

Risk affects all aspects of the gathering of audit evidence.

At the planning stage

- The audit procedures adopted are chosen in response to the assessed risk.

- The quantity of evidence required is decided on based on the level of risk.

However, remember that ISA 330 says that gathering more, poor quality evidence will probably do nothing to reduce the level of risk.

At the review stage

- Has the evidence gathered actually reduced the level of risk (after evaluating the results of the testing)?

- If not, should we do more tests or look at evidence from a different source?

Sampling risk

'Sampling risk' arises from the possibility that the auditor's conclusion, based on a sample, may be different from the conclusion reached if the entire population were subjected to the same audit procedure. There are two types of sampling risk:

(1) The risk the auditor will conclude, in the case of a test of controls, that controls are more effective than they actually are, or in the case of a test of details, that a material error does not exist when in fact it does. This type of risk affects audit effectiveness and is more likely to lead to an inappropriate audit opinion.

(2) The risk the auditor will conclude, in the case of a test of controls, that controls are less effective than they actually are, or in the case of a test of details, that a material error exists when in fact it does not. This type of risk affects audit efficiency as it would usually lead to additional work to establish that initial conclusions were incorrect.

The mathematical complements of these risks are termed confidence levels.

Non-sampling risk

'Non-sampling risk' arises from factors that cause the auditor to reach an erroneous conclusion for any reason not related to the size of the sample. For example, ordinarily the auditor finds it necessary to rely on audit evidence that is persuasive rather than conclusive, the auditor might use inappropriate audit procedures, or the auditor might misinterpret audit evidence and fail to recognise an error.

Test your understanding 3

(1) **List three qualities audit evidence must have?**

(3 marks)

(2) **List two reasons why audit evidence is likely to be persuasive rather than conclusive.**

(2 marks)

(3) **List two examples where it would be appropriate to use statistical sampling.**

(2 marks)

9 Audit documentation

Why do we need working papers?

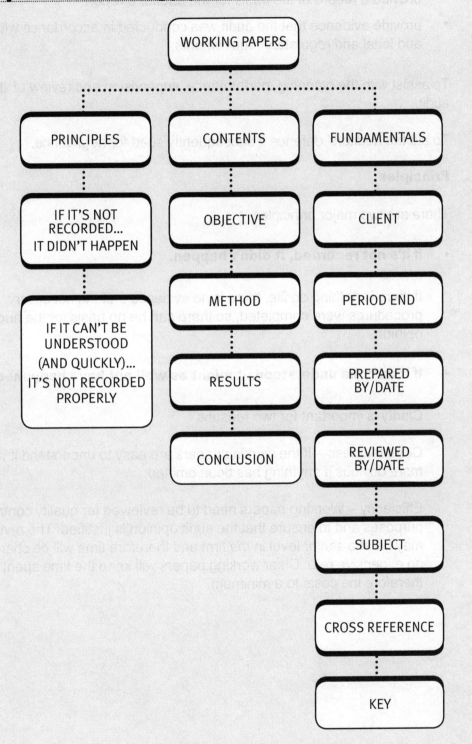

The job of working papers is to:

- provide a record of the basis for the auditor's report

- provide evidence that the audit was conducted in accordance with ISAs and legal and regulatory requirements.

To assist with the planning, performance, supervision and review of the audit.

To aid the auditors' defence if subsequently sued for negligence.

Principles

There are two major principles

- **If it's not recorded, it didn't happen.**

   If there is nothing on file, there is no evidence that the necessary procedures were completed, so there can be no basis for the audit opinion.

- **If it can't be understood, it might as well not have happened.**

   Clarity is important for two reasons

   Completeness – If the working papers are easy to understand it will be more obvious if anything has been omitted.

   Efficiency – Working papers need to be reviewed for quality control purposes and to ensure that the audit opinion is justified. The reviewer may be at a senior level in the firm and therefore time will be charged at an expensive rate. Clear working papers will keep the time spent and therefore the costs to a minimum.

Structure and layout

The file

There are two broad areas to the file.

- The control part consisting of:
  - the planning section
  - the completion and review section.

- The main working papers are divided into the relevant sections of the financial statements, e.g. non-current assets, inventories, receivables, etc.

Expandable Text - Lead schedule and working papers

This represents a hierarchical or pyramid structure so that:

- the figures in the financial statements are supported by the detailed working papers in the various sections

- the matters arising and errors revealed on each section are summarised at the review and completion stage

- the audit strategy and plan, recorded in the planning section, are translated into action in the underlying sections

- each working paper on file either summarises the information on other working papers or supports the conclusions reached on another working paper and this is demonstrated by a system of indexation and cross referencing.

Individual sections of the file

Each section of the file also follows hierarchical principles with:

- lead schedule
- section summary/matters arising
- supporting schedules
- transactions/other detailed testing.

The working papers in each section will normally include:

The lead schedule

Client: XYZ Ltd

Year ended: 31 December 2009

Subject: receivables

Reference J1

Prepared by: AB   Date

Reviewed by   Date

	Ref	This year Draft $	Adjustments $	Final $	Last Year Final $
Trade receivables					
Less irrecoverable debt					
Other receivables					
Prepayments					

Summary of work done	Ref
Circularisation of material receivables carried out	J10
Receivables ageing reviewed and discussed with xx	J20
Correspondence with disputed accounts reviewed	J21
Material other receivables agreed to confirmation or after date receipts	J30
Material invoices agreed to invoices and payment and calcualtions checked	J40

Conclusion

Subject to satisfactory resolution of dispute with CDE Ltd (J2) receivables are fairly stated

This is an example of the lead schedule for the accounts receivable section.

Note

- The headings – client, year end, subject, preparer, reviewer.

- The account headings, which correspond to the analysis of accounts receivable in the note to the financial statements.

- Comparative figures.

- The suggested column headings, draft, adjustments and final, which allow the reviewer to see adjustments made to the client's original figures, while ensuring the final column agrees to the financial statements.

- Cross-references to supporting schedules.

- Brief summary of work done.

- Conclusion.

Section summary (matters arising)

- A schedule that summarises:
  - what you did
  - why you are confident in your conclusions
  - Iimportant issues for the partner and manager to consider.

Supporting schedules

Either:

Sub-categories, e.g. For non-current assets:

- land and buildings
- plant and machinery
- IT equipment
- motor vehicles.

Or:

Transaction testing schedules.

Client Year end Subject				Ref Initials Reviewed							
						Tests					
Item No	Details	£	£	A	B	C	D	E	F	G	

Note:

- Item numbering so that problem items can easily be referred to.
- Details column – showing nature of transaction, customer, supplier name etc.
- $ columns for recording amounts.

- Testing grid – each test will be specified on the audit programme, or specific schedule drawn up for the purpose and can be ticked off in the grid when completed. This makes it clear what has and has not been done. Problems encountered are explained on the matters arising schedule.

Audit programmes

These may be:

- a pre-printed (or IT based) schedule or checklist detailing the detailed tests to be completed – if so, it needs to be tailored for the requirements of the client
- a specifically drafted list of the tests to be completed.

Audit packs

Most firms use 'audit packs', which:

- ensures a consistent approach to planning, completion and individual sections of the file
- but can lead to a 'box ticking' approach to the audit, which is not sufficiently responsive to the specific risks of the assignment.

Audit packs may be:

- proprietary, off the shelf, sets of stationery or audit software
- developed in house by the individual audit firm.

The use of IT in the administration of audits

IT may be used in two ways to assist with the administration of audit assignments:

- For budgeting, time recording and billing purposes.
- IT-based audit packs.

Budgeting, time recording and billing

Requires:

- the setting of charge out rates
- recording of hours worked, usually via timesheets
- accumulation of costs on individual assignments through a coding system to arrive at a work in progress figure that can be billed to the client in due course.

Costs on assignments need to be monitored on a regular basis and the implications of overruns understood and dealt with.

IT-based working paper systems

Advantages

- Takes the conformity advantages of audit packs to another level.
- Cross-referencing and compliance with indexation system become automatic.
- Incomplete work is highlighted automatically.

Disadvantages

- can be expensive to install.
- Need for extensive (and costly) training.

Test your understanding 4

(1) **Why do auditors prepare working papers?**

(1 mark)

(2) **List six things which appear usually at the top of every working paper.**

(3 marks)

(3) **What is the purpose of a lead schedule?**

(1 mark)

(4) **Why should all working papers be easy to review?**

(1 mark)

Custody and retention of working papers

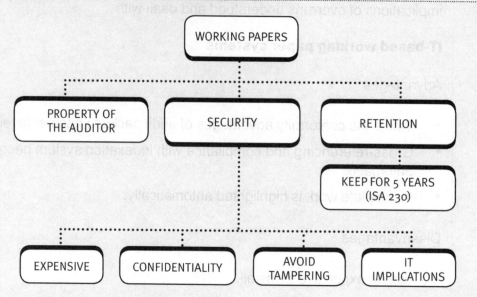

Who owns the working papers?

The auditor does. This is important because:

*   Access to the working papers is controlled by the auditor, not the client, which is an element in preserving the auditor's independence.

*   In some circumstances care may need to be taken when copies of client generated schedules are incorporated into the file.

Security

Working papers must be kept secure.

*   Audits are expensive exercises. If the files are lost or stolen, the evidence they contain will need to be recreated, so the work will need to be done again. The auditors may be able to recover the costs from their insurers, but otherwise it will simply represent a loss to the firm. Either way, prevention is better than cure.

*   By its nature, audit evidence will comprise much sensitive information that is confidential. If the files are lost or stolen, the auditor's duty of confidentiality will be compromised.

*   There have been cases of unscrupulous clients altering auditors' working papers to conceal frauds.

The implications of IT based audit systems are also far reaching.

*   By their nature, laptops are susceptible to theft, even though the thief may have no interest in the contents of the audit file. Nevertheless, all the problems associated with re-performing the audit and breaches of confidentiality remain.

- It is more difficult to be certain who created or amended computer based files than manual files – handwriting, signatures and dates have their uses – and this makes it harder to detect whether the files have been tampered with.

This means that the following precautions need to be taken.

- If files are left unattended at clients' premises – overnight or during lunch breaks – they should be securely locked away, or if this is impossible, taken home by the audit team.
- When files are left in a car, the same precautions should be taken as with any valuables.
- IT-based systems should be subject to passwords, encryption and backup procedures.

Retention

ISA 230 states that audit documentation should be retained for five years from completion of the audit. Many firms keep working papers for longer than this because information may still be required for tax purposes.

All of this means that firms need to make arrangements for:

- secure storage of recent files
- archiving older files
- archiving and backup of IT-based files.

10 Smaller entities

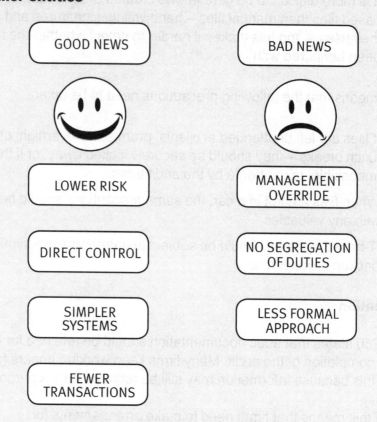

Smaller commercial entities will usually have the attributes above most of which are double edged in a good news/bad news kind of way:

- **Lower risk**: Smaller entities may well be engaged in activity that is relatively simple and therefore lower risk. However, this will not be true for small – often one person businesses – where there is a high level of expertise in a particular field, e.g. consultancy businesses, creative businesses, the financial sector.

- **Direct control by owner managers** is a strength because they can know what is going on and have the ability to exercise real control. They are also in a strong position to manipulate the figures or put private transactions 'through the books'.

- **Simpler systems**: Smaller entities are less likely to have sophisticated IT systems, but pure, manual systems are becoming increasingly rare. This is good news in that many of the bookkeeping errors associated with smaller entities may now be less prevalent. However, a system is only as good as the person operating it.

Evidence implications

- The normal rules concerning the relationship between risk and the quality and quantity of evidence apply irrespective of the size of the entity.
- The quantity of evidence may well be less than for a larger organisation.
- It may be more efficient to carry out 100% testing in a smaller organisation.

Small not-for-profit organisations

Small not for profit organisations have all the attributes of other small entities. Arguably, however, the position is more difficult for the auditor because:

- While most small businesses are under the direct management of the owner, small not-for-profit organisations tend to be staffed by volunteers and the culture is more likely to be one of trust rather than accountability.

Problems

- **Management override** – Smaller entities will have a key director or owner who will have the authority to do what they want. Therefore could override the systems with ease.
- **No segregation of duties** – Smaller entities tend to only have one accounts clerk that processes all information, therefore having a lack of segregation of duties. To overcome this issue the director should authorise and review the accounts clerk work.
- **Less formal approach** – Smaller entities tend to have simple systems and very few controls due to the lack of complexity and trust, therefore it would be difficult to test the reliability of the systems, therefore substantive testing, tends to be used more.

Expandable Text- Small not for profit organisations

- Therefore documentation and controls may be less formal, e.g.
    - The mother of a child at a toddlers' playgroup agrees to go to the next town by car to collect some new outdoor activity equipment. She is reimbursed for the cost of her petrol and the amount is agreed informally, based on the estimated distance and fuel consumption of her car. She submits no receipt for her petrol and is reimbursed in cash from the box where the money taken each day for children attending the playgroup is kept.

    - The collection after a religious service is counted each week by one person – a retired bank manager – who then pays the amounts into the organisation's bank account.

- In both of these examples, the auditor is in a difficult position:
    - The petrol claim may be right or it may be wrong – the auditor has no evidence. The auditor can re-perform the mileage calculation, or compare the total of such reimbursements, the amounts in the previous year's financial statements. In the end, the auditor will decide whether the risk of material misstatement is sufficient to consider qualifying the audit report.

    - The retired bank manager (used as an example of respectability and trustworthiness) may be skimming off a small amount each week, or he may not. The only evidence the auditor has is likely to be the analytical procedures performed on the collections over time, adjusted for seasonal fluctuations, etc.

    It may be possible to compare the amounts collected when the usual counter is away on holiday, but even this is of questionable reliability.

11 Chapter summary

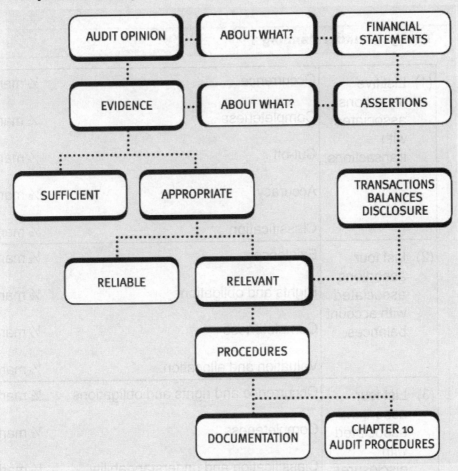

Test your understanding answers

Test your understanding 1		
(1) List five assertions associated with transactions.	Occurrence	½ mark
	Completeness	½ mark
	Cut-off	½ mark
	Accuracy	½ mark
	Classification	½ mark
(2) List four assertions associated with account balances.	Existence	½ mark
	Rights and obligations	½ mark
	Completeness	½ mark
	Valuation and allocation	½ mark
(3) List four assertions associated with disclosures in financial statements.	Occurrence and rights and obligations	½ mark
	Completeness	½ mark
	Classification and understandability.	½ mark
	Accuracy and valuation	½ mark

KAPLAN PUBLISHING

Test your understanding 2

(1) List the eight types of audit procedure?	Inspection of records or documents.	½ mark
	Inspection of assets.	½ mark
	Observation.	½ mark
	Enquiry.	½ mark
	Confirmation.	½ mark
	Recalculation.	½ mark
	Reperformance.	½ mark
	Analytical procedures.	½ mark
(2) Why does the auditor need to obtain management representations?	Where the issue is material.	1 mark
	Where other sources of evidence cannot reasonably be expected to exist.	1 mark
	Where other evidence is of lower quality.	1 mark
	Where it is specifically required by an ISA.	1 mark
(3) List three examples where an auditor might use confirmations.	Circularisation of receivables.	1 mark
	Confirmation of bank balances.	1 mark
	Confirmation from legal advisers of actual or contingent liabilities arising from legal proceedings.	1 mark
	Confirmation of inventory held by third parties.	1 mark
	Confirmation of investment portfolios by investment managers.	1 mark

Test your understanding 3

(1)	List three qualities audit evidence must have.	It must be: • Sufficient. • Relevant. • Reliable.	1 mark 1 mark 1 mark
(2)	List two reasons why audit evidence is likely to be persuasive rather than conclusive.	The auditor gathers evidence on a test basis (the sample may or may not be representative). • People make mistakes (both client and auditor). • Documents could be forged (increasingly easy with digital technology). • The client's personnel may not always tell the truth.	½ mark ½ mark ½ mark ½ mark
(3)	List two examples where it would be appropriate to use statistical sampling.	Purchases transaction testing Revenue transactions testing Payroll transactions testing, etc.	1 mark 1 mark 1 mark

KAPLAN PUBLISHING

Test your understanding 4

Solution

(1)	Why do auditors prepare working papers?	To provide a record of work done and evidence that the work was performed in accordance with auditing standards, to assist in the planning, performance and review of the audit.	1 mark
(2)	List the six things which appear usually at the top of every working paper.	Client name / Year end / Subject / Prepared by / Reviewed by / Reference.	½ mark each
(3)	What is the purpose of a lead schedule?	To provide a summary of each area.	1 mark
(4)	Why should all working papers be easy to review?	To make it easier to spot anything that has been omitted, to ensure that the time spent by senior staff reviewing the audit file is minimised.	1 mark

KAPLAN PUBLISHING

10

Audit procedures

Chapter learning objectives

When you have completed this chapter you will be able to:

- explain the purpose of substantive procedures in relation to financial statements assertions

- explain the substantive procedures used in auditing each balance

- tabulate those substantive procedures in a work program, for the following areas:
  - inventories
  - receivables
  - payables
  - bank and cash
  - non current assets
  - non current liabilities
  - accounting estimates

- explain the use of computer assisted audit techniques in the context of an audit

- discuss and provide relevant examples of the use of test data and audit software for the transaction cycles and statement of financial position items

- discuss the use of computers in relation to the administration of the audit

- discuss and provide examples of how analytical procedures are used as substantive procedures

- compute and interpret key ratios used in analytical procedures

- discuss the problems associated with the audit of accounting estimates

- discuss the extent to which auditors are able to rely on the work of experts and internal audit

- discuss the audit considerations relating to entities using service organizations

- discuss why auditors rely on the work of others

- explain the extent to which reference to the work of others can be made in audit reports

- apply audit techniques to small not for profit organisations

- explain how the audit of a small not for profit organisation differs from the audit of for profit organisations.

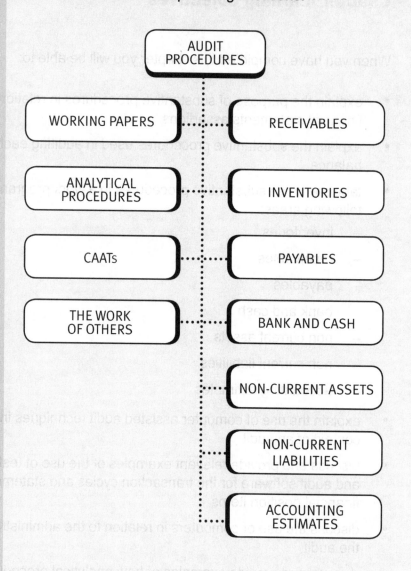

1 General principles

A word of warning: chapter 9 dealt with the principles of audit evidence. This chapter deals with how those principles are applied.

In the sections that follow, we will examine a number of specific audit areas and deal with how these are usually tested. You may be tempted to learn these by heart. Whatever you do,

DO NOT DO THIS!!!!

The audit of any item is based on:

- the risk of misstatement
- the nature of the item
- the assertion you are testing.

The examiner is not stupid. He or she knows that auditing is a matter of professional skill and judgement. If you can answer an exam question simply by learning a few pages of a book, it is not a very good test of whether you are a competent auditor.

So the questions may not ask about standard situations and you will have to apply your knowledge to the demands of the question.

Things you always have to do

Nevertheless, there are some things which, one way or another, will always apply (and which, if you mention them, will gain you marks):

- understand the system
- analytical procedures
- document your work.

Things you will always have to consider

What are you being asked to test?

- A transaction or event that took place during the year.
- An account balance at the period end.
- Presentation or disclosure.

What is the nature of the item you are testing?

- Asset
- Liability
- Revenue
- Expense

What assertion(s) are you testing?

- Existence
- Occurrence
- Valuation
- Cut-off, etc.

Things you may have to do

- If you rely on controls, you will have to test them.
- Management representations are required for some items by ISA 580 and by a number of other ISAs.
- If there are high volumes of transactions, consider using computer assisted audit techniques (CAATs).

2 Analytical procedures

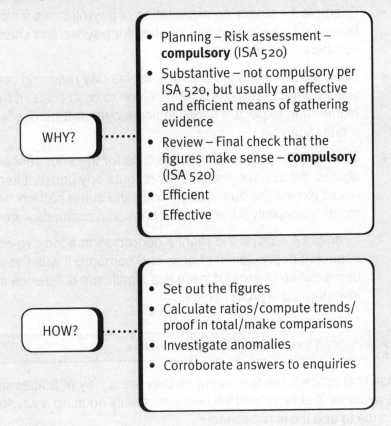

WHY?

- Planning – Risk assessment – **compulsory** (ISA 520)
- Substantive – not compulsory per ISA 520, but usually an effective and efficient means of gathering evidence
- Review – Final check that the figures make sense – **compulsory** (ISA 520)
- Efficient
- Effective

HOW?

- Set out the figures
- Calculate ratios/compute trends/ proof in total/make comparisons
- Investigate anomalies
- Corroborate answers to enquiries

Why do them?

Analytical Procedures as substantive evidence

ISA 520 states that analytical procedures must be used at the planning stage to identify risks, and at the completion stage of the audit as a final review of the FS.

They may also be used at the substantive stage when the auditor is auditing the draft financial statements.

Analytical procedures are not just the comparison of one year with another. AP's can be used in the following ways:

- Ratio analysis
- Trend analysis
- Proof in total

In order to use analytical procedures the following process should be followed:

- Create your own expectation of what you think the figure should be
- Compare your expectation to the actual figure

- Investigate any significant differences
  - Example 1 - create an expectation of payroll costs for the year by taking last year's cost and inflating for payrise and change in staff numbers – proof in total.

  - Example 2 – calculate the receivables day ratio and compare it with prior year and credit terms given to customers. If the figure is higher than expected it may indicate overstatement of receivables – ratio analysis.

  - Example 3 – plot monthly sales data for the prior year and plot against the current year and investigate any unusual trends. You would expect the business to follow the same pattern month on month especially if they have a seasonal business – trend analysis.

  - Example 4 – using the client's depreciation policy, re-compute the expected depreciation charge and compare it with the actual depreciation charge. If there is a significant difference it should be investigated – proof in total.

Expandable Text - Analytical procedures

Analytical procedures are useful as they are a way of addressing several FS assertions at once and you are essentially auditing a whole balance at once to see if it is reasonable.

You can use them to corroborate other audit evidence obtained. By using analytical procedures you identify unusual items that can then be further investigated to ensure that a misstatement doesn't exist in the balance.

In order to use analytical procedures effectively you need to be able to create an expectation. It will be difficult to create an expectation if operations are significantly different from last year, more so if the changes haven't been planned for. If the changes were planned, we can compare the actual with the forecast. However, there is no point comparing actual with prior year since it bears no relation to the current year.

It will also be difficult to use analytical procedures if there have been lots of one-off events in the year as there will be nothing to compare them with.

The ratios

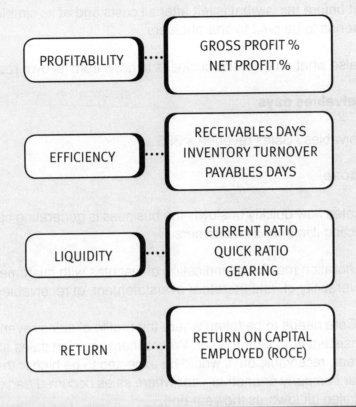

PROFITABILITY ···· GROSS PROFIT %
NET PROFIT %

EFFICIENCY ···· RECEIVABLES DAYS
INVENTORY TURNOVER
PAYABLES DAYS

LIQUIDITY ···· CURRENT RATIO
QUICK RATIO
GEARING

RETURN ···· RETURN ON CAPITAL
EMPLOYED (ROCE)

Expandable Text - Ratios

Gross margin

Gross profit / Sales revenue × 100%

Purpose

For most business – main exceptions are consultancies and some businesses in the service sector – the margin between sales revenue and cost of sales is what generates the profits the business needs to pay the wages, service any debt and eventually pay dividends to shareholders.

The lower the margin, the greater the volume of sales revenue needed.

Net margin

Profit before tax / Sales revenue × 100%

Purpose

Profit before tax is what is left after all costs and at its simplest enables dividends to be paid to shareholders.

It is also what enables the business to grow from its own resources.

Receivables days

Receivables / Sales revenue × 365

Purpose

Indicates how quickly or slowly the business is generating cash by collecting it in from its customers.

Deterioration may be an indication of disputes with customers or non-recoverability of, and therefore overstatement, of receivables.

NB. Care needs to be taken where the profile of sales revenue is inconsistent from year to year. Where there are high sales at the end of the year, receivable days would be expected to be higher than for a similar company or another year where sales occurred earlier in the year and tailed off towards the year end.

Payables days

Payables / Purchases × 365

Purpose

To show how long the company is taking to pay its suppliers.

May be indicative of cash-flow problems, or, extended credit terms taken.

Inventory turnover

Inventory / Cost of sales × 365

(How many days worth of cost of sales are tied up in inventory.)

Or

Cost of sales / Inventory

(How many times the year end inventory could have been sold in the year.)

Purpose

To show how much the business has invested in its inventory.

Slower inventory turnover may indicate excessive inventory holdings, over optimistic valuation or building up inventory for the launch of a new product.

The current ratio

Current assets / Current liabilities

Purpose

Indicates the business' ability to settle its current liabilities.

The quick ratio

Current assets − inventory / Current liabilities

Purpose

A refinement of the current ratio, which eliminates less liquid assets, inventory, from the equation.

Leverage or gearing

Share capital + reserves / Borrowings

Or

Borrowings / Share capital + reserves + borrowings × 100

Purpose

To show the relative reliance of the business on external or internal sources of finances.

Businesses with higher leverage are usually regarded as more risky – greater danger of being financially overstretched, but the opportunity of greater rewards for individual shareholders.

Return on capital employed (ROCE)

Profit before interest and tax / Share capital + reserves + borrowings.

Purpose

Is the business giving sufficient return compared with other possible investments?

ROCE is a useful measure for a large diversified group that can switch where it invests its funds. It is of less use for a small, owner-managed business where choice of investment is limited.

How are analytical procedures used?

Calculating the ratios is just the start. Analytical procedures are audit procedures in their own right, designed to enable the auditor to reduce the risk of coming to the wrong opinion about the financial statements.

This means that the auditor needs to use analytical procedures to identify anomalies in the figures, which may indicate problems.

To do this, the auditor will make comparisons:

- between the current year and previous year(s)
- between actual figures and budgets, forecasts or client's expectations
- with similar companies

Analytical procedures as substantive procedures

ISA 520 states that the auditor may use analytical procedures as substantive procedures.

The suitability of this approach depends on four factors:

- The suitability of using substantive analytical procedures given the assertions.
- The reliability of the data.
- The degree of precision possible.
- The amount of variation which is acceptable.

Some examples.

(1) Suitability

- Analytical procedures are clearly unsuitable for testing the – existence of inventories – to do this you need to go and count the items on the shelves in the warehouse.

- Analytical procedures may well be suitable for testing the value–of labour carried forward in inventory – by comparing direct labour costs for the year with value in inventory, in the context of the costs of raw materials and overheads in inventory.

(2) Reliability

- If controls over sales order processing are weak, it will –probably be necessary to rely on tests of details rather than analytical procedures.

(3) Precision

- There is likely to be greater consistency in gross margins over – time than in discretionary expenditure like advertising or R&D.

(4) Acceptable variation

- Variations in sales revenue, which may have a minor impact–on the results for the year, will be regarded differently from receivables, which, if uncollectible will have a proportionately greater impact.

Expandable Text - Analytical procedures

(1) **Viola Ltd has Sales revenue of $1m and a gross margin of 35%. What is the value of its cost of sales?**

(2) **French Horn Ltd has sales revenue of $3m and receivables of $500,000. Calculate its receivables period.**

(3) **Oboe Ltd has inventories of $1m at the beginning of the year and $2m at the end of the year and purchases of $9m for the year. Calculate its inventory turnover period.**

Solution –

(1) Viola Ltd has Sales revenue of $1m and a gross margin of 35%. What is the value of its cost of sales?	$650,000
(2) French Horn Ltd has sales revenue of $3m and receivables of $500,000. Calculate its debtor's period.	61 days

(3) Oboe Ltd has inventory of $1m at the beginning of the year and $2m at the end of the year and purchases of $9m for the year. Calculate its inventory turn period.	91 days Inventory turns over four time in the year Purchases + opening inventory less closing inventory = cost of sales = $8m 0.25 x 365 = 91 days

3 The audit of receivables

WHAT ARE THEY?

- PEOPLE WHO OWE US MONEY (trade and loan receivables, etc.)
- PEOPLE WHO OWE US SERVICES (prepayments)

KEY QUESTIONS

- Trade: Are they going to pay and fairly soon?
- Prepayments: Did we make the payment?
  - Is it accounted for in the correct period?
  - i.e. is the calculation correct?

PROCEDURES

- Trade: Ask them (circularisation)
  - See if they pay (after date receipts)
  - Review ageing
- Prepayments: Verify payment
  - Review invoices, etc. for cut-off

Key assertions

Assertions – receivables

- **Existence** – The receivable actually exists.
- **Rights and obligations** – The receivable belongs to the company.
- **Valuation and allocation** – Receivables are included in the financial statements at the correct amount.
- **Cut-off** – Transactions and events have been recorded in the correct accounting period.

Audit procedures

- Obtain a list of receivables balances, cast this and agree it to the receivables control account total at the end of the year. Ageing of receivables may also be verified at this time.
- Determine an appropriate sampling method (cumulative monetary amount, value-weighted selection, random, etc.) using materiality for the receivable balance to determine the sampling interval or number of receivables to include in the sample.
- Select the balances to be tested, with specific reference to the categories of receivable noted below.
- Extract details of each receivable selected from the ledger and prepare circularisation letters.
- Ask the chief accountant at the company (or other responsible official) to sign the letters.
- The auditor posts or faxes the letters to the individual receivables.
- Obtain a list of credit balances in the receivables ledger and obtain explanations from management.

Receivables circularisation – procedures

Purpose:

- Direct third party confirmation to give evidence of existence and valuation.

Advantages:

- Independent evidence.
- External evidence.
- Relatively efficient (if successful).

Disadvantage

* Those circularised may not reply.

Method

* Select sample of receivables to be circularised.
* Inform client of intended list of those to be circularised.
* Consider implications if client objects to any of the accounts selected being circularised.
* Record names and amounts circularised.
* Record replies received and consider implications of any accounts not agreed.
* For non-replies perform alternative procedures (other evidence in relation to accounts receivable).

Expandable Text - Confirmation letter example

Example of wording of an accounts receivable confirmation letter

Note. This letter is an example of **positive** confirmation – we think you owe this much, please confirm – which is usually used for circularising receivables.

Negative confirmations – please tell us if you owe our client any money and how much – are of less use in this context.

Typed on client's letterhead

Customer Ltd

Customer's address

Date of circularisation

Dear Sirs

As part of their normal audit procedures we have been requested by our auditors, Auditor & Co, to ask you to confirm the balance on your account with us at Year End Date.

> The balance on your account as shown by our records is shown below. After comparing this with your records will you please be kind enough to sign the confirmation below and return a copy to them in the enclosed prepaid envelope. We shall be grateful if you would do this even if the account has since been settled. If the balance is not in agreement with your records, will you please note on the confirmation the details of the items making up the difference in the space provided.
>
> Please note that this request is made for audit purposes only and has no further significance. Remittances should be sent to us in the normal way.
>
> Your kind co-operation in this matter will be greatly appreciated.
>
> Yours faithfully
>
> Chief Accountant
>
>
> Auditor & Co
>
> Auditor's address
>
> Dear Sirs
>
> We confirm that, except as noted below[x], a balance of \$xxxxx
>
> was owing by us to Client Limited at Year End Date.
>
> Name of company or Individual Customer Ltd
>
> Signed
>
> Position held
>
> [x]Details of differences if any

Recoverability/Provision for doubtful debts [Valuation]

- Discuss the assumptions underlying the general provision with management to ensure reasonable

- Recalculate the provision based on management's assumptions and agree to the figure in the financial statements

- Compare the prior year provision to the amounts actually written off as bad in the year to test how accurate management usually are in estimating possible bad debts

- Obtain a list of aged receivables and investigate the recoverability of any old balances

- For a sample of year end balances, agree outstanding invoices to remittance advices/bank statement showing receipt of money after year end Discuss invoices more than 3 months old with management to consider recoverability of amount

- Where overdue receivables have not paid, trace the balances to the provision for doubtful debts. Where the balances are not included in the provision discuss with management the basis on which they believe the debtor to be recoverable

Presentation and disclosure

- Agree receivables figure in the financial statements to the receivables control account total and the nominal ledger

Analytical review

- Calculate the trade receivables collection period and compare to last year to assess reasonableness

Cut-off

- Select a sample of GDN's immediately prior to the year-end and immediately after the year end and and ensure that they have been recorded in the correct period.

- For prepayments review relevant invoices to check calculation of prepayment and ensure that payment has actually been made by agreeing it to the bank statements.

Income statement entries related to accounts receivable

Check postings and validity of:

- bad debt write offs

- movements on bad debt provision

- recoveries from receivables previously written off.

Ensure doubtful receivables and recoveries identified from other audit work are properly reflected in the income statement.

4 The audit of inventories

Overview

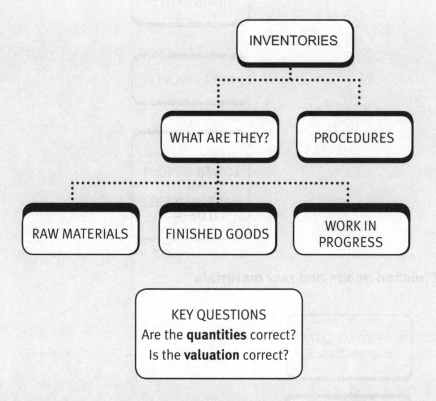

The audit of inventories is usually regarded as one of the higher risk areas of the audit:

*   It is usually crucial to assurance about an entity's profit.
*   It may be complex.
*   It is usually subject to a degree of estimation.

They can also be very varied, e.g.:

*   sheep or cows on a farm
*   jewellery
*   the costs of developing a computer game
*   cars
*   food and drink
*   chemicals
*   petrol.

That's probably enough to be going on with!

How are inventories valued?

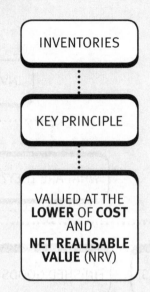

INVENTORIES

KEY PRINCIPLE

VALUED AT THE **LOWER** OF **COST** AND **NET REALISABLE VALUE** (NRV)

Finished goods and raw materials

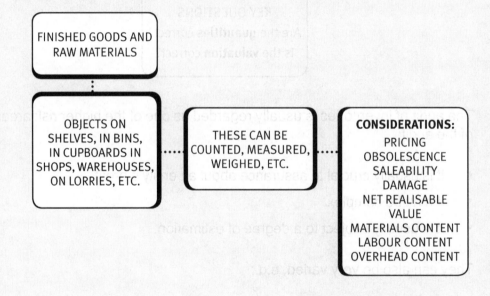

FINISHED GOODS AND RAW MATERIALS

OBJECTS ON SHELVES, IN BINS, IN CUPBOARDS IN SHOPS, WAREHOUSES, ON LORRIES, ETC.

THESE CAN BE COUNTED, MEASURED, WEIGHED, ETC.

CONSIDERATIONS:
PRICING
OBSOLESCENCE
SALEABILITY
DAMAGE
NET REALISABLE VALUE
MATERIALS CONTENT
LABOUR CONTENT
OVERHEAD CONTENT

Work in progress

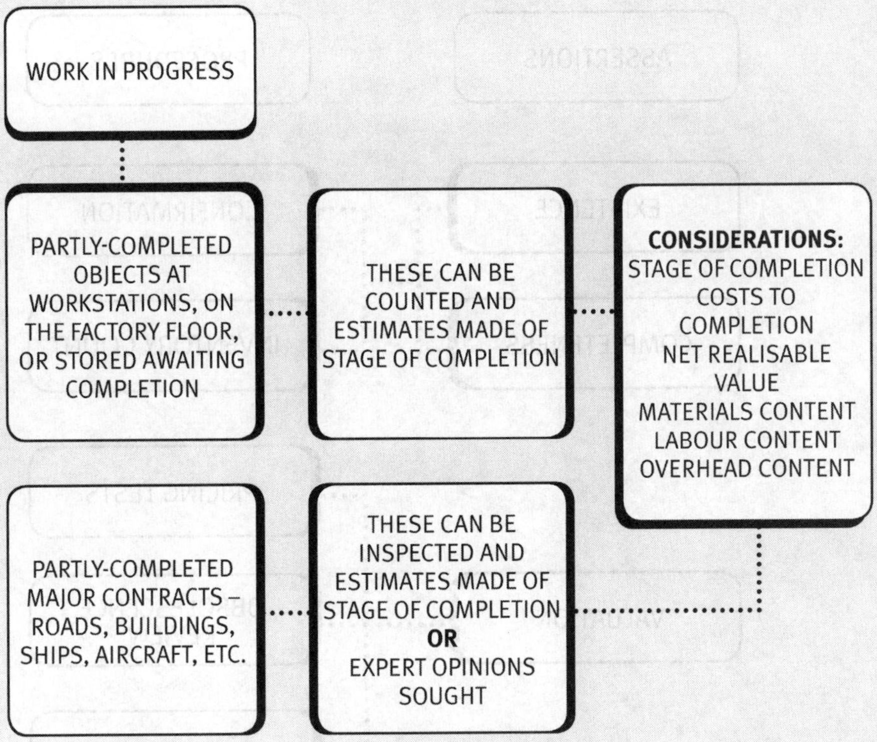

WORK IN PROGRESS

PARTLY-COMPLETED OBJECTS AT WORKSTATIONS, ON THE FACTORY FLOOR, OR STORED AWAITING COMPLETION

THESE CAN BE COUNTED AND ESTIMATES MADE OF STAGE OF COMPLETION

CONSIDERATIONS:
STAGE OF COMPLETION
COSTS TO COMPLETION
NET REALISABLE VALUE
MATERIALS CONTENT
LABOUR CONTENT
OVERHEAD CONTENT

PARTLY-COMPLETED MAJOR CONTRACTS – ROADS, BUILDINGS, SHIPS, AIRCRAFT, ETC.

THESE CAN BE INSPECTED AND ESTIMATES MADE OF STAGE OF COMPLETION
OR
EXPERT OPINIONS SOUGHT

Assertions again

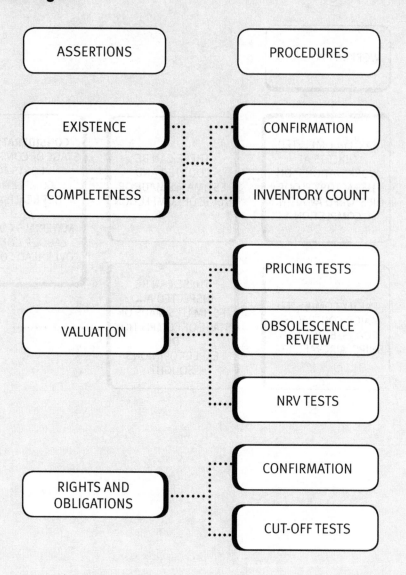

ASSERTIONS	PROCEDURES
EXISTENCE	CONFIRMATION
COMPLETENESS	INVENTORY COUNT
	PRICING TESTS
VALUATION	OBSOLESCENCE REVIEW
	NRV TESTS
RIGHTS AND OBLIGATIONS	CONFIRMATION
	CUT-OFF TESTS

KAPLAN PUBLISHING

Inventory

Procedures

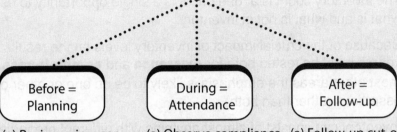

Before = Planning

(a) Review prior year working papers
(b) Discuss instructions
(c) Familiarisation, nature, value, location etc.
(d) Arrange third party certificates
(e) Consider need for expert(s)
(f) Role of internal audit
(g) Extract representtive sample

During = Attendance

(a) Observe compliance with instructions
(b) Make test counts (from physical to recorded and *vice versa*)
(c) Take copies of inventory take sheets
(d) Obtain more detasils of damaged inventory
(e) Note cut-off details

After = Follow-up

(a) Follow-up cut-off tests
(b) Ensure all copies of inventory take sheets from inventory day agree to client inventory sheet and check sequencing is complete
(c) Ensure continuous inventory records adjusted
(d) Follow-up third party certificates
(e) Conclude on reliability of quantities used as a basis for computing inventory
(f) Valuation review lower of cost and NRV

The inventory count

Principles

- The inventory count is a 'one off'. It is a single opportunity to establish what is and what is not in inventory

- Because of the crucial impact of inventory levels on the results for the year, it must be tested both for **existence** and **completeness.** (For most other areas the emphasis is likely to be on one or other of these assertions rather than both)

- Inventory can consist of almost anything with different properties (see the list above). It can therefore be quite complex and so needs to be well organised by the client. The auditor needs to be equally well organised to ensure that sufficient, appropriate evidence is gathered

- It is the client's responsibility to establish the correct value of the inventory. The auditor's job is to form an opinion as to whether that value is materially correct or not. It is therefore **not** the auditor's responsibility to count the inventory, only to check that it has been done correctly.

Procedures

Before the count

- Obtain clients' instructions for the count and review them :
  - for obvious flaws
  - to ensure that the logistics for the audit team have been thought through
  - to obtain awareness of where the most material or otherwise risky inventory lines are to be found.

On the count (inventory count)

- Observe the count as it proceeds to ensure:
  - the client's instructions are being followed
  - everything is counted and recorded
  - there is no risk of anything being included more than once
  - evidence of damaged or slow moving inventory is being recorded
  - cut-off is observed – no despatches or deliveries occur while the count is taking place, and there is no movement of inventory within the client's premises which may confuse the count
  - inventory sheets (or whatever method is used to record the count – handheld devices, barcode readers, etc.) are properly controlled.

KAPLAN PUBLISHING

- Conduct test counts on a suitably random basis whilst gearing the tests towards material items:
  - **Existence** – it will be necessary to check from the client's inventory records to your test data, so you need to ensure that you record sufficient details of the location and the items to be able to trace them later.

  - **Completeness**– you will need to be able to trace the items from your counts, into the client's inventory records and will therefore need to record sufficient details to enable you to do this.

    Note. These aspects of the count are crucial – the auditor needs to know in advance:

    - the details of the inventory
    - how the inventory will be recorded in the client's system.

Record cut-off information:

- the last goods received record of the year
- the last despatch record of the year.

Audit procedures at the final audit stage

- Obtain a list showing each individual line of inventories categorised between finished goods, WIP and raw materials. Cast and agree the total to the inventories figures in the financial statements.

Presentation and disclosure

- Check that the figures disclosed in the financial statements agree to the audited figures and that inventories have been correctly analysed between finished goods, raw materials and work in progress.

Valuation

- Trace some items of inventory in the inventory sheets back to original purchase invoices to agree the cost
- Trace the same items of inventory to post-year-end sales to determine the net realisable value of inventory
- For items that have not yet been sold trace to the provision for slow-moving inventory or discuss with management why these have not been provided for

- Ensure that inventory is stated in the accounts at the lower of cost and net realisable value by reviewing the relevant purchase invoices and after year end sales invoices.

Analytical review

- Calculate inventory turnover and compare to last year to assess reasonableness

- Calculate gross profit percentage and compare to prior year to assess reasonableness

Cut-off

- Select a sample of GRN's from immediately prior to the year end and included in year-end payables, and ensure that the goods are included in year-end inventories.

- Select a sample of GDN's from immediately prior to the year end and included in year-end receivables, and ensure that the goods are not included in year-end inventories and that the invoice was raised in the correct period.

Year end counts and continuous inventory systems

The procedures suggested above apply to all inventory counts whether as a one-off year end exercise or where inventory is counted on a rolling basis throughout the year.

The objective is the same:

- To know what the client has in inventory at the time the count took place.

Continuous inventory systems

Where the client has a continuous inventory system, where a theoretical 'book inventory figure' is always known, there are both advantages and disadvantages for the auditor.

Advantages

- The auditor is less time constrained and can pick and choose particular locations and inventory lines at any time to ensure the system is working properly.

- Slow moving and damaged inventory should be identified and adjusted for in the clients' records on a continuous basis therefore the inventory valuation should be more reliable.

Disadvantages

- The auditor will need to gain sufficient evidence that the system operates correctly at all times, not just at the time of the count.

- Additional procedures will need to be devised to ensure that the year end inventory figure is reliable, even though it may not have been counted at that date.

Inventory held at third parties

- Where the client has inventory at locations not visited by the auditor, the auditor normally obtains confirmation of the quantities, value and condition from the holder. The auditor needs to consider whether the holder is sufficiently independent to be able to provide relevant, reliable evidence.

- As with confirmations from receivables, the auditor requests details from the party holding the inventory on behalf of the client to confirm its existence.

- The confirmation request will be sent by the client to those parties identified by the auditor.

- The reply should be sent directly to the auditor to prevent it being tampered with by the client.

- Problems can occur if the third party uses a different description to that of the client and as always, a response is not guaranteed.

Other audit evidence about inventory

- For specialised inventory – livestock, property, food in restaurants, significant work in progress – it will be necessary to obtain evidence from experts – see section 9 of this chapter.

- The auditor needs to obtain evidence of the value of the inventory.
    - Cost information can be obtained from invoices and price lists.
    - The costs of manufactured inventory can be obtained from invoices and costing records.
    - The opinion of independent experts may be obtained.

Test your understanding 1

(1) **List the audit procedures before the inventory count.**

(3 marks)

(2) **List the audit procedures to test for existence and completeness on inventory.**

(2 marks)

(3) **Saxophone Ltd runs a petrol filling station. List the audit procedures to test the quantities of petrol in inventory.**

(2 marks)

(4) **Flute Ltd makes large machines out of very heavy lumps of steel. List the audit procedures to test its inventory of sheet and bar steel.**

(2 marks)

(5) **Piccolo Ltd has a sheep farming business. List the audit procedures to verify the number of animals it owns at the year end.**

(2 marks)

5 The audit of payables and accruals

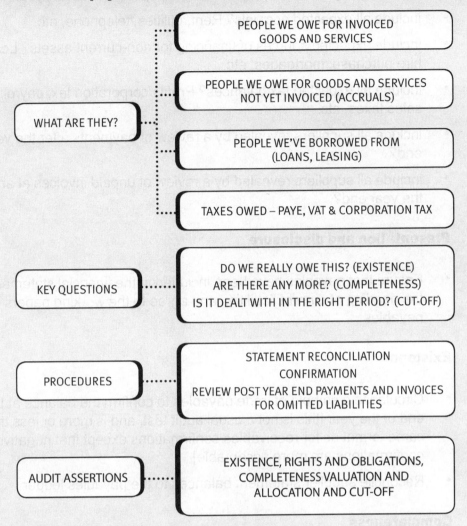

Principles

- The main thrust of the testing of payables is usually to test for completeness.
- Testing for existence, valuation, etc. is still important, but the major consideration, is for the auditor to gain assurance that all liabilities which should be included, are included.

You therefore have to think of the best indicators that additional liabilities may exist. If as a result of this, none are revealed, the testing of the values, rights and obligations of the payables we know about is relatively straightforward.

Possible indicators of additional liabilities

Does the list of payables at the year end:

- include all the major suppliers the client dealt with during the year?

- include all significant suppliers from the equivalent list last year?

- include all expected accruals? Rent, utilities, telephone, etc.

- include expected sources of financing for non-current assets? Leasing, hire purchase, mortgages, etc.

- include all expected tax balances? Profits/corporation tax, payroll taxes, sales taxes, etc.

- include all suppliers revealed by a review of payments after the year end?

- include all suppliers revealed by a review of unpaid invoices at and after the year end?

Presentation and disclosure

- Ensure that payables have been included in the financial statements in the heading of current liabilities and agree to the working papers of payables

Existence

- Circularise a sample of trade payables to confirm the balance at the end of the year [this is not a usual audit test, and is more or less the same format as for receivables confirmations except that negative confirmations are more acceptable]

- Reconcile supplier statement balances to the payables ledger

Completeness

- Investigate any supplier names that were shown on last year's payables listing but do not have a balance showing in this year's list of balances

- Review after date invoices and payments and ensure they have been provided for at the year-end as appropriate

- Perform analytical procedures on the list of payables. Determine reasons for any unusual changes in the total balance of individual payables in the list

- Calculate the trade payables payment period and compare to last year to assess reasonableness

- Obtain a list of the individual balances from the payables ledger, check the cast and agree the total to the trade payables figure in the draft financial statements

- Obtain a list of debit balances in the payables ledger and obtain explanations from management

- Agree brought forward figures to last year's audit file

Cut-off

- Select a sample of GRN's immediately prior to the year end and to test that they are in year-end payables, and ensure that the goods are in year-end inventories, also test GRN's post year end to test that they are not in inventory at the year end

Supplier statement reconciliations

For those suppliers' balances selected for testing:

- obtain supplier statements at the statement of financial position
- compare with balance according to the client's records
- seek explanation for differences from client staff.

Expandable Text - Explanation of differences

There are generally two main explanations for differences:

(1) **Timing differences:**

- Invoices not yet received by the client.
- Payments not yet received by the supplier.
- Returns and credit notes not yet appearing on the supplier's statement.

(2) **Errors**

- Supplier errors that will remain as part of the reconciliation until the supplier corrects them.
- Client errors, which the client needs to adjust.

Note. It is possible that there are administrative reasons at the client for some of the differences:

- **Goods received accrual**– invoices received but not yet processed – perhaps awaiting authorisation, or perhaps 'Mary does the postings on Tuesdays' which means that invoices arriving between Wednesday and Monday are known about but not yet entered on the system.

- **Goods received not invoiced**– the client accrues for all goods received but does not post to the purchase ledger until the invoice is received.

- **Cheques in the drawer**– not a good idea to have signed cheques lying around, but sometimes for relatively short periods there may be a delay in sending out the cheque. Sometimes, with systems with automated payment runs, the accounts staff do not know how to prevent cheques being produced and the number of 'cheques in the drawer' can be quite substantial for long periods. This is a very bad idea, raises questions about the accounting staff's competence, and, on the assumption the amounts are material, will mean the amounts will have to be added back to both bank and payables.

Suggested layout for a supplier's statement reconciliation

Supplier's statement reconciliation Supplier Limited	Year end date	
	$	$
Balance per supplier statement		xxxx
Less:		
Returns/credit notes not yet credited	xx	
Payments not yet received by supplier	xx	

		(xx)
		————
		xxx
		————
Balance per purchase ledger		xxx
Invoices not yet posted		xxx
Goods received not invoiced		xxx
		————
Reconciled balance		xxx
		————

These figures should be the same!

Expandable Text - Supplier reconciliation example

Tuba Ltd

You are auditing the payables of Tuba Ltd and have found that the balance according to Tuba's purchase ledger does not agree to the statement from its supplier Trombone Ltd.

The following is relevant:

	$
Balance per Tuba Ltd's purchase ledger	350
Balance per Trombone Ltd's statement	1,500
Invoices in file on purchase ledger clerks' desk awaiting posting	150
Goods returned by Tuba to Trombone in last week of the year, not yet reflected on Trombone's statement	200
Value of goods from Trombone received by Tuba's goods inwards department and invoiced by Trombone on the very last day of the year (invoices are sent by mail)	50
Payment by cheque sent by mail by Tuba to Trombone on the very last day of the year	750

What is the correct figure for the balance between Tuba and Trombone that should form part of Tuba's payables figure in its financial statements?

Solution

Trombone Ltd statement reconciliation

	$	$
Balance per supplier statement		1,500
Less:		
Returns/credit notes not yet credited	200	
Payments not yet received by supplier	750	
Agreed balance		950
		_____
		550
		_____
Balance per purchase ledger		350
Invoices not yet posted		150
Goods received not invoiced		50
		_____
Reconciled balance		550
		_____

Accruals

- Review relevant invoices when received after the statement of financial position date. If none are received, compare with previous periods
- Obtain the list of accruals from the client, cast it to confirm arithmetical accuracy
- Agree the figure per the schedule to the general ledger and financial statements
- Agree the calculation of the accrual by reference to supporting documentation e.g. previous period invoice

Tax balances

- Corporation/Profits taxes – agree computations.
- Payroll taxes – agree to payroll records.

Overdrafts, loans, etc.

- Agree to bank confirmations.

Leases, hire purchase

- Agree details to underlying agreement.

Income statement entries related to accounts payable

- Accruals will have a direct impact on the income statement accounts they relate to – ensure the postings have been put through correctly and any opening accruals have been properly reversed.
- Some accruals may themselves lead to additional accruals, e.g. accrued bonuses payable to directors and staff, may lead to additional employer's social security charges.
- For all interest bearing accounts, loans, overdrafts, etc., ensure the correct accrual is made for interest payable.

6 The audit of bank and cash

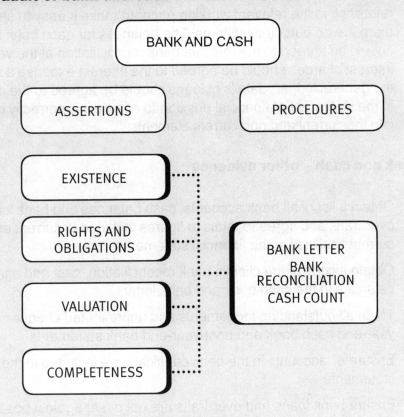

The bank letter (bank confirmation reports)

- Direct confirmation of bank balances gives the auditor independent, third-party evidence.

- The format of the letter is usually standard and agreed between the banking and auditing professions.

- Issues covered are:
  - the client's name
  - the confirmation date
  - balances on all bank accounts held
  - any documents or other assets held for safekeeping
  - details of any security given
  - details of any contingent arrangements – guarantees, forward currency purchases or sales, letters of credit.

- The auditor needs the client to give the bank authorisation to disclose the necessary information (In some jurisdictions such disclosures are illegal so bank letters cannot be used at all).

- Ensure that all banks that the client deals with are circularised.

- When items on the bank letter are dealt with, tick them off and cross-reference to the relevant working paper to make it easy to see that there are no outstanding items. The balances for each bank account should be agreed to the relevant bank reconciliation at the year end; interest charges should be agreed to the interest expense account in the general ledger; details of loans should be agreed to the disclosure in the statement of financial position to ensure it is correctly classified into the current and non current elements.

Bank and cash – other evidence

- Obtain a list of all bank accounts, cash balances and bank loans and overdrafts and agree to totals to figures included in current assets and current liabilities in the financial statements

- Obtain a copy of the client's bank reconciliation, cast and agree the balances to the cash book and bank letter

- Trace all outstanding lodgements and unpresented cheques to pre-year-end cash book and post-year-end bank statements

- Ensure all accounts in the bank certificate are included in the financial statements

- Ensure bank loans and overdrafts are not offset against positive bank balances in the financial statements

- Count the petty cash in the cash tin at the end of the year and agree the total to the balance included in the financial statements

- Note. It is vital for an auditor conducting a cash count to do so in the presence of a member of the client's staff and to obtain a signature for the amounts handed back into the client's custody

- Where there are multiple cash balances – a number of tills in a department store, etc. – it is important to ensure amounts cannot be moved between tills and that proper cut-off procedures are in place.

Income statement and other account entries related to bank and cash

- Clearly, bank loans, overdrafts and bank deposits all have interest implications.

- The bank letter may reveal details of security, borrowings and contingent liabilities which need to be disclosed in the financial statements.

Presentation and disclosure

- Ensure that bank and cash have been included in the financial statements in the heading of current assets and overdraft loans presented in current liabilities and non-current liabilities.

- Ensure the financial statement amounts agree back to the trial balance amount.

7 The audit of tangible non-current assets

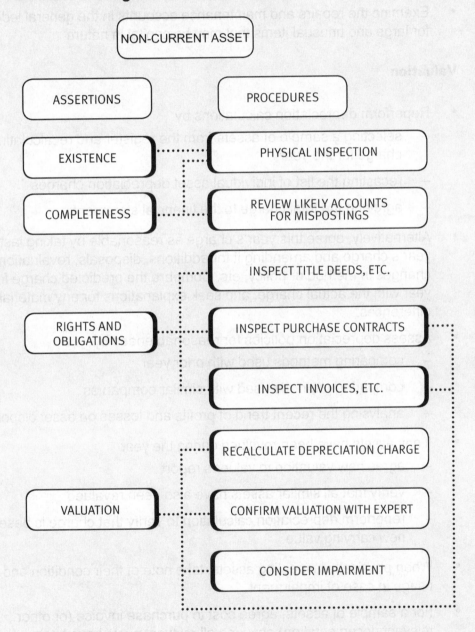

Existence

- Select a sample of assets from the **non-current asset register** and physically inspect them.

Completeness

- Select a sample of assets visible at the client premises and inspect the asset register to ensure they are included.

- Examine the repairs and maintenance accounts in the general ledger for large and unusual items that may be capital in nature.

Valuation

- Reperform depreciation calculations by:
  - selecting a sample of assets from the register and recalculating the charge for the year
  - recasting the list of individual asset depreciation charges
  - agreeing the total charge to the financial statement.

- Alternatively, agree this year's charge as reasonable by taking last year's charge and amending it for additions, disposals, revaluations, changes in method or policy, etc. Compare the predicted charge for the year with the actual charge, and seek explanations for any material differences.

- Assess depreciation policies for reasonableness by:
  - comparing methods used with prior year
  - comparing methods used with similar companies
  - analysing the recent trend of profits and losses on asset disposals.

- If any assets have been revalued during the year:
  - agree new valuation to valuer's report
  - verify that all similar assets have also been revalued
  - reperform depreciation calculation to verify that charge is based on new carrying value.

- When physically inspecting assets, take note of their condition and usage in case of impairment.

- For a sample of assets, agree cost to purchase invoice (or other relevant documentation) ensuring all relevant costs have been included.

- If any assets have been constructed by the company, obtain analysis of costs incurred and agree to supporting documentation (timesheets, materials invoices, etc.).

Rights and Obligations

- For a sample of recorded assets, obtain and inspect ownership documentation:
  - title deeds for properties
  - registration documents for vehicles
  - insurance documents may also help to verify ownership (and asset values).

- Where assets are leased, inspect the lease document to assess whether the lease is operating or finance (if the latter, the asset should be included on the company's statement of financial position).

Disclosure

- Agree opening balances with prior year financial statements.
- Compare depreciation rates in use with those disclosed.
- For revalued assets, ensure appropriate disclosures made (e.g. name of valuer, revaluation policy).
- Agree breakdown of assets between classes with the general ledger account totals.

8 The audit of non-current liabilities

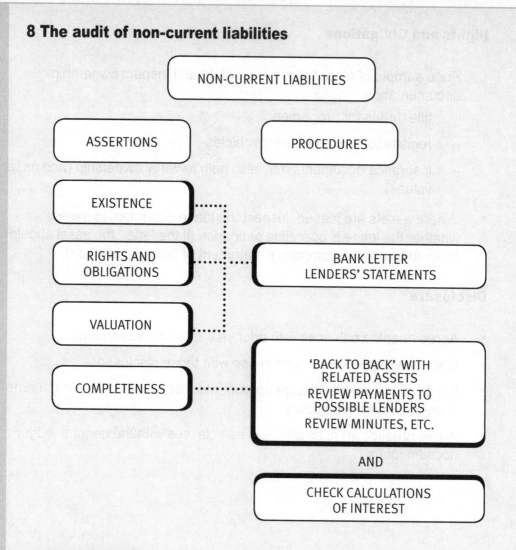

Loan payables

- Agree loan balance to the loan statement confirms rights and obligation and valuation.

- Agree interest payments to the loan agreement and the bank statements, to confirm rights and obligations.

- Analyse relevant disclosures of interest rates, amounts due (e.g. between current and non-current payables) to ensure complete and accurate.

- Recalculate the interest accrual to ensure arithmetical accuracy.

Provisions and contingencies

Provisions are a form of payable where the amount or timing of payment is uncertain. As such they are harder to audit.

Where the likelihood of payment is only **possible**, rather than **probable**, no amounts will be entered in the accounts. However, the matter (**contingent liability**) must be adequately disclosed.

- Discuss the matter giving rise to the provision with the client to verify whether an obligation exists.

- Obtain confirmation from the clients lawyers as to the possible outcome and probability of having to make a payment.

- Review subsequent events. By the time the final audit is taking place the matter may have been settled.

- Obtain a letter of representation from the client as the matter is one of judgement and uncertainty. For more on representation letters see chapter 11.

Test your understanding 2

(1) **Describe the audit procedures to confirm unpresented cheques are included on a client's bank reconciliation.**

(1 mark)

(2) **List 4 things that might be included on a bank letter besides the balances on a client's accounts.**

(2 marks)

(3) **Describe an audit procedure to test the rights and obligations assertion for a freehold property.**

(1 mark)

(4) **Describe an audit procedure to test the completeness of a client's hire purchase and leasing liabilities.**

(1 mark)

9 Relying on the work of others

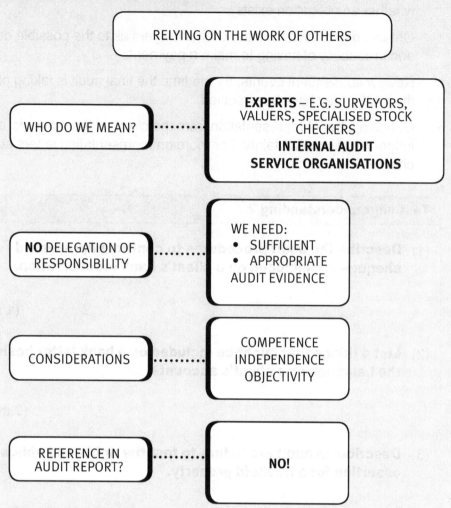

RELYING ON THE WORK OF OTHERS

WHO DO WE MEAN? .... **EXPERTS** – E.G. SURVEYORS, VALUERS, SPECIALISED STOCK CHECKERS
INTERNAL AUDIT
SERVICE ORGANISATIONS

NO DELEGATION OF RESPONSIBILITY .... WE NEED:
- SUFFICIENT
- APPROPRIATE
AUDIT EVIDENCE

CONSIDERATIONS .... COMPETENCE
INDEPENDENCE
OBJECTIVITY

REFERENCE IN AUDIT REPORT? .... **NO!**

Why rely on the work of other people?

- Auditors may **need** to rely on the work of others. (The ISAs stress the need for auditors to consult with others in appropriate circumstances.)
- Auditors may **choose** to rely on the work of others because they find it effective and efficient to do so.

The need to consult others

Auditors do not need to be experts in all aspects of their clients' business.

Where they are unable to form an opinion without expert help the auditors will need to consult. Examples are:

- property valuations
- construction work in progress

- specialist inventory – livestock, food and drink in the restaurant trade, technically complex inventory

- actuarial valuations for pension schemes.

Choosing to consult others

Because of the circumstances at a particular client, it may be effective and efficient for the auditor to rely on the work of others. Examples are:

- internal audit (see below)

- confirmation from external holders of the client's inventory

- another firm of auditors for assurance on an overseas branch or subsidiary

- service organisations (see below).

What attributes do these 'other people' need?

ISA 620 Using the Work of an Expert states that the auditor should obtain sufficient and appropriate evidence that the work of the expert is adequate for the purpose of the audit.

In making this assessment the external auditor must assess the expert's:

- independence and objectivity

- competence – consider:
  - qualifications
  - experience.

For example, the auditor might inspect a valuation report to provide evidence of a revaluation of land and buildings. However, this report might be have been produced by a qualified valuer who is a close friend or relative of one of the directors.

The auditor will have to decide whether:

- the valuer is sufficiently independent

- the report provided is reliable or not.

Relying on internal audit

- Internal audit forms a part of the client's system of internal control.

- It may well therefore reduce control risk.

- The auditor will take this into consideration when planning audit procedures and reduced levels of substantive testing may therefore be appropriate.

The auditor cannot devolve responsibility for the audit opinion onto the internal audit department.

ISA 610 Considering the Work of Internal Audit states that before relying on the work of internal audit, the external auditor must first assess the internal audit function with regard to:

- the objectivity and technical competence of the internal audit staff

- whether the internal audit function is carried out with due professional care

- the effect of any constraints or restrictions placed on the internal function by management or those charged with governance.

If the function is assessed and is found not to be sufficiently independent of the management structure or the staff are not suitably qualified and trained, there is no point in the external auditor going to the trouble of assessing the work that has been performed by the function during the year as it will not be considered reliable enough for external audit purposes.

However, if the internal audit function has been assessed as reliable, the specific work should be evaluated to ascertain its adequacy. The external auditor must consider whether:

- the work is properly supervised, reviewed and documented

- the persons performing the work have relevant experience and training

- sufficient and appropriate evidence has been obtained

- the conclusions drawn are valid given the results of the work performed

- recommendations made have been acted on by management.

If the auditor assesses both the function and the specific work to be reliable and adequate, the work will be relied on and reduced levels of testing will be performed.

Service organisations

The client may outsource certain functions to another company – a service organisation, e.g.

- payroll
- receivables collection
- the entire finance function
- internal audit.

Advantages from the auditor's point of view

- The independence of the service organisation may give increased reliability to the evidence obtained.
- Specialist skills readily available and tend to have a broader range of expertise
- Less detailed work may therefore be required.

Disadvantages

- May not obtain information readily
- Difficulties in assessing the reliability of the outsource company
- Lack of sufficient appropriate evidence.

Other considerations

- The auditor will need to be confident of the reliability and the independence of the service organisation.
- If the audit firm provides some of these services itself – e.g. bookkeeping or payroll services – it will need to ensure that it can maintain its own independence and objectivity as auditor.

Reference to the work of others in the audit report

It is the auditors' responsibility to obtain sufficient and appropriate audit evidence in order to arrive at the correct audit opinion.

Therefore, no reference should be made in the audit report to the use of others during the audit.

If the auditors cannot satisfy themselves that the work of others is sufficiently reliable then the auditor must find another means of obtaining the required level of comfort.

They cannot pass the blame onto another party.

10 Accounting estimates

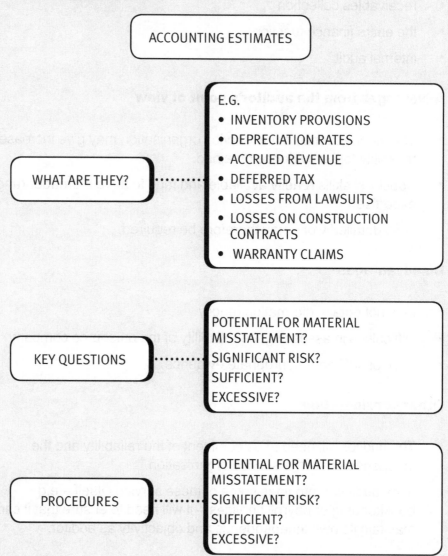

ACCOUNTING ESTIMATES

WHAT ARE THEY?

E.G.
- INVENTORY PROVISIONS
- DEPRECIATION RATES
- ACCRUED REVENUE
- DEFERRED TAX
- LOSSES FROM LAWSUITS
- LOSSES ON CONSTRUCTION CONTRACTS
- WARRANTY CLAIMS

KEY QUESTIONS

POTENTIAL FOR MATERIAL MISSTATEMENT?
SIGNIFICANT RISK?
SUFFICIENT?
EXCESSIVE?

PROCEDURES

POTENTIAL FOR MATERIAL MISSTATEMENT?
SIGNIFICANT RISK?
SUFFICIENT?
EXCESSIVE?

Accounting estimates are of particular concern to the auditor as by their nature there may not be any physical evidence to support them. They are subjective and judgemental and therefore prone to management bias. If the directors wish to manipulate the accounts in any way, accounting estimates are the easy way for them to do this. The auditor must take care when auditing estimates to ensure this has not been the case.

Procedures used by the auditor in respect of estimates are:

- Discuss with management their process for calculating the estimate and assess whether this appears reasonable.

- For estimates such as provisions it may be possible to obtain an independent expert opinion for example correspondence from lawyers regarding a legal provision or a surveyor's report for evidence of an environmental provision.

- Review subsequent events, for example if there is a pending legal case with a legal provision at the statement of financial position date, the case may have been settled by the time of the audit and therefore will provide evidence as to whether the provision was reasonably stated. An accrual can be compared with the actual invoice if the invoice has been received by the client by the time of the audit.

11 Computer assisted audit techniques (CAATs)

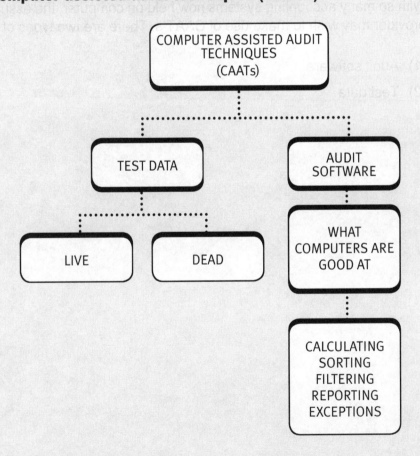

The use of a computer to either perform, be tested or to assist the auditors in carrying out their audit procedures.

When planning the audit the partners need to make sure they have enough resources, this could be done by using software to identify who is free at that time to do the audit. The computer software may have a schedule of who is available and when.

Reports can be generated on the computer, they look more professional and can aid in more complex work, in the form of Excel helping you calculate and outcome or an amount.

Computers also store documentation and is to refer back to and tends to be a safe location for documents as long as the relevant controls are in place.

With so many accounting systems now held on computer, the assurance provider may wish to make use of CAAT's. There are two types of CAAT's

(1) Audit software

(2) Test data

Auditing around the computer?

This term means that the 'internal' software of the computer is not documented or audited by the auditor, but the inputs to the computer are agreed to the expected outputs to the computer.

Audit outcome

Increase the AUDIT RISK Why?

The actual computer files and programs are NOT TESTED.

Therefore no DIRECT evidence that the programs are working as documented

Where errors are found it maybe difficult or even impossible to determine why those errors have occurred.

If amendments cannot be made, there is an increased likelihood of audit qualifications.

Since controls are being tested, all discrepancies between predicted and actual results must be fully resolved and documented, irrespective of financial amounts involved.

Audit software

Description

This is software specifically designed for audit purposes, there are a number of off-the-shelf packages available, or the auditor could have a tailor-made system. It is used to process the client's data in order to check that the figures themselves are correct. It can therefore carry out a whole range of substantive procedure, across all sorts of different data.

Examples of what audit software can do include:

* Extract a sample according to specified criteria
    - Random
    - Over a certain amount
    - Below a certain amount
    - At certain dates

- Calculate ratios and select those outside the criteria
- Check calculations (for example additions)
- Prepare reports (budget vs actual)
- Produce letters to send out to customers suppliers
- Follow items through a computerised system

Package programmes are generally designed to;

- read computer files
- select information
- perform calculations
- create data files, and
- print reports in a format specified by the auditor

Test data

The assurance provider supervises the process of running data through the clients system. To do this the auditor would have to

- Note controls in the clients system
- Decide upon the test data

It maybe processed during a normal production run ('live' test data) or during a special run at a point in time outside the normal cycle ('dead' test data), either with real data or dummy data.

- Run the test data
- Compare results with those expected
- Conclude on whether controls are operating properly

Through test data. This is data generated by the auditor in order to test the systems, processing logic, calculations and controls, to ensure that the controls within the system are operating properly.

An auditor would take a transaction through a system, testing the systems limits. So you would have 'normal' transactions and invalid transactions to test that the system work. If the results are positive that means the auditor can rely on the system and have more confidence that the output is accurate.

What are the benefits of CAAT's?

Benefits / Advantages	Examples
CAAT's force the auditor to rely on programmed controls during the audit. Sometimes it may be the only way to test controls within a computer system, therefore enables the auditor to test program controls	Credit limits within a system can only be changed by the accountant. A computer assisted check will test that this is the case.
Using CAAT's enables the auditors to comply with ISA of obtaining appropriate audit evidence increasing the overall confidence for the audit opinion	
Large number of items can be tested quickly and accurately	Checking the depreciation charged on each asset would be quicker with a computer assisted program than manually
CAAT's test original documentation instead of print outs, therefore the authenticity of the document is more valid this way.	Actual wages will be tested instead of paper copies.
After initial set up costs, using CAAT's are likely to be cost effective, as the same audit software can be used each year as long as the system doesn't changed	Examples of use or audit tests (1) Calculation checks (2) Reviewing lists of old or outstanding items and investing those specifically (3) Detecting for unreasonable items (4) Detecting violation of the system rules (5) New analysis (6) Completeness checks (7) Selects samples (8) Identifying exception reporting facilities
Allow the results from using using CAATs to be compared with 'traditional' testing,	If the two sources of evidence agree then this too will increase the overall audit confidence

What are the weaknesses, or problems with CAAT's, and how can they be resolved?

Weaknesses / problems	Recommendations / resolve
Limitations CAAT's will be limited depending on how well the computer system is integrated. The more integrated the better the use of CAAT's. For example the invoices should be computer generated and then processed through the accounts system to feed in to the financial statements. The existing system made do some of the functions of the CAAT, for example highlight old balances or obsolete inventory.	Ensure you understand the system to assess whether audit software will be relevant for the company. Need to assess whether there is a need for the audit software.
Reliability CAAT's are only useful methods of testing if you can rely on the system, so the auditor would have to assess the reliability first, before use.	Assess the reliability, document and then make a decision whether it's relevant to use audit software as part of the evidence collected.
Cost It takes time to design CAAT's tests therefore may not be cost effective if the auditor is dealing with a bespoke system, as there maybe a lot of set up costs. The reason for this is it takes time to write specific test data or to program the audit software to the needs of the client.	A cost benefit analysis from the audit point of view should be carried out prior to deciding to use the audit software.
Lack of software documentation If the company you are auditing can not confirm all system documentation is available, then the auditors will be unable to do the tests effectively due to lack of understanding.	Shouldn't use audit software until these have been identified. Hold until this point.
Change to clients systems If there is a change in the accounting year or from the previous year then the audit software will have to be reset and designed, therefore may be costly.	A cost benefit analysis from the audit point of view should be carried out prior to deciding to use the audit software. Or if you know there to be a change in the near future hold the audit software until that year.

Lack of direction and useless results Audit tests may be done just because the auditors have the facility to do them, therefore the output of results will either be inconclusive or not required. Therefore having an inefficient and costly audit.	The audit manager needs to be clear exactly what audit assertions are being tested, and what the expected outputs are.
Use of copy files Clients tend to provide the auditors with copies of the system notes and any other relevant information. The problem here is do we know if those are the actual files?	To ensure the files are genuine either the auditor should supervise the copying or use the originals in the first place.
Test data – problems	
Damage of computer system Because we are testing the limits of the system the dummy process may damage the computer system.	Ensure as auditors we understand the system and have support if need be form software experts.
Need to reverse or remove dummy transactions Ideally test data should be run 'live' if not possible then the 'dead' test data needs to be used under identical systems for it to be valid, and enough computer time should be provided. The transactions may be incorrectly or incompletely removed, leaving dummy data in a live system.	Ensure there is a process for ensuring all dummy transactions are cleared and the auditor has discussed when they can use the computer and for what test specifically.

Examples of Test Data

Tests	Reason for the Test
Revenue	
Input an order into the clients system that would cause a customer to exceed their credit limit	The order should not be accepted, or should raise a query whether you are sure you wish to proceed. If this happens then the auditors will have confidence the system is working properly
Input a negative number of items on an order	Ensures only positive quantities are accepted
Input incomplete customer details	The system should not process the order unless all information is completed
Input an excessive amount	There are reasonable checks in the system to identify possible input errors. A warning should appear on the screen confirming the number
Input and invalid inventory code	Ensures that the computer detects the invalid code and presents an error message rather than taking the nearest code and accepting it
Input of invalid details	Ensures that no errors are made for sipping and payment
Purchases	
Raise an order from a supplier not on the preferred supplier list	A query should be raised as to whether you want to proceed with this transaction
Process an order with an unauthorised staff ID	The system should reject the process altogether or send the request through to an appropriate person for authorisation
Try and make changes to the supplier standing data using the ID of someone who is not authorised to do so	The system should reject the process altogether or send the request through to an appropriate person for authorisation
Payroll	
Try and set up a new employee up on the payroll system using an unauthorised ID	The system should reject the process altogether or send the request through to an appropriate person for authorisation
Try and make employee changes of detail using an unauthorised ID	The system should reject the process altogether or send the request through to an appropriate person for authorisation

Make an excess change for example increase someone's salary by $1,000,000 by someone authorised	The system should have parameters in place to question this amount, and maybe reject it due to it being outside the normal range
Receivables	**Audit software examples**
Cast the receivables ledger to ensure it agrees with the total on the receivables control account	To ensure the completeness and accuracy of the items on the receivables control account
Compare the balances to the credit limits to ensure they haven't been exceeded	To check or violation of the system rules
Review the balances to ensure they don't exceed the total sales to that customer	To check for unreasonable items in the ledger
To review the receivable days on a monthly basis and compare to year	To obtain new / relevant statistical information
To form receivable balances to show all material items and select appropriate sampling for testing.	To select specific items for the audit test.
To produce an aged receivables analysis to assist with identification of irrecoverable receivables.	To assist in the receivables valuation testing.

Test your understanding 3

Give examples of test using CAATs when dealing with orders received, goods despatched, and invoices raised.

12 Not for profit organisations

A not for profit organisation is an organisation whose primary objective is other than making a profit, examples being:

- charities
- clubs
- public schools.

Audit techniques

- The auditor will test the utilisation of funds to ensure they are being spent correctly.

- Tend to perform substantive procedures due to lack of systems, evidence being analytical procedures, discussion and regulations.

- Sample size tends to be high, due to the volume of transactions being low. In some cases populations can be tested 100%.

- Observation presents its self as a problem, due to people acting in good behaviour when observed. Therefore the auditor may not obtain a true reflection of what's going on.

Differences

- Not for profit organisations tend to have poor systems due to
  - lack of segregation of duties, as the organisation will be restricted with the amount of staff who work
  - people tend to be volunteers, therefore likely to be unqualified and have an unawareness of the importance of controls.

- Whereas profit organisations do.

- In not for profit organisations the transactions tend to be less formal, so there maybe no receipt for expenses or receipts of money. Whereas a profit organisation will document all communication and transactions.

- Revenue is unpredictable in non profit organisations, so if difficult to forecast, unlike profit organisations who tend to hold contracts and orders, so difficult to test the going concern basis.

13 Chapter summary

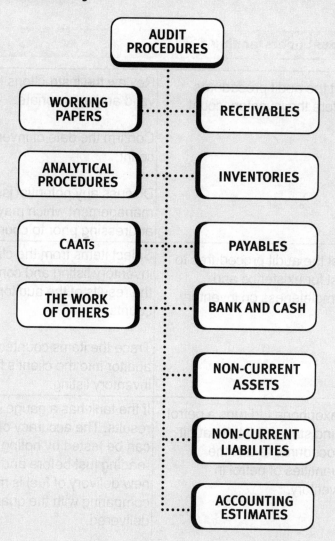

Test your understanding answers

Test your understanding 1

(1)	List the audit procedures before the inventory count.	Review the instructions to ensure valid and appropriate.
		Confirm the date of inventory count.
		Discuss any potential issues with management which may need addressing prior to count.
(2)	List the audit procedures to test for existence and completeness on inventory.	Select items from the client's final inventory listing and compare with the results of the auditor's test counts
		Trace the items counted by the auditor into the client's final inventory listing.
(3)	Saxophone Ltd runs a petrol filling station. List the audit procedures to test the quantities of petrol in inventory.	If the tank has a gauge – read the results. The accuracy of the gauge can be tested by noting the reading just before and after a new delivery of fuel is made and comparing with the quantity delivered.
		If there is no gauge, it will be necessary to 'dip the tank' using a measuring stick.
(4)	Flute Ltd makes large machines out of very heavy lumps of steel. List the audit procedures to test its inventory of sheet and bar steel.	Test count bars sheets of steel.
		Assess average weights of bars and sheets from delivery/ weighbridge records
(5)	Piccolo Ltd has a sheep farming business. List the audit procedures to verify the number of animals it owns at the year end.	Count them at dipping time or when they are herded together for some purpose.
		Or (preferably) use the report of a relevant expert.

The marks (1 each) appear beside the answer cells:
- Review the instructions... — 1
- Confirm the date... — 1
- Discuss any potential issues... — 1
- Select items from the client's final inventory listing... — 1
- Trace the items counted... — 1
- If the tank has a gauge... — 1
- If there is no gauge... — 1
- Test count bars sheets of steel. — 1
- Assess average weights of bars... — 1
- Count them at dipping time... — 1
- Or (preferably) use the report of a relevant expert. — 1

Test your understanding 2

(1)	Describe the audit procedures to confirm unpresented cheques are included on a client's bank reconciliation.	Review post-year-end bank statements to test that all cheques drawn before year end but clearing after the statement of financial position date are included on the reconciliation.	1
(2)	List 4 things that might be included on a bank letter besides the balances on a client's accounts.	Deeds and other documents or assets held.	½
		Guarantees.	½
		Forward currency contracts	½
		Bills of exchange and letters of credit.	½
(3)	Describe an audit procedure to test the rights and obligations assertion for a freehold property.	Review title deeds and register of charges, for owners details and ensure they agree.	1
(4)	Describe an audit procedure to test the completeness of a client's hire purchase and leasing liabilities.	For all assets acquired in the year review correspondence to ensure there are no hire purchase or leasing liabilities in relation to the asset.	1

Test your understanding 3

Solution

Orders
Place orders on the website using test data.

Goods dispatched
Programme audit software to select a sample of customer orders, obtain the GDN number from each order, and verify that each GDN number exists in the GDN file.

Invoice
Programme audit software to select a sample of GDNs, obtain the invoice numbers from each order and verify that each invoice number exists in the invoice file.

(GDN – goods despatch note)

KAPLAN PUBLISHING

11

Completion and review

Chapter learning objectives

Upon completion of this chapter you will be able to:

Subsequent events

- explain the purpose of a subsequent events review

- discuss the procedures to be undertaken in performing a subsequent events review.

Going concern

- define and discuss the significance of the concept of going concern

- explain the importance of and the need for going concern reviews

- explain the respective responsibilities of auditors and management regarding going concern

- discuss the procedures to be applied in performing going concern reviews

- discuss the disclosure requirements in relation to going concern issues

- discuss the reporting implications of the findings of going concern reviews.

Management representations

- explain the purpose of and procedures for obtaining management representations

- discuss the quality and reliability of management representations as audit evidence

- discuss the circumstances where management representations are necessary and the matters on which representations are commonly obtained.

Audit Finalisation and review

- discuss the overall review of evidence obtained
- explain the significance of unadjusted differences.

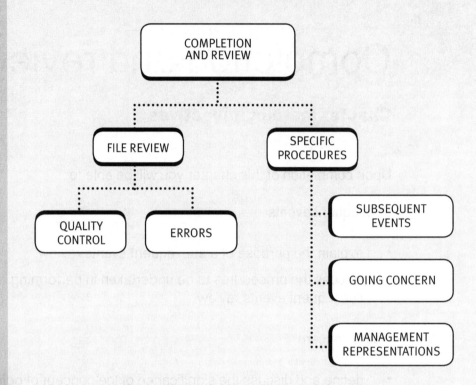

1 Introduction

This chapter deals with some of the procedures which happen at the completion stage of the audit.

It deals with:

- the significance of the partner's file review
- what to do about errors
- subsequent events (events after the reporting period)
- going concern
- management representations.

It does not deal with the technicalities of how to carry out a file review or some of the other issues which tend to arise at the completion stage. You will come across these later in your studies.

2 Overall review of evidence

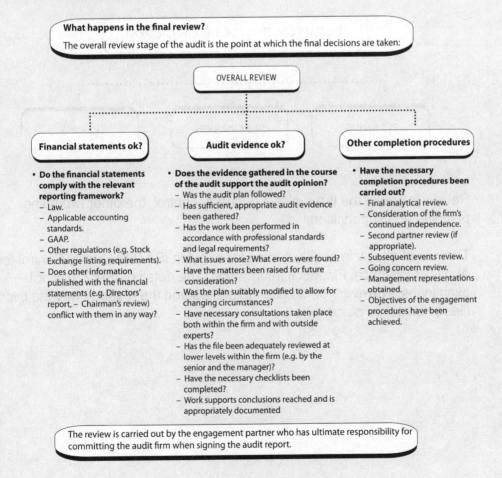

What happens in the final review?

The overall review stage of the audit is the point at which the final decisions are taken:

OVERALL REVIEW

Financial statements ok?

- **Do the financial statements comply with the relevant reporting framework?**
  - Law.
  - Applicable accounting standards.
  - GAAP.
  - Other regulations (e.g. Stock Exchange listing requirements).
  - Does other information published with the financial statements (e.g. Directors' report, – Chairman's review) conflict with them in any way?

Audit evidence ok?

- **Does the evidence gathered in the course of the audit support the audit opinion?**
  - Was the audit plan followed?
  - Has sufficient, appropriate audit evidence been gathered?
  - Has the work been performed in accordance with professional standards and legal requirements?
  - What issues arose? What errors were found?
  - Have the matters been raised for future consideration?
  - Was the plan suitably modified to allow for changing circumstances?
  - Have necessary consultations taken place both within the firm and with outside experts?
  - Has the file been adequately reviewed at lower levels within the firm (e.g. by the senior and the manager)?
  - Have the necessary checklists been completed?
  - Work supports conclusions reached and is appropriately documented

Other completion procedures

- **Have the necessary completion procedures been carried out?**
  - Final analytical review.
  - Consideration of the firm's continued independence.
  - Second partner review (if appropriate).
  - Subsequent events review.
  - Going concern review.
  - Management representations obtained.
  - Objectives of the engagement procedures have been achieved.

The review is carried out by the engagement partner who has ultimate responsibility for committing the audit firm when signing the audit report.

What is the purpose of a final review?

From the above list you can probably gather that the review is a highly significant part in the whole audit process. This can best be summarised by stating that the overall review is the point where the decision is taken that:

- the firm's procedures have been followed properly
- the quality of the work done is up to standard

and either the financial statements:

- give a true and fair view and
- comply with the applicable accounting framework or they do not.

Overall review – quality control

The three pillars of quality control

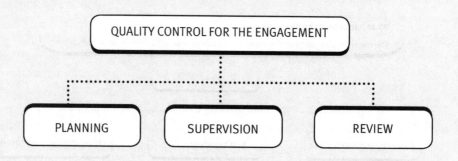

Review is one of the three pillars of quality control, the other two being planning and supervision.

The role of review in quality control is set out in ISA 220 Quality Control for Audits of Historical Financial Information. The detail of ISA 220 is not examinable however you do need to understand the reasons why the overall file review takes place.

3 Unadjusted differences

During the course of the audit, the auditor will have identified errors within the account balances and transactions. How these differences are dealt with impacts on their significance to the financial statements.

- All identified errors should be recorded on a working paper set up for the purpose. Often referred to as:
  - errors summary
  - overs and unders
  - schedule scoresheet.

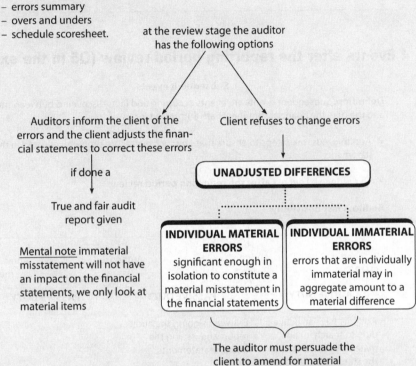

at the review stage the auditor has the following options

Auditors inform the client of the errors and the client adjusts the financial statements to correct these errors

Client refuses to change errors

if done a

UNADJUSTED DIFFERENCES

True and fair audit report given

Mental note immaterial misstatement will not have an impact on the financial statements, we only look at material items

INDIVIDUAL MATERIAL ERRORS
significant enough in isolation to constitute a material misstatement in the financial statements

INDIVIDUAL IMMATERIAL ERRORS
errors that are individually immaterial may in aggregate amount to a material difference

The auditor must persuade the client to amend for material errors otherwise a qualifieid report will be given

- Errors identified through sampling need to be extrapolated so that the potential error in the population as a whole can be estimated. If such errors reveal a potentially material adjustment, the audit team should have carried out additional work to determine whether or not the error actually is material, before the assignment reaches the review stage.

- **ISA 260 Communication of audit matters with those charged with governance** states that the auditors would normally report:
  - material audit adjustments **whether or not recorded by the entity** and

  - aggregate uncorrected misstatements

  to those charged with governance. ISA 260 allows for a threshold to be set to avoid the necessity for reporting errors which are clearly trivial, but this reinforces the need for the 'errors schedule' to be completed methodically as the audit progresses.

  - Consideration of errors identified in the course of the audit will often provide useful input to the planning process for the following year's audit.

Test your understanding 1

List three examples of findings that could result in unadjusted differences (material or immaterial).

(3 marks)

4 Events after the reporting period review (Q5 in the exam)

Subsequent events

Definition: Subsequent events are events occurring and facts discovered between the period end and the date the financial statements are authorised for issue.

✓ Auditors must take steps to ensure that any such events are properly reflected in the financial statements.

✓ This is done by **events after the reporting period review**.

Auditors responsisibltiy

Year end 31/12/09	Auditors sign	Authorised issue	Annual General meeting
ACTIVE DUTY	**PASSIVE DUTY**		**PASSIVE DUTY**

• Auditors have an active duty to search for all material events between the statement of financial positon date and the date the audit report is signed.	Between signing the audit report and issuing the financial statements. • Auditors have a passive duty. • Auditors only have to act if they are made aware of something – but once they are aware, they have a duty to take the necessary action.	

ACTIONS	**ACTIONS**	**ACTIONS**
✓ Discuss with management ask them to revise Financial Statements ✓ If client updates the financial statements the auditor would give a clean audit report ✓ If the client refuses to change the financial statements the audit report will need to be qualified	✓ Discuss with management ✓ Review the financial statements to ensure revised and redraft audit report ✓ If client refuses – seek legal advice – attend Annual General Meeting – resign	✓ Discuss with management but the directors will have to recall the financial statements ✓ Review the financial statements to ensure revised and redraft audit report ✓ If client refuses – seek legal advice – attend Annual General Meeting – resign

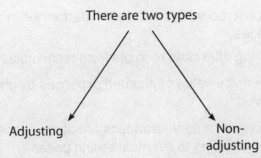

The auditor has done the subsequent event review and has found a material event

There are two types

Adjusting   Non-adjusting

- **Adjusting** – events providing additional evidence relating to conditions existing at the balance sheet date; they require **adjustments** in the financial statements.

- **Non-adjusting** – events concerning conditions which arose after the statement of financial position date, but which may be of such materiality that their **disclosure** is required to ensure that the financial statements are not misleading.

Examples

✓ Trade receivables going bad
✓ Credit notes relating to sale invoices in the year end
✓ Inventory at the year end sold lower than cost

Examples

✓ Take over
✓ Legal issues after the year end
✓ A fire happening after the B/S date which had to impact on the inventory because it was sold prior to the fire

ISA 560 Subsequent Events details the responsibilities of the auditors with respect to subsequent events and the procedures they can use. As auditors are responsible for their audit work right up to the date that the financial statements are issued, they should perform subsequent event reviews until that date has passed.

However, the nature of their responsibility changes at the point the audit report is signed – see section 'Going concern reviews – the auditor's role' below.

Audit procedures undertaken in performing a subsequent events review might include any of the following:

- Enquiring into management procedures/systems for the identification of subsequent events.

- Reading minutes of members' and directors' meetings, and of audit and executive committee meetings, and enquiring about matters not yet minuted.

- Reviewing accounting records including budgets, forecasts and interim information.

- Making enquiries of directors to ask if they are aware of any subsequent events, adjusting or non-adjusting, that have not yet been included or disclosed in the financial statements.

- 'Normal' post reporting period work performed in order to verify year-end balances:
  - checking after date receipts from receivables
  - verifying the value of accrued expenses by checking invoices when received
  - checking inventory valuations are at lower cost and net realisable value by testing to eventual selling prices.

- Obtaining, from management, a letter of representation.

Illustration 1 – Events after the reporting period review

A few days after signing an audit report, but before the client's financial statements have been approved by the shareholders at the AGM, the auditors receive a phone call from a director indicating a material error in the financial statements.

In such circumstances, a number of things may happen.

- Client produces a revised set of financial statements.

Where this happens, the auditor needs to produce a new audit report, as the audit report must always be dated on or after the date that the financial statements are signed by the directors. The auditor will therefore need to extend 'active duties' on all other matters from the original date of the audit report to the new date.

- Client refuses to change the financial statements.

Now the financial statements are materially wrong, but the initial audit report said they were true and fair. The auditor should ask for the audit report back, so that a new qualified report can be issued. However, the client may refuse this as well.

In such circumstances, the auditor should obtain legal advice, consider resignation, and speak at the AGM to notify shareholders.

Test your understanding 2

The date is 3 September 2008. The audit of Brand Co is nearly complete and the financial statements and the audit report are due to be signed next week. However, the following additional information on two material events has just been presented to the auditor. The company's year end was 30 June 2008.

Event 1 – Occurred on 6 July 2008

The filiments in a new type of light bulb have been found to be defective making the light bulb unsafe for use. There have been no sales of this light bulb; it was due to be marketed in the next few weeks. The company's insurers estimate that inventory to the value of $600,000 has been affected. The insurers also estimate that the light bulbs are now only worth $125,000. No claim can be made against the supplier of filiments as this company is in liquidation with no prospect of any amounts being paid to third parties. The insurers will not pay Brand for the fall in value of the inventory as the company was underinsured. All of this inventory was in the finished goods store at the end of the year and no movements of inventory have been recorded post year-end.

Event 2 – Occurred 3 August 2008

Production at the Bask factory was halted for one day when an oil truck reversed into a metal pylon, puncturing the vehicle allowing oil to spread across the factory premises and into a local reservoir. The Environmental Agency is currently considering whether the release of oil was in breach of environmental legislation. The company's insurers have not yet commented on the event.

Required:

(a) **For each of the two events above:**

   (i) **Explain whether the events are adjusting or non-adjusting according to IAS 10 Events After the Reporting Period.**

       (4 marks)

   (ii) **Explain the auditors' responsibility and the audit procedures and actions that should be carried out according to ISA 560 (Redrafted) Subsequent Events.**

       (12 marks)

(b) Assume that the date is now 15 September 2008, the financial statements and the audit report have just been signed, and the annual general meeting is to take place on 10 October 2009. The Environmental Agency has issued a report stating that Brand Co is in breach of environmental legislation and a fine of $800,000 will now be levied on the company. The amount is material to the financial statements.

Required:

Explain the additional audit work the auditor should carry out in respect of this fine.

(4 marks)

(20 marks)

Expandable Text - Answer plan

The date is <u>3 September 2008</u>. The audit of Brand Co is nearly complete and the financial statements and the audit report are due to be signed next week. However, the following additional <u>information on</u> **two material events** has just been presented to the auditor . The company's year end was <u>30 June 2008</u>.

<u>Event 1</u> – Occurred on <u>6 July 2008</u>

The filiments in a new type of light bulb have been found to be <u>defective</u> making the light bulb unsafe for use. There have been no sales of this <u>light bulb</u>; it was due to be marketed in the next few weeks. The company's insurers estimate that inventory to the value of <u>$600,000</u> has been <u>affected</u>. The insurers also estimate that the light bulbs are now only worth <u>$125,000</u>. No claim can be made against the supplier of filiments as this company is in liquidation with no prospect of any amounts being paid to third parties. The <u>insurers</u> will <u>not</u> pay Brand for the fall in value of the inventory as the company was underinsured. All of this inventory was in the <u>finished goods store</u> at the <u>end of the year</u> and <u>no movements</u> of inventory have been recorded post year-end.

Event 2 – Occurred <u>3 August 2008</u>

Production at the Bask factory was halted for <u>one day</u> when an oil truck <u>reversed</u> into a metal pylon, puncturing the vehicle allowing oil to spread across the factory premises and into a local reservoir. The Environmental Agency is currently considering whether the <u>release of oil</u> was in <u>breach</u> of <u>environmental legislation</u>. The company's insurers have not <u>yet commented on the event</u>.

Required:

(a) For each of the two events above:

    (i)   <u>Explain</u> whether the <u>events</u> are <u>adjusting</u> or <u>non-adjusting</u> <u>according</u> to IAS 10 *Events After the Reporting Period*.

                   (4 marks)

    (ii) Explain the <u>auditors' responsibility</u> and the <u>audit procedures</u> and <u>actions</u> that should be carried out according to ISA 560 *(Redrafted) Subsequent Events*.

                   (12 marks)

(b) Assume that the date is now <u>15 September 2008</u>, the financial statements and the audit report have just been signed, and the annual general meeting is to take place on <u>10 October 2009</u>. The Environmental Agency has issued a report stating that Brand Co is in <u>breach</u> of environmental legislation and a fine of <u>$800,000</u> will now be levied on the company. The amount <u>is material</u> to the financial statements.

Required:

<u>Explain</u> the <u>additional audit work</u> the auditor should carry out in respect <u>of this fine</u>.

                   (4 marks)
                 (20 marks)

5 Going concern

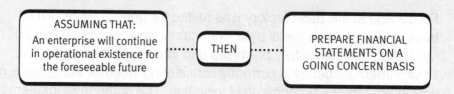

ASSUMING THAT:
An enterprise will continue in operational existence for the foreseeable future

.... THEN ....

PREPARE FINANCIAL STATEMENTS ON A GOING CONCERN BASIS

The going concern concept – definition

According to IAS1 financial statements should be prepared on the basis that the company is a going concern unless it is inappropriate to do so.

- The **going concern concept** is defined in IAS1 as the assumption that the enterprise will continue in operational existence for the foreseeable future.

- Any consideration involving the 'foreseeable future' involves making a judgement about future events, which are inherently uncertain.

- Uncertainty increases with time and judgements can only be made on the basis of information available at any point – subsequent events can overturn that judgement.

- Management (and auditors) should generally look ahead **at least one year** from the date of the directors' approval of the financial statements, in assessing the validity of the going concern basis.

- There may be circumstances in which it is appropriate to look further ahead. This depends on the nature of the business and the associated risks.

The going concern concept – significance

Whether or not a company can be classed as a going concern affects how its financial statements are prepared.

- Financial statements are usually prepared on the basis that the reporting entity is a going concern.

- IAS1 states that 'an entity should prepare its financial statements on a going concern basis, unless
  - the entity is being liquidated or has ceased trading, or
  - the directors have no realistic alternative but to liquidate the entity or to cease trading.'

- Where the assumption is made that the company will cease trading, the financial statements are prepared using the **break-up basis** under which:
  - assets are recorded at likely sale values
  - inventory and receivables are likely to require more provisions, and
  - additional liabilities may arise (severance costs for staff, the costs of closing down facilities, etc.).

Going concern reviews – the auditor's role

Auditors are concerned with ensuring that financial statements give a 'true and fair' view, which includes being satisfied that they have been prepared using the correct basis.

- A set of financial statements is typically put together on the presumption that the company will continue trading for the foreseeable future (as a guide, at least one year).

- Auditors may appear negligent if they issue a 'clean' audit report on a company's financial statements that paint a positive picture, only for that company to quickly go out of business.

- Hence it is important for auditors to be assured that the company is a going concern, to confirm that the correct basis of preparation has been used.

- Auditors undertake 'going concern reviews' to obtain this assurance.

Going concern – responsibilities

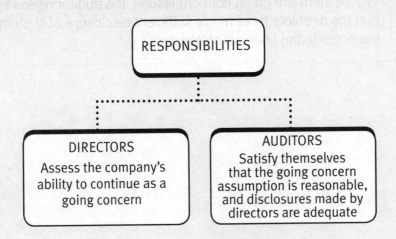

Expandable Text - Directors and Auditors responsibilities

Both directors and auditors of an entity have responsibilities regarding going concern.

Directors

- It is the directors' responsibility to assess the company's ability to continue as a going concern when they are preparing the financial statements.

- If they are aware of any material uncertainties which may affect this assessment, then IAS 1 requires them to disclose such uncertainties in the financial statements.

- When the directors are performing their assessment they should take into account a number of relevant factors such as:
    - current and expected profitability
    - debt repayment
    - sources (and potential sources) of financing.

Auditors

- ISA 570 Going Concern states that the auditor needs to consider the appropriateness of management's use of the going concern assumption. The auditors need to assess the risk that the company may not be a going concern.

- Where there are going concern issues, the auditor needs to ensure that the directors have made sufficient disclosure of such matters in the notes to the financial statements.

KAPLAN PUBLISHING

Going concern – what the auditor has to do (Audit procedures)

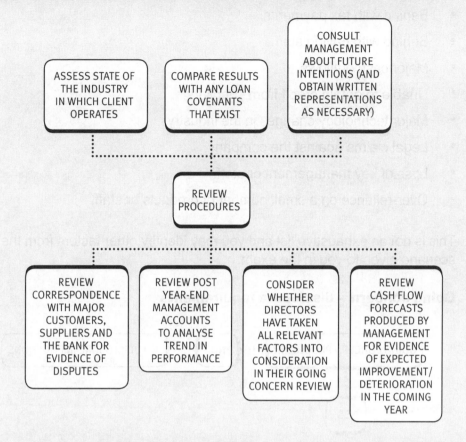

The procedures that the auditors undertake for their going concern review will depend on the risk that the company may not be a going concern.

- In a company where profits are high, cash flows are positive, finance is in place, and there is no obvious exposure to large losses, going concern procedures are likely to be minimal.

- Where any doubts regarding going concern exist, procedures are more extensive.

- When companies go out of business, it is more likely to be due to a lack of **cash** than a lack of **profits**. However, in the long term, profits are of course essential for survival.

- The auditor should remain alert for evidence of events or conditions which may cast significant doubt on the entity's ability to continue as a going concern, both in the planning stage and throughout the audit.

Indicators of going concern problems

Typical indicators of going concern problems include the following:

- Net current liabilities (or net liabilities overall!).

- Borrowing facilities not agreed.

- Default on loan agreements.

- Unplanned sales of non-current assets.
- Behind with tax payments.
- Behind with paying staff.
- Major cash outflows.
- Unable to obtain credit from suppliers.
- Major technology changes in the industry.
- Legal claims against the company.
- Loss of key management or staff.
- Over-reliance on a small number of products or staff.

This is not an exhaustive list and you may identify other factors from the scenario given to you in the exam.

Going concern – disclosure requirements

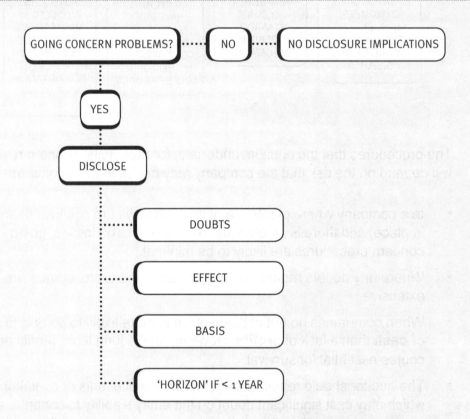

Where there is any doubt over the going concern status of a company, the directors should include disclosures in the financial statements explaining:

- the doubts
- the possible effect on the company.

Where the directors have been unable to assess going concern in the usual way (e.g. for less than one year beyond the date on which they sign the financial statements), this fact should be disclosed.

Where the financial statements are prepared on a basis other than the going concern basis, the basis used should be disclosed.

Going concern reviews – reporting implications

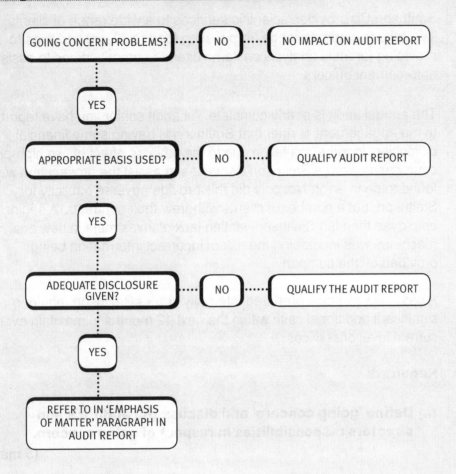

We will look at the detail of the contents of the auditor's report in Chapter 12.

Here it is important for you to understand the following.

- Financial statements are normally prepared on the going concern basis.

- Where the going concern basis is used and is appropriate, the auditors **do not** need to mention the fact in their report.

- If the auditors believe that the going concern basis is inappropriate, or the disclosures given by management about the going concern issues are inadequate, but the directors do not, the audit report will need to be qualified, i.e. the auditors will be saying that the financial statements do not give a true and fair view.

- If the going concern basis is not appropriate and the directors prepare the financial statements on some other, appropriate basis, the auditors would normally refer to this in their report because it is a matter of extreme significance – this is called an 'emphasis of matter paragraph' for obvious reasons.

FIXED TEST 3 - Smithson

Smithson Co provides scientific services to a wide range of clients. Typical assignments range from testing food for illegal additives to providing forensic analysis on items used to commit crimes to assist law enforcement officers.

The annual audit is nearly complete. As audit senior you have reported to the engagement partner that Smithson is having some financial difficulties. Income has fallen due to the adverse effect of two high-profile court cases, where Smithson's services to assist the prosecution were found to be in error. Not only did this provide adverse publicity for Smithson, but a number of clients withdrew their contracts. A senior employee then left Smithson, stating lack of investment in new analysis machines was increasing the risk of incorrect information being provided by the company.

A cash flow forecast prepared internally shows Smithson requiring significant additional cash within the next 12 months to maintain even the current level of services.

Required:

(a) **Define 'going concern' and discuss the auditor's and directors responsibilities in respect of going concern.**

(5 marks)

(b) **State the audit procedures that may be carried out to try to determine whether or not Smithson Co is a going concern.**

(10 marks)

(c) **Explain the audit procedures the auditor may take where the auditor has decided that Smithson Co is unlikely to be a going concern.**

(5 marks)

Expandable Text - Answer plan

Smithson Co provides scientific services to a wide range of clients. Typical assignments range from testing food for illegal additives to providing forensic analysis on items used to commit crimes to assist law enforcement officers.

The annual audit is nearly complete. As audit senior you have reported to the engagement partner that Smithson is having <u>some financial difficulties</u>. <u>Income</u> has <u>fallen</u> due to the adverse effect of two <u>high-profile court cases</u>, where Smithson's services to assist the prosecution were <u>found to be in error</u>. Not only did this provide <u>adverse publicity</u> for Smithson, but a <u>number</u> of <u>clients withdrew</u> their <u>contracts</u>. A <u>senior employee</u> then <u>left Smithson</u>, stating <u>lack of investment</u> in new analysis machines was <u>increasing</u> the <u>risk</u> of <u>incorrect</u> information being provided by the company.

A cash flow forecast prepared internally shows Smithson requiring <u>significant additional cash within</u> the <u>next 12 months</u> to maintain even the current level of services.

Required:

(a) Define '<u>going concern</u>' and <u>discuss</u> the auditor's and <u>directors responsibilities</u> in respect of going concern.

(5 marks)

(b) State the <u>audit procedures</u> that may be <u>carried out</u> to try to determine <u>whether or not Smithson Co</u> is a <u>going concern</u>.

(10 marks)

(c) Explain the <u>audit procedures</u> the auditor may take where the auditor has decided that Smithson Co is <u>unlikely</u> to be a <u>going concern</u>.

(5 marks)

6 Management representations

What are management representations?

Management representations are a particular type of enquiry, whereby the auditor asks management to confirm, in writing, a number of issues covered by or surrounding the financial statements.

- These may be general matters such as:
  - the directors' understanding that it is their responsibility to produce financial statements that show a true and fair view or
  - whether all information that the auditors need for the purpose of the audit has been communicated to the auditors.

- They may be specific to the client or this particular year's financial statements such as:
  - confirmation of values where there is a significant degree of estimation or judgement involved, e.g. development expenditure on new products or the outcome of litigation
  - formal confirmation of the directors' judgement on contentious issues, e.g. the recognition of revenue, or the value of assets where there is a risk of impairment.

How are management representations obtained?

As the audit progresses, the audit team will assemble a list of those items about which it is appropriate to seek management representations.

As part of the completion process the auditors will write to the client's management stating the issues about which they are seeking representations.

The representations themselves may take any of the following forms.

- A letter from the client's management to the auditors covering the necessary points. Usually the auditors will provide management with a draft of the letter for them to produce on the client's letterhead and sign.

- A letter from the auditors to management setting out the necessary points, which management signs in acknowledgement and returns to the auditors.

- Minutes of the meeting at which representations were made orally which can be signed by management as a true record of what was discussed.

Why do auditors need management representations?

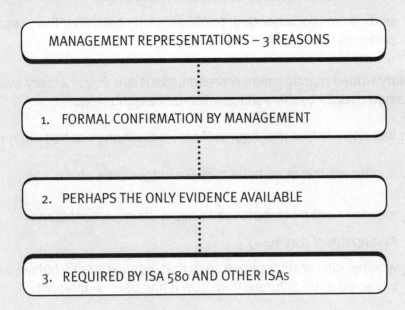

MANAGEMENT REPRESENTATIONS – 3 REASONS

1. FORMAL CONFIRMATION BY MANAGEMENT

2. PERHAPS THE ONLY EVIDENCE AVAILABLE

3. REQUIRED BY ISA 580 AND OTHER ISAs

You may think that as the auditor's job is to form an independent opinion about whether or not the financial statements prepared by management give a true and fair view, the value of representations from management might be questionable.

However, there are three good reasons why management representations are necessary:

(1) Precisely because it is management's responsibility to produce financial statements that show a true and fair view, the most obvious first source of audit evidence is to ask them whether or not they have done so.

(2) There may be circumstances where no other sufficient, appropriate audit evidence may reasonably be expected to exist – the issues concerning estimation and judgement mentioned above are the most obvious examples.

(3) **ISA 580 Management representations** and the requirements of a number of other ISAs make it compulsory for the auditors to obtain management representations on a number of specific issues.

The quality and reliability of management representations

We have seen in Chapter 9 on audit evidence that the quality and reliability of audit evidence depends on a number of issues, in particular:

• its source (independent, external or auditor generated evidence is better than evidence generated internally by the client)

- how it is obtained (evidence obtained directly by the auditor is better than evidence obtained indirectly by inference)

- its medium (documentary, particularly original rather than copied, evidence is better than oral evidence).

Clearly written management representations are documentary evidence obtained directly by the auditor which is the good news.

The bad news is that management representations are **not** independent.

The auditor will therefore have to make judgements about:

- management's competence to make the representations

- management's integrity

- whether circumstances are such that management's behaviour may be expected to be different from how it has been in the past.

If, for example the client was:

- under increased financial pressure because of difficult trading conditions

- subject to being taken over, where the value of managements' shareholdings could vary widely depending on the terms of the takeover

the auditors might revise their judgement about the reliability of management representations.

Expandable Text - Examples in a management letter

Representations about what exactly?

In the section above about the nature of management representations, we considered examples of the types of representations which might be appropriate.

In the extended text below is a checklist from a UK-based audit pack of possible items on which management representations might be obtained.

If you have access to ISA 580 you will find that it has an additional appendix which summarises the requirements of other ISAs for representations.

It is not really appropriate or necessary for you to learn all of these things by heart. You do, however, need to understand the type of things about which representations are usually obtained.

Exam hint

Always consider whether obtaining management representations is appropriate in answer to a question about designing audit procedures or gathering audit evidence. It very often will be.

Possible representations to be obtained from management

1	Directors acknowledge responsibility for financial statements.
2	Directors acknowledge responsibility for design and implementation of internal control procedures.
3	All books of account and relevant supporting information made available.
4	Directors have assessed the risk of fraud and regard it as low.
5	No irregularities involving management or employees with significant role in preparing financial statements.
6	All allegations of fraud have been disclosed.
7	All related parties have been identified.
8	There has been full compliance with contractual obligations.
9	There has been full compliance with laws and regulations.
10	Financial statements are free from material misstatements including omissions.
11	Uncorrected errors are immaterial.
12	All balances and transactions with related parties have been suitably disclosed.

Test your understanding 3

(1) **List three reasons why auditors obtain management representations.**

(3 marks)

(2) **List six items that could be in a management representation letter.**

(3 marks)

7 Chapter summary

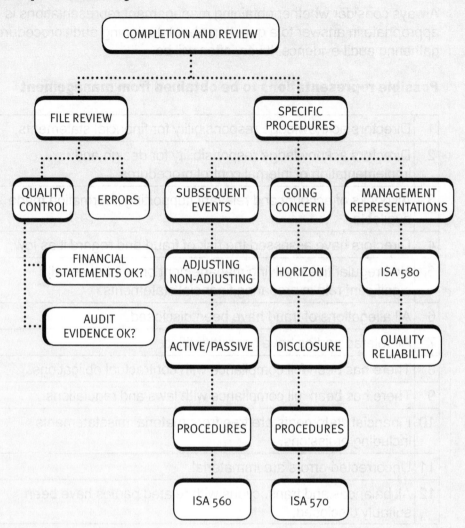

Test your understanding answers

Test your understanding 1

| List three examples of findings which could result in unadjusted differences (material or immaterial). | Lots of possibilities – some suggestions:

• year-end inventory counted incorrectly
• trade receivables unrecoverable
• over-provisions
• under-provisions
• depreciation incorrectly calculated
• cash book/payables ledger/ receivables ledger closed too early/ late
• sales revenue cut-off incorrectly applied
• accruals and prepayments calculated incorrectly
• interest charge/income not recognised. | 1 mark each |

Test your understanding 2

Answer

(a) **Event 1**

   (i) The problem with the light bulb inventory provides additional evidence of conditions existing at the end of the reporting period as the inventory was in <u>existence</u> and the faulty filiments were included in the inventory at this time.

   1 mark

   The value of the inventory is overstated and should <u>be reduced</u> to the <u>lower of cost</u> and <u>net realisable</u> value in accordance with IAS 2 *Inventories*.

   1 mark

	An <u>adjustment</u> for this decrease in value must <u>be made</u> in the financial statements.	1 mark
	The inventory should therefore be valued at <u>$125,000</u> being the net realisable value.	1 mark
(ii)	The decrease in value of inventory took place after the end of the reporting period but before the financial statements and the audit report were signed.	1 mark
	The auditor is therefore <u>still responsible</u> for identifying material events that affect the financial statements.	1 mark
	Audit procedures are therefore required to determine the net book value of the inventory and check that the $125,000 is the sales value of the light bulbs.	1 mark

Audit procedures will include:

–	Obtain <u>documentation</u> from the <u>insurers</u> confirming their estimate of the value of the light bulbs and that no further <u>insurance claim</u> can be made for the loss in value.	1 mark
–	Obtain the amended financial statements and ensure that the directors have included $125,000 as at the end of the reporting period.	1 mark
–	Ensure that the year-end value of inventory has been decreased to $125,000 on the statement of financial position, statement of financial position note and the income statement.	1 mark
–	Review inventory lists to ensure that the defective filiments were not used in any other light bulbs and that further adjustments are not required to any other inventory.	1 mark
–	Obtain an additional management representation point confirming the accuracy of the amounts written-off and confirming that no other items of inventory are affected.	1 mark

Event 2

(i) The release of oil occurred after the end of the reporting period, so this is indicative of conditions existing after the end of the reporting period – the event <u>could not</u> be foreseen at the end of the reporting period.

1 mark

In this case, <u>no adjustment</u> to the financial statements appears to be necessary.

1 mark

However, the investigation by the Environmental Agency could result in legal claim against the company for illegal pollution so as a material event it will need <u>disclosure</u> in the financial statements.

1 mark

(ii) As with event 1, the event takes place before the signing of the audit report, therefore the auditors have a <u>duty to identify</u> <u>material events affecting</u> the financial statements.

1 mark

Audit procedures will include:

- Obtain any <u>documentation</u> on the event, for example <u>board minutes</u>, copies of environmental legislation and possibly interim reports from the Environmental Agency to determine the extent of the damage.

1 mark

- <u>Inquire</u> of the directors whether they will disclose the event in the financial statements.

1 mark

- If the directors plan to make disclosure of the event, ensure that disclosure appears appropriate.

1 mark

- If the <u>directors do not plan</u> to make any disclosure, consider whether disclosure is necessary and inform the directors accordingly.

1 mark

- Where disclosure is not made and the auditor <u>considers disclosure is necessary, modify the audit opinion</u> on the grounds of disagreement and explain the reason for the qualification in the report. This will be for lack of disclosure (not provision) even though the amount cannot yet be determined.

1 mark

> – Alternatively, if the auditor considers that the release of oil and subsequent fine will affect Brand's ability to continue <u>as a going concern</u>, draw the members' attention to this in an <u>emphasis of matter paragraph</u>.
>
> 1 mark

(b) The notification of a fine has taken place after the audit report has been signed.

Audit procedures will include:

> – Discuss the matter with the directors to determine their course of action.
>
> 1 mark

> – Where the directors decide to amend the disclosure financial statements, audit the <u>amendment</u> and <u>then</u> <u>re-draft</u> and re-date the audit report as appropriate.
>
> 1 mark

> – Where the directors decide not to amend the financial statements as the disclosure the auditor can <u>consider</u> other methods of <u>contacting the</u> <u>members</u>. For example the auditor can speak in the upcoming general meeting to inform the members of the event.
>
> 1 mark

> – Other options such as <u>resignation</u> seem inappropriate due to the proximity fo the annual general meeting (AGM). Resignation would allow the auditor to ask the directors to convene an extraordinary general meeting, but this could not take place before the AGM so the auditor should speak at the AGM instead.
>
> 1 mark

FIXED TEST 3 - Smithson

THIS IS A FIXED TEST – Please answer the question in full (long form written). Then log on to en-gage at the following address: www.en-gage.co.uk. Follow the link to 'Fixed Test 3' and answer the questions based on your homework answer.

Once you have answered the questions on en-gage a model answer will be available for your reference.

Test your understanding 3

(1) Formal confirmation by management of their responsibilities.	1 mark
Perhaps the only evidence available.	1 mark
Required by ISA 580 and other ISAs.	1 mark
(2) No irregularities involving management or employees that could have a material effect on the financial statements	½ mark
All books of account and supporting documentation have been made available to the auditors	½ mark
Information and disclosures with reference to related parties is complete	½ mark
Financial statements are free from material misstatements including omissions	½ mark
No non-compliance with any statute or regulatory authority	½ mark
No plans that will materially alter the carrying value or classification of assets or liabilities in the financial statements	½ mark
No plans to abandon any product lines that will result in any excess or obsolete inventory	½ mark
No events, unless already disclosed, after the end of the reporting period that need disclosure in the financial statements	½ mark

Reporting

Chapter learning objectives

Upon completion of this chapter you will be able to:

- describe and analyse the format and content of unmodified and modified audit reports

- discuss the type of opinion provided in statutory audits.

1 The audit opinion

A company's auditor must report their opinions to shareholders/members on two primary matters:

(1) Whether the financial statements give a **true and fair** view (or present fairly in all material respects).

(2) Whether the financial statements have been **properly prepared** in accordance with relevant rules, e.g.

- International Accounting Standards,

- a particular country's legal requirements.

Expandable Text - Additional requirements

In some jurisdictions there may be additional requirements.

- In the UK there is a requirement to express an opinion on whether the Directors' Report is consistent with the financial statements.

- In Ireland there is a requirement to report on the adequacy of a company's capital.

These considerations are assessed on the basis of the audit work carried out and the evidence obtained from this.

In addition, certain other matters may have to be **reported by exception.** These matters, which are also referred to as **implied reporting**, are laid down by a country's laws.

In the UK, these matters are:

- where **R**eturns are not received from all branches of the company

- where **A**ccounting records are inconsistent with the FS

- where **P**roper accounting records have not been kept

- where all **I**nformation and explanations were not received

- where **D**irector transactions with the company are missing from FS.

The above can be remembered using the mnemonic RAPID.

Reporting by exception is **not** the same as a qualification; however, as the matters dealt with are usually legal requirements, non-compliance will probably lead to a qualification anyway. For instance, if all informations and explanations have not been received, there will most likely be a limitation of scope. This term is explained later in the chapter.

2 The auditor's report on financial statements

ISA 700 The Auditor's Report on Financial Statements, explains the basic principles of audit reporting and identifies the elements of the auditor's report.

Contents of an audit report	Example of a clean audit report
Title	**INDEPENDENT AUDITOR'S REPORT**
Addressee	**(APPROPRIATE ADDRESSEE)**
	Report on the financial statements
Introductory paragraph	We have audited the accompanying financial statements of the ABC Company, which comprise the statement of financial position as at 31 December, 20X9, and the income statement, statement of changes in equity and statement of cash flow for the year then ended, and a summary of significant accounting policies and explanatory notes.
Management responsibility	**Management's responsibility for the financial statements** Management is responsible for the preparation and fair presentation of these financial statements in accordance with International Financial Reporting Standards. This responsibility includes, designing, implementing and maintaining internal control relevant to the preparation and fair presentation of financial statements that are free from material misstatement, whether due to fraud or error; selecting and applying appropriate accounting policies; and making accounting estimates that are reasonable in the circumstances.
Auditor's responsibility	**Auditor's responsibility** Our responsibility is to express an opinion on these financial statements based on our audit.

Scope paragraph

We conducted our audit in accordance with International Standards on Auditing. Those Standards require that we comply with ethical requirements and plan and perform the audit to obtain reasonable assurance about whether the financial statements are free of material misstatement.

An audit involves performing procedures to obtain audit evidence about the amounts and disclosures in the financial statements. The procedures selected depend on the auditor's judgement, including the assessment of the risks of material misstatement of the financial statements, whether due to fraud or error. In making those risk assessments, the auditor considers internal control relevant to the entity's preparation and fair presentation of the financial statements in order to design audit procedures that are appropriate in the circumstances, but not for the purpose of expressing an opinion on the effectiveness of the entity's internal control. An audit also includes evaluating the appropriateness of accounting policies used and the reasonableness of accounting estimates made by management, as well as evaluating the overall financial statement presentation.

We believe that the audit evidence we have obtained is sufficient and appropriate to provide a basis for our audit opinion.

Opinion

Opinion

In our opinion, the financial statements give a true and fair view of **(or 'present fairly, in all material respects',)** the financial position of the Company as of 31 December, 20X9, and of its financial performance and its cash flows for the year then ended in accordance with International Financial Reporting Standards.

Other reporting responsibility	Report on other Legal and Regulatory Requirements
	[Form and content of this section of the auditor's report will vary depending on the nature of the auditor's other reporting responsibilities.]
Auditor signature	Auditor's signature
Date of report	Date of the auditor's report
Auditors address	Auditor's address

Preparing the audit report

ISA 700 describes the elements that make up the audit report as:

Title

- The title should be 'appropriate'. The use of 'Independent Auditor's Report' distinguishes this report from any other report produced internally or by other non-statutory auditors.

Addressee

- The report should be addressed to the intended user of the report which is usually the shareholders, board of directors or other party defined in the engagement or local regulations.

- This varies from country to country, but is usually addressed to the members of the company. This is to prevent other parties relying on the report when it is not intended for their use.

Introductory paragraph

- Identifies the financial statements which have been audited (see below), by name or by the use of page numbers, and stating the period they cover. This is in order to distinguish such information from other documents that have not been subject to audit (e.g. the Directors' Report).

Statement of responsibilities of management

- Preparation of the financial statements which show a true and fair view or present fairly in all material respects and in accordance with the applicable financial framework.

- Designing and implementing an effective internal control system.
- Applying appropriate accounting policies.
- Making reasonable accounting estimates.

Statement of responsibilities of the auditors

- Express opinion.
- Assess the risk of material misstatement.
- The fact that the audit was planned and performed to obtain reasonable assurance about whether the financial statements are free from material misstatement.
- Consider internal control as a basis for preparing financial statements without responsibility for implementing it.
- Obtain sufficient, appropriate audit evidence on which to base the opinion.

Scope Paragraph

- The standards under which the audit was conducted i.e. ISAs.
- A summary of audit processes and procedures in general terms e.g. examining on a test basis, evidence to support the financial statement amounts and disclosures.
- Evaluate the appropriateness of accounting policies.
- Evaluate the overall presentation of the financial statements.

Opinion

- This covers the primary statements and associated notes referred to in the introductory paragraph (even though only the first two are referred to explicitly).
- Truth and fairness (or presented fairly in all material respects).
- Preparation in accordance with the financial reporting framework – applicable legislation and accounting standards.
- If applicable, any other matters required under a country's regulations. Such a statement would be made at the end of the opinion paragraph.

Auditor's signature

- This should include reference to the auditor's status as a Registered Auditor.
- The report may be signed by the firm, by the auditor individually or both. Normally the firm's signature is given as the firm as a whole assumes responsibility for the audit.

Date of report

- The audit report must be signed **after** the directors have approved the financial statements and preferably on the same day.

- It is not necessary that the final typewritten copies of financial statements are available for signature – draft copies may be signed, provided the draft documents are sufficiently clear to enable a proper overall assessment of presentation to be made.

Auditor's address

- The audit report should name a specific location, which is normally the city where the auditor maintains the office that has responsibility for the audit.

Test your understanding 1 (All Q2 types)

(1) **List the main contents of an unmodified audit report?**

(3 marks)

(2) **What opinion does the auditor give in an unmodified audit report?**

(2 marks)

(3) **When should the audit report be signed?**

(1 mark)

(4) **Who should sign the audit report and what further information about the signatory should be provided?**

(1 mark)

Audit reports

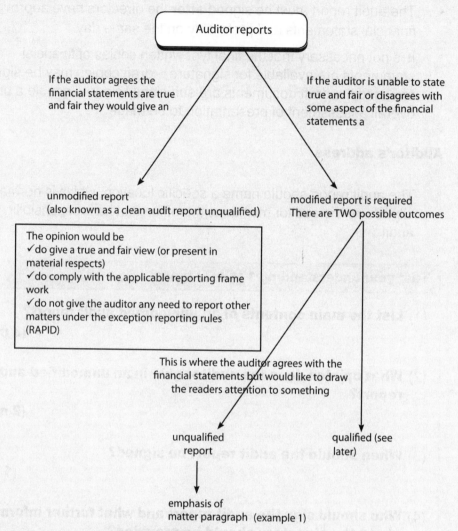

Auditor reports

If the auditor agrees the financial statements are true and fair they would give an

If the auditor is unable to state true and fair or disagrees with some aspect of the financial statements a

unmodified report
(also known as a clean audit report unqualified)

modified report is required
There are TWO possible outcomes

The opinion would be
✓ do give a true and fair view (or present in material respects)
✓ do comply with the applicable reporting frame work
✓ do not give the auditor any need to report other matters under the exception reporting rules (RAPID)

This is where the auditor agrees with the financial statements but would like to draw the readers attention to something

unqualified report

qualified (see later)

emphasis of matter paragraph (example 1)

Examples of emphasis of matters

Where there are particular circumstances surrounding the financial statements, e.g.

- significant uncertainties whose outcome depends on future events

- going concern problems

- material misstatements in prior period figures

- the financial statements have been prepared on a break up basis not a going concern.

and they are fully disclosed, the auditors may wish to draw the reader's attention to them in the audit report.

KAPLAN PUBLISHING

Exam hint

In the examination, you might be asked to describe the type of report that would be appropriate, to draft sections from the opinion paragraph or to comment on whether a given example is appropriate in the circumstances. The following sections guide you through the process.

The production of a full report will not be asked.

The 'emphasis of matter' paragraph

Example 1

'Without qualifying our opinion we draw attention to Note X to the financial statements. The Company is the defendant in a lawsuit alleging infringement of certain patent rights and claiming royalties and punitive damages. The Company has filed a counter action, and preliminary hearings and discovery proceedings on both actions are in progress. The ultimate outcome of the matter cannot presently be determined, and no provision for any liability that may result has been made in the financial statements.'

There are some further things to note.

- The emphasis of matter paragraph is placed after the opinion paragraph.
- The auditor makes it clear in the paragraph that the opinion is not qualified.
- The sections of the report prior to the paragraph are unchanged.
- Where possible, the potential financial effect on the financial statements should be quantified (not possible in the example given).
- The paragraph is given a separate heading.

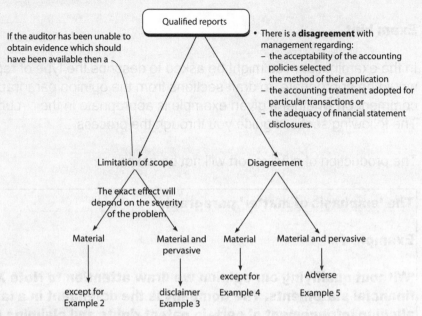

Note: Material and pervasive (definition)

- ISA 700 uses the phrase 'material and pervasive' and we know that unless the matter is material, it will not cause the report to be qualified at all. (Although you should remember that materiality can be about an item's nature as well as its value.)
- So the nature of the qualification depends on the degree of effect that the auditor considers it may have on the financial statements.
  To be considered pervasive, it must affect the view given by the financial statements as a whole. As such:
  – if the circumstance is a limitation of scope it will leave the auditor unable to form an opinion at all
  – if it is a disagreement, it will be of such significance that the financial statements do not give a true and fair view.

Effect on the audit report

The result of these matters on the audit report is shown below. Note the circumstances given at the top of the example reports that will give you an indication of when each type will be appropriate.

Limitation of scope – material but not pervasive

Example 2

Previous paragraphs as per standard report ...

Auditor's responsibility

Our responsibility is to express an opinion on these financial statements based on our audit. **Except as discussed in the following paragraph**, we conducted our audit in accordance with ...

We did not observe the counting of the physical inventories as of 31 December 20X9, since that date was prior to the time we were initially engaged as auditors for the Company. Owing to the nature of the company's records, we were <u>unable</u> to satisfy ourselves as to <u>inventory quantities</u> by other audit procedures.

Opinion

In our opinion, **except for the effects of such adjustments, if any, as might have been determined to be necessary had we been able to satisfy ourselves as to physical inventory quantities,** the financial statements give a true and …

Example 3

Limitation of scope – pervasive therefore a disclaimer

'We were engaged to audit the accompanying financial statements of the ABC Company, which comprise the statement of financial position as of 31 December, 20X9 and the income statement, the statement of changes in equity and the cash flow statement for the year then ended, and a summary of the significant accounting policies and other explanatory notes.

Management responsibility paragraph as per standard report (omit the sentence stating the responsibility of the auditor).

(The paragraph discussing the scope of the audit would either be omitted or amended according to the circumstances.)

(Add a paragraph discussing the scope limitation as follows.)

We were not able to observe all physical inventories and confirm accounts receivable due to limitations placed on the scope of our work by the Company.

Because of the significance of the matters discussed in the preceding paragraph, we do not express an opinion on the financial statements.'

Example 4

Disagreement – material but not pervasive

Previous paragraphs as per standard report ...Opinion

As discussed in Note X to the financial statements, no depreciation has been provided in the financial statements which practice, in our opinion, is not in accordance with International Financial Reporting Standards. The provision for the year ended 31 December, 20X9, should be XXX based on the straight-line method of depreciation using annual rates of 5% for the building and 20% for the equipment. Accordingly, the non-current assets should be reduced by accumulated depreciation of XXX and the loss for the year and accumulated deficit should be increased by XXX and XXX, respectively.

In our opinion, **except for the effect on the financial statements of the matter referred to in the preceding paragraph**, the financial statements give a true and ...'

Example 5

Disagreement – pervasive therefore adverse opinion

Previous paragraphs as per standard report ...

Opinion paragraph

'In our opinion, because of the effects of the matters discussed in the preceding paragraph(s), **the financial statements do not give a true and fair view of (or do not "present fairly") the financial position of the Company as of 31 December, 20X9**, and of its financial performance and its cash flows for the year then ended in accordance with International Financial Reporting Standards.'

As you can see, there is a potentially difficult decision process to go through when deciding what kind of modified audit report may be appropriate.

Question approach

(1) Ask yourself what the directors have disclosed in the financial statements.

(2) Ask yourself, do we as the auditors agree or have we obtained sufficient evidence to give a clean audit report.

(3) Give opinion.

(4) State why.

Test your understanding 2

Exam type question (normally Q5)

Taylor (Profit before tax $750,000)

On 5 January 2009 a customer sued the company for personal damages arising from an unexpected defect in one of its products. Shortly before the year end the company made an out-of-court settlement with the customer, which is not material of $10,000, although this agreement is not reflected in the financial statements as at 31 December 2008. Further, the matter was reported to the press and was extensively reported. Subsequently, the matter became known and the company's legal advisers have now informed you that further claims have been received following the publicity, although they are unable to place a figure on the potential liability arising from such claims which have not yet been received. The company had referred to the claims in a note to the financial statements stating, however, that no provision had been made to cover them because the claims were not expected to be material.

Discuss the effect on the audit report.

(10 marks)

Answer plan

Taylor (Profit before tax) $\dfrac{\$750,000}{\text{materiality}}$ 5% 37,500
10% 75,000

On 5 January 2009 a customer sued the company for personal damages arising from an unexpected defect in one of its products. Shortly before the year end the company made an out-of-court settlement with the customer, which is not material of $10,000, although this agreement is not reflected in the financial statements as at 31 December 2008. Further, the matter was reported to the press and was extensively reported. Subsequently, the matter became known and the company's legal advisers have now informed you that further claims have been received following the publicity, although they are unable to place a figure on the potential liability arising from such claims which have not yet been received. The company had referred to the claims in a note to the financial statements stating, however, that no provision had been made to cover them because the claims were not expected to be material.

(The underlined words are the key words/information to take away from the scenario.)

Test your understanding 3

(1) **List four types of qualified audit report?**

(2 marks)

(2) **Give an example of when each type of report would be appropriate.**

(4 marks)

(3) **What is an 'emphasis of matter' paragraph?**

(3 marks)

3 The impact of auditors' reports

- The unqualified report is a summary of the auditor's work and conclusions. It adds <u>credibility</u> to the contents of the financial statements.

- Clearly, if the audit report has any impact, the <u>management</u> should be <u>reluctant</u> to get themselves into a position where a <u>qualification</u> is required.

- If the subject matter of the qualification is a disagreement, then a large or public company faces possible/probable investigation. In the UK this will be by the Financial Reporting Review Panel. This can require a company to reissue its accounts with the ultimate sanction that it can take the company to court if it does not comply with its wishes.

- If the subject matter is a limitation of scope, the company may find itself in financial difficulties. Trade payables may be reluctant to supply goods on credit terms and the bank may call in any overdraft. It should be appreciated that overdrafts are technically repayable on demand.

- The severity of these potential effects helps to ensure that the auditor decides very carefully whether a qualification is required and ensures that management take the 'threat' of qualification seriously.

4 Chapter summary

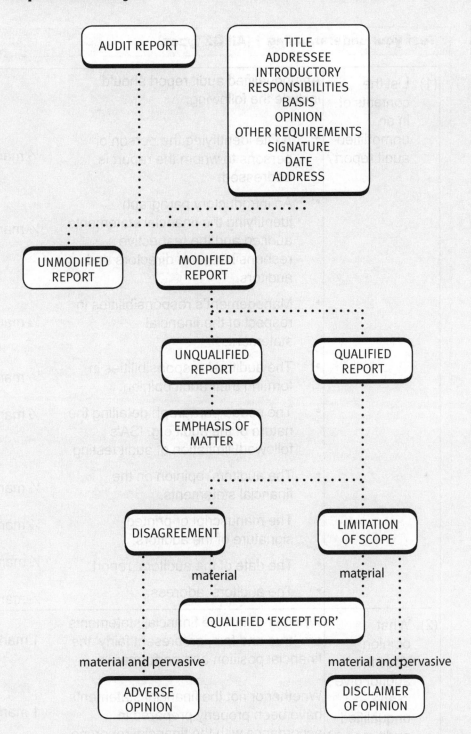

AUDIT REPORT

TITLE
ADDRESSEE
INTRODUCTORY
RESPONSIBILITIES
BASIS
OPINION
OTHER REQUIREMENTS
SIGNATURE
DATE
ADDRESS

UNMODIFIED REPORT

MODIFIED REPORT

UNQUALIFIED REPORT

QUALIFIED REPORT

EMPHASIS OF MATTER

DISAGREEMENT

LIMITATION OF SCOPE

material

material

QUALIFIED 'EXCEPT FOR'

material and pervasive

material and pervasive

ADVERSE OPINION

DISCLAIMER OF OPINION

Test your understanding answers

Test your understanding 1 (All Q2 types)

(1) List the contents of in an unmodified audit report?	An unqualified audit report should include the following.	
	• A title identifying the person or persons to whom the report is addressed.	½ mark
	• An introductory paragraph identifying the financial statements audited and the respective responsibilities of directors and auditors.	½ mark
	• Management's responsibilities in respect of the financial statements.	½ mark
	• The auditors' responsibilities in forming their audit opinion.	½ mark
	• The scope paragraph detailing the nature of the audit e.g. ISA's followed, limitation of audit testing.	½ mark
	• The auditors' opinion on the financial statements.	½ mark
	• The manuscript or printed signature of the auditors.	½ mark
	• The date of the auditors' report.	½ mark
	• The auditors' address.	½ mark
(2) What opinion does the auditor give in an unqualified audit report?	Whether or not the financial statements are 'true and fair', or 'present fairly' the financial position and performance.	1 mark
	Whether or not the financial statements have been properly prepared in accordance with the financial reporting framework and statutory requirements where appropriate.	1 mark
(3) When should the audit report be signed?	The audit report should be signed after the directors have signed the financial statements (preferably same day).	1 mark

(4) Who should sign the audit report and what further information about the signatory should be provided?	The auditor's signature should refer to Registered Auditor status and be signed either by the firm or the auditor individually.	1 mark

Test your understanding 2

Answer

Out of court settlement

The out of court settlement is <u>not material</u> (10K/950K) is <u>less than 5%</u>, therefore there will be no impact on the audit report (a clean audit report will be given).   1 mark

If we look at this transaction on its own the financial statements <u>will show a true and fair view</u> (materially).   1 mark

Further claims

Materiality is questionable here, if we <u>agree with</u> the directors and its <u>not material</u> then again there would give a <u>clean audit report</u>.   1 mark

If the two issues became material in total then I would <u>ask</u> the <u>director</u> to <u>amend</u> the financial statements, if the   1 mark
director <u>did so</u>, and the auditor reviewed updates and agreed the updates were accurate then an <u>unmodified</u> <u>report</u> would be given.   1 mark

Remembering clean audit report, unmodified report is the opinion the financial statements show a true and fair view (they represent the same thing).   Remember

The bad publicity could affect the going concern of the business.

If the directors <u>used</u> the <u>going concern basis</u> but we as the <u>auditors</u> feel the business will not continue for the foreseeable future we as the auditors would disagree, as it should be on a break up basis.	1 mark
The effect on the opinion would be <u>adverse</u>.	
If the <u>directors prepared</u> the financial statements on a <u>break up basis</u> and the <u>auditor agreed</u> we would give a modified, <u>unqualified report</u>, <u>emphasis of matter</u>.	1 mark
Drawing the attention of this matter to the readers.	1 mark
If the <u>directors</u> have prepared the financial statement on a <u>going concern basis</u> and the going concern status is <u>uncertain</u>, as long as the issue was <u>adequately disclosed</u> the effect on the audit report would be <u>unqualified</u>, with an <u>emphasis of matter paragraph</u>.	1 mark 1 mark
If the directors <u>didn't adequately</u> disclose then this would be one disagreement therefore the effect on the audit report would be <u>qualified except for</u>.	1 mark 1 mark

Test your understanding 3

(1) List four types of qualified audit report?	**Limitation of scope** • Except for. • Disclaimer. **Disagreement** • Except for. • Adverse.	½ mark ½ mark ½ mark ½ mark
(2) Give an example of when each type of report would be appropriate?	Examples of the above could be: **Limitation in scope – material** No inventory count carried out at a branch. **Limitation in scope – pervasive** Destruction of accounting records. **Disagreement – material** Difference of opinion between directors and auditor as to whether to provide for a doubtful debt. **Disagreement – pervasive** Inappropriate basis of preparation used e.g. if the going concern basis has been used when the break up basis should have been used.	 ½ mark ½ mark ½ mark ½ mark ½ mark ½ mark ½ mark ½ mark ½ mark

(3)	What is an emphasis of matter paragraph?	An 'emphasis of matter' highlights a matter affecting the financial statements and draws the reader's attention to a note that more fully explains the position.	1 mark
		An emphasis of matter does not constitute a qualified opinion. It is usually situated after the opinion paragraph and states that the opinion is not qualified with regard to that matter. It is used when there is a significant uncertainty or going concern issue that has been fully disclosed in the notes to the financial statements and the outcome of the issue is dependent on events yet to happen.	1 mark 1 mark

Index

Index

Index

Index